The People's Pope

THE PEOPLE'S POPE

The Story of Karol Wojtyla of Poland

James Oram

Chronicle Books • San Francisco

Chronicle Books
870 Market Street
San Francisco, California 94102

Designed by Chan Israel Graphic Design.
Printed by Fremont Litho with Peter Levison Associates.

Picture Acknowledgements:
Photos of contemporary Poland by Neil Duncan.
Additional material by Adam Bujak, L' Osservatore Romano, Rome and
Interpress, Poland.

Many people gave of their time and knowledge to help me prepare this book ... too many to name individually, especially those living in Poland. But I would like to mention in gratitude Juliusz Kydrynski of Krakow, a distinguished writer and a passionate Pole, who guided me through the early life of John Paul II, and Boleslaw Taborski, now living in London, who introduced me to the world of Polish prose and poetry. I thank also Michael Wilson and Malcolm Farr in Rome, Leo Chapman and Rosalie George in London, Peter Brennan in New York, and Jozef Drewniak in Sydney. A special thanks to my editor, Geoffrey Moon, who helped me over ecclesiastical hurdles, and Marie Ussher, who had to put up with the outrageous moods of a writer hammering at a deadline. I would also like to acknowledge the kind permission of Hutchinson and Company in the United Kingdom and Random House in the USA in allowing me to use excerpts from the poetry of Pope John Paul II translated by Jerzy Peterkiewicz.

James Oram,
Sydney, 1979.

For the people of Poland who have suffered too much.

The Body of John Paul I lying in state in the Vatican.

CHAPTER ONE

Five a.m. For six hours the Roman Catholic Church had been without a leader, the miniscule and powerful, walled Vatican state without a ruler, the world without a Pope, God without a vicar on an increasingly godless earth. The light was burning in the papal apartment high above St Peter's Square but it was shining on the face of a dead man and at five a.m. there was none that knew the heart of John Paul I had stopped beating six hours before.

The first of the early morning traffic was rumbling along the Via Della Conciliazione, the wide street sweeping towards the warm embrace of Bernini's colonade on each side of St Peter's Square, but in the Vatican apartments it was muffled and far off; faint irritations heard through the old walls, the thick drapes.

The nuns were bustling in the kitchen preparing early coffee and in other rooms the hierarchy of the Church was preparing for the day. At ten minutes past five a nun placed a cup of coffee, as was the custom, outside the door of the Pope's apartment. John Paul I was precise in his routine. He woke at five. He drank his coffee ten minutes later. She was surprised when at twenty past five she went back for his empty cup to find the coffee still untouched outside the door, but it was not her position to question the Pope's routines, even to mentally scold him for staying in bed when all around him the ritual of the day was beginning as it had, in an almost unbroken pattern, for centuries.

In the chapel within the Apostolic Palace, Father John Magee, private secretary to the Pope, a priest of Irish stock and a man with a deep appreciation of the arduous papal duties, looked at his watch. It was five thirty. The Pontiff should now have been in the chapel to begin Mass. It was unlike John Paul I to be late, for he found intense satisfaction in the quiet early hours of the day before Rome turned into a cacophony of blaring horns, screeching brakes, colourful torrents of abuse from one motorist to another, before the hordes of tourists invaded St Peter's Square until even the pigeons were outnumbered.

Walking the few yards to the Pope's bedroom, he knocked on the door and, finding no answer, entered the room. John Paul I was still in bed. He was propped up by pillows, his head drooped forward on to his chest. One hand clutched sheets of paper. The reading lamp beside the bed was burning.

Moving quickly to the side of the bed, Magee knew in his heart, even though his mind rejected the idea, that the Pope was dead. Magee was stunned. It had seemed but a few days ago that he had watched John Paul I installed in the ancient office, had noted with pleasure how the Pope shunned the traditional extravagance and pomp of the coronation ceremony and instead allowed only a simple Mass in St Peter's Square. He remembered how the Pope had refused the elaborate triple-tiered papal tiara and had worn, as the symbol of attaining power, a plain woollen pallium around his shoulders.

He felt grief for a man who had, in a short time, with his smile and his compassion and his honesty, broken down many of the barriers of conservatism that surrounded the Vatican like stone walls. In his tears he remembered the simplicity of the man who once said: "I am only a poor man, accustomed to small things and silence".

Still shocked, still unbelieving, Magee immediately contacted the French-born Vatican Secretary of State, Cardinal Jean Villot who was at the Pope's bedside within minutes. Villot confirmed that John Paul I was dead and once more, in so short a time, he immediately became administrator, or Camerlengo, of the Holy See a position he would hold until the day that another cardinal would wear the Shoes of the Fisherman.

The roster list of papal physicians was consulted and Dr Renato Buzzonnetti rushed to the bedside. A check showed that John Paul I had died of an acute coronary thrombosis and that death had occurred around eleven p.m. the previous night.

There was much to be done, duties and traditions that could not be put aside because of grief, old rituals that were a part of *sede vacante* (a break in the papal rule). The seal in the Ring of the Fisherman, engraved with an image of St Peter in a boat fishing, a symbol of Papal power, had to be broken with a hammer. There was also the tradition of tapping the dead Pope's forehead three times with a silver hammer, calling his name and asking: "Are you dead?"

By now the word that the Church was without a Pope had spread through the Apostolic Palace. Faces were streaked with tears as they remembered Albino Luciani, the 263rd successor to St Peter.

Some remembered his humility, even the words he once said: "I must explain that, just as there are different writers so there are different bishops. Some resemble eagles, who soar with high level magisterial documents. Others are like nightingales who sing the praises of the Lord in marvellous fashion. Others, instead, are poor wrens, who, on the lowest branch of the episcopal tree, only squeak. I am one of the latter kind".

Some of the older priests recalled he was born in the small town of Forno di Canale, near Belluno, in the Italian Dolomites, on 17 October 1912. His father, Giovanni, was a determined socialist and young Albino shared many of his father's beliefs, with such intensity, in fact, that when he was a young curate he horrified his parish priest with his socialist, even revolutionary ideas. But as he worked more for the Church he became more conservative, although he still believed that wealth should be shared, that the poor were entitled to the riches of the world. When he was Patriarch of Venice, he shocked many of the older members of the Church—"ancients" he called them—by selling several antique possessions of the Patriarchate to found a home for handicapped children. He also put his own property up for sale, including two pectoral crosses on gold chains and a ring given him by a previous Pope. He explained, without apology, his actions with the words: "Real treasures of the Church are the poor, the disinherited, the small ones who must be helped".

There were others that day who recalled the Pope's writings, in which he penned letters to famous people in literature, history and fable, to such diverse characters as Mark Twain, Sir Walter Scott, Charles Dickens, G. K. Chesterton, Jesus Christ, even to Pinocchio of the long and growing nose.

His letter to Jesus began: "I have been criticised. 'He's a bishop, he's a cardinal,' people have said. 'He's been writing letters to all kinds of people: to Mark Twain, to Péguy, to Casella, to Penelope, to Dickens, to Marlowe, to Goldoni and Heaven knows how many others. And not a line to Jesus Christ.'

"You know this. With you, I try to keep talking continuously. It's hard to translate this into letters, though; I talk to you about personal things. Such small things, too. And then, what could I write to You, or about You, after all the books that have been written about You?

"And then, we already have the Gospel. As lightning is greater than all fires and radium than all metals and as the missile flies faster than the poor savage's arrow, so is the Gospel greater than all other books.

"All the same, here is my letter. I write it trembling, feeling like a poor deaf-mute trying to make himself understood, or like Jeremiah who, when he was asked to preach, said to you, very reluctantly, 'Ah, Lord God, behold. I cannot speak: for I am a child.' "

To Charles Dickens he wrote: "In your day, social injustices were of a single kind—they were suffered by the workers who could accuse the employers. Today, all sorts of people accuse all sorts of others. Workers in the country say they are much less well paid than workers in industry. Here in Italy, the south is against the north. In Africa, Asia and Latin America, the nations of the Third World are against the rich nations.

"But even in the rich nations there are plenty of pockets of poverty and insecurity. Many workers are unemployed or uncertain of their jobs. They are not always protected properly against accidents. Often they feel they are treated merely as means of production, not as a central part of it.

"Then, too, the frantic rush to grow rich, and the exaggerated crazy use of unnecessary things has used up necessities—clear air and pure water, silence, inner peace, rest . . ."

In his letter to Pinocchio, John Paul recalled the pleasures of being a boy with the words: "You used to go and watch carriages arriving in the main square, and so did I. You wriggled and made faces and put your head under the bedclothes before taking a glass of nasty medicine and so did I. A slice of bread buttered on both sides, a sweet with a soft middle, a sugar lump and sometimes even an egg, or a pear, even the skin of a pear, were wonderful treats for the greedy, hungry boy you were. And so they were for me.

"I too was involved in fights on the way to and from school: with snowballs in winter and fisticuffs at every other season. I took a bit and gave a bit, trying to keep my end up and not cry when I got home, because if I'd complained they'd have certainly finished off what the others had started!"

As the shock waves of the Pope's death, the rumours and the truth, rolled through the close confines of the Vatican, there were some members of the hierarchy who felt concern for the Church itself. The celebrations, the joy surrounding the election of John Paul I a month earlier, had been an obscuring mist over the problems that beset the Church. Now the mist had been blown away. Young people were not being attracted into the Church to do its work, there was revolt from the right on some aspects of papal teaching and a radical, questioning movement by priests on the left. There was also the strain on Vatican coffers, with the cost of one papal funeral a few weeks earlier, followed by a conclave, and now it was to be repeated. The election of a new Pope does not come cheaply, there is no cut-price way around the affair. Some Vatican observers have put the cost of a conclave at between four and five million dollars, much of it going to pay bonuses to Vatican dependants each time a Pope dies and again when one is elected. Each employee, from cardinal to street cleaner, receives a bonus of $250. And then there is the cost of fares and accommodation for many of the 110 conclavists who cannot afford to pay themselves, as well as the expense of preparing the Sistine Chapel, the robes and the papal apartments.

A cardinal remarked later: "A mourning on top of another mourning—it is a very grave trial for the Church and we must truly pray. Who knows what awaits us now?"

And all those who wept that morning remembered that it had been only 33 days since Albino Luciani took the name of John Paul I.

They asked what had gone wrong. Was the strain of office too much? Was the task of being leader to the 700 million Roman Catholics of the world, of being the ruler of the Vatican, too arduous a task for any one man?

In some ways it is. As leader of the church he must consult, write, talk, teach, and make contact with Church hierarchy from around the world. He must tread the minefield of international diplomacy, must question, learn, face the rapidly changing patterns of science and patiently argue the position of the church to a political world that is frequently hostile. He must also pacify the conservatives within the Church who want no change and appease the radicals who have an entirely new vision of the future of Catholicism. It is not a task for those faint of heart.

The Pope must also rule Vatican City, an independent and sovereign state, which mints its own coins and prints stamps, and has its own yellow and white flag bearing the crossed keys and the tiara. It is even entitled to its own fleet, though the nearest water is the muddy flow of the Tiber.

Three thousand people work within the walls of the Vatican, although only a few live there or are citizens. The citizens are not born into the status, but are created because of the work they do or once did. All cardinals resident in Rome, whether employed or not, have citizenship, as do active members of the papal diplomatic corps and the Swiss Guards.

All these are the Pope's responsibility, although he does not attend to ordinary administrative details himself. The actual running of the state is in the hands of a commission of cardinals headed by the Cardinal Secretary of State who is assisted by a cardinal pro-president who follows the city's affairs on a daily basis. But Popes can and do make their wishes and their personality felt. They do take an interest in their state, in many of the hundreds of daily problems that arise in running what is virtually an independent country. It is a self-imposed burden to be added to the already excessive weight the Pope must carry as head of the Catholic Church.

The weight sometimes crushes completely.

It is also a lonely task. Even though the Lateran Treaty of 1939 between the church and the Italian Government allowed the Pope to move from the confines of the Vatican City, he could not travel with the freedom of the ordinary man. All was planned. All had to go through official channels.

Author Lawrence Elliott, in his book *I Will Be Called John*, tells of the problems caused when Pope John XXIII decided to slip out of the Vatican in his black Mercedes-Benz. Elliott quotes the Holy Father's chauffeur, Guido Gusso, as saying: "According to the rules, he was supposed to announce his intention of going out at least two hours in advance so that the *carabinieri* could be informed. But that meant that a big train of autos and motorcycle police would go with him and he didn't like that because then he would cause traffic jams and the police wouldn't let the people come near him and the monsignori were always rushing him to go back. What he liked was to stop at the red lights, like everyone else, and if it happened that the people recognised him he would wave and bless them. So sometimes, when he wanted to visit somebody, he quietly sent me for the car and we just went out by ourselves".

The same sense of frustration, of confinement, of loneliness, is expressed by Kiril I, the fictitious Pope in Morris West's penetrating look at pontifical life, *The Shoes of the Fisherman*. Kiril writes in his diary: "I find myself wishing for an agreeable companion to spend the vacation with me, but I have not yet found time to cultivate any real friendship. My isolation is all the greater because I am so much younger than the members of the Curia, and—God help me—I do not want to become an old man before my time. I understand now how some of my predecessors have lapsed into nepotism and surrounded themselves with relatives, and how others have cultivated favourites in the Vatican. It is not good for any man to be wholly alone ..."

John XXIII did much to break down the old rules that helped cause the isolation, that created a vast and unreal gulf between the Pope and even his most intimate aides. Before John XXIII wore the Ring of the Fisherman, the aides were required to drop to their knees each time they came into the Pope's presence. It was said in the time of Pius XII that officials knelt even when the Pope called them on the telephone.

"John could not abide that sort of exaggerated ceremony," Elliott wrote. "It ran counter to his Bergamesque sense of brotherhood and he was continually ordering people to their feet. When an aged reporter from *L'Osservatore Romano* assured him that he was perfectly comfortable conducting an interview from his knees, John threatened to leave the room unless the man sat in a chair".

John also detested the tradition that a Pope must eat alone, which was established centuries earlier to prevent gluttonous feasts. He changed this ritual after a week, saying: "I searched all through the sacred scripture for whatever it is that requires the Pope to eat alone and I found nothing. So now I have an occasional guest and am much more comfortable".

But there was still enough ritual, enough of the old ways, to cause John Paul I to be lonely. He often reached for the telephone as solace for his isolation. Almost every second day he telephoned Cardinal Pericle Felici, a man of wit and conversation. It made the isolation within the Apostolic Palace seem less.

At other times he called the mothers superior of religious orders for a chat, and would talk at length to priests and bishops. On one occasion a seminarian in Venice answered his telephone to find, to his astonishment, Pope John I on the other end of the line. The seminarian had written to John Paul long before he became Pope and the Holy Father used the letter as an excuse to make contact with an old familiar voice.

There was also the question of John Paul's health, whether he was strong enough to move from his diocese in Venice which had 600 000 Catholics to a position where he was leader of 700 million.

"His health has always caused concern," said his niece, Pia Luciani, several days after he was elected Pope. "He is delicate, but, I advise you, he is not a travelling hospital".

When he was born he was sickly and his parents summoned a priest to baptise him fearing he might not live through the day. He had been in a sanatorium twice for treatment of a lung condition, and underwent surgery four times: to remove his tonsils; to set a broken nose after a fall and twice for gallstones.

Only five days before his death, an old friend, Dr Antonio da Ros, who had treated the Pope for 20 years, warned him: "Holiness, you can't continue at this pace".

John Paul I shook his head. "What can I do? I can't do anything else".

And at his last public audience, where he appeared to be in good health, he told the sick who were among the crowd: "Know that the Pope understands and loves you. The Pope has been in the hospital eight times and has had four operations".

He worked hard and he expected Vatican officials to be early at their desks and work with equal fervour. So began his last day—28 September 1978.

He arose at five a.m., attended Mass, had breakfast and, after working in his bedroom until eight a.m., went down to his office for the start of his official day. Another demanding papal day.

He met in private audience the Most Reverend Carmine Rocco, of Brazil, the Most Reverend John Gordon, titular Archbishop of Nicopolis ad Nestum, Cardinal Bernardin Gantin, president of the Pontifical Commission of Justice and Peace, the Reverend Roger Heckel, secretary of the Justice and Peace Commission and the Reverend Henri de Riedmatten, secretary of the Vatican's charity council.

"Pope John Paul looked quite well," de Riedmatten said later. "He spoke a lot about the need for all Catholics to put up all possible efforts to promote justice and peace in the Christian way. He insisted that priority must be given to evangelisation, to spreading the message of Christ."

Then ushered into his presence was a group of bishops from the Philippines, led by Cardinal Julio Rosales, Archbishop of Cebu, who were making their *ad limina*, the modern day version of the old pilgrimage to the tombs of St Peter and St Paul in Rome.

John Paul I said in halting English: "In welcoming you with deep affection, we wish to recall a passage found in the Breviary. This passage has struck us forcefully. It concerns Christ and was spoken by Paul VI on his visit to the Philippines. 'I must bear witness to his name: Jesus is the Christ, the Son of the living God. He is the king of the new world; He is the secret of history; He is the key to our destiny'.

"On our part we hope to sustain you, support you, and encourage you in the great mission of the episcopate: to proclaim Jesus Christ and to evangelise His people. Among the rights of the faithful, one of the greatest is the right to receive God's word in all its entirety and purity, with all its exigencies and power. A great challenge of our day is the full evangelisation of all those who have been baptised. In this, the Bishops of the Church have a prime responsibility. Our message must be a clear proclamation of salvation in Jesus Christ. With Peter we must say to Christ in the presence of our people: 'You have the words of eternal life'."

He paused briefly, but there was no strain showing on his face, only the smile that had become familiar to millions. Then he went on, carefully selecting the correct English pronunciation from the catalogue of his mind: "For us, evangelisation involves an explicit teaching about the name of Jesus, His identity, His teaching, His Kingdom and His promises. And His chief promise is eternal life. Jesus truly has words that lead us to eternal life. Just recently at a general audience we spoke to the faithful about eternal life. We are convinced that it is necessary for us to emphasise this element,

The house in Wadowice where Karol Wojtyla
(John Paul II) was born.

in order to complete our message and to model our teaching on that of Jesus.

"From the days of the Gospel, and in imitation of the Lord who 'went about doing good' the Church is irrevocably committed to the relief of physical misery and need. But her pastoral charity would be incomplete if she did not point out even 'higher deeds'. In the Philippines Paul VI did precisely this. At a moment when he chose to speak about the poor, about justice and peace, about human rights, about economic and social liberation—at a moment when he also effectively committed the Church to the alleviation of misery he did not and could not remain silent about the 'higher good', the fullness of life in the Kingdom of Heaven."

John Paul looked at the faces before him, the representatives of the Church in the most Catholic of countries in South-East Asia, and for a moment pondered the way the Church had spread throughout the world. It also made communication difficult. Did not the Almighty strike at the Tower of Babel to undo the ungodly and not to hinder those who were attempting to spread His word?

"More than ever before," he continued, slowly, "we must help our people to realise just how much they need Jesus Christ, the Son of God and the Son of Mary. He is their Saviour, the key to their destiny and to the destiny of all humanity.

"Dear brothers, we are spiritually close to you in all the efforts you are making on behalf of evangelisation; as you train catechists, as you promote the biblical apostolate, as you assist and encourage all your priests in their great mission at the service of God's word, and as you lead all your faithful to understand and to fulfill the requirements of justice and Christian love. We greatly esteem these and all your endeavours on behalf of the Kingdom of God. In particular, we fully support the affirmation of the missionary vocation, and earnestly hope that it will flourish among our youth.

"We are aware that the Philippines has a great vocation in being the light of Christ in the Far East: to proclaim His truth, His love, His justice and salvation by word and example before its neighbours, the peoples of Asia. We know that you have a privileged instrument in this regard: Radio Veritas. It is our hope that the Philippines will use this great means and every other means to proclaim with the entire Church that Jesus Christ is the Son of God and Saviour of the world.

"Our greetings go to all your local Churches, especially to the priests and religious. We encourage them to even greater holiness of life as a condition for the supernatural effectiveness of their apostolate. We love and bless the families of your dioceses and all the laity. We ask the sick and the handi-

The Black Madonna at Jasna Gora
Monastery...Poland's holiest relic.

capped to understand their important part in God's plan, and to realise just how much evangelisation depends on them.

"To all of you, brothers, we impart our special apostolic blessing, invoking upon you joy and strength in Jesus Christ."

Cardinal Rosales broke the language barrier by speaking in Italian in his reply, an action which delighted the Pope, and then the church leaders filed out to continue their rounds of the Vatican. John Paul I had less than twelve hours to live.

He ate lunch, meagre as were all his midday meals, then retired to the plain wooden bed in his room for a siesta. Not even the vast amount of work placed before a Pontiff can take away the custom of Italy, born of hot impossible summer days and carried through in Rome to the cooler autumn weeks. After his siesta he spoke by telephone to Cardinal Giovanni Colombo and talked business in his office with Cardinal Sebastiano Baggio, head of the Congregation for Bishops.

As was the custom, he met with Cardinal Villot at seven thirty to discuss the routine business of the Vatican. Villot was to recall later that the Pope showed no signs of fatigue. John Paul I then went to the chapel for evening prayer and as he bade staff members goodnight, he was told of yet another political killing in Rome, where so much blood had been spilled on the streets over the last two years in the name of hopeless causes and insane dreams. The latest death was that of a Communist youth who had been killed in an ambush by Fascists.

John Paul shook his head, saying sadly: "They kill each other—even the young people".

No one would hear John Paul I speak again. He went to bed to work on papers and there he died.

Cardinal Villot knew the routine of a papal death and, sadly, knew it too well for not two months had passed since the last time he had assumed the title and responsibilities of Camerlengo of the Holy Roman Church following the death of Paul VI. A tall, widely-travelled and well-read man, Villot was once described by a Vatican observer as being "exasperatingly courteous in the French manner, insistingly righteous, efficient, with his own lines of communication to France, progressive, tolerant of weakness, humanistic".

Villot held considerable power in his elegant hands in his position of Secretary of State. He was also Prefect of the Council for the External Affairs of the Church; a member of the Congregations for the Doctrine of the Faith, for the Bishops, for the Evangelisation of Peoples (Propaganda Fide), for the Causes of Saints; of the Commissions for the Revision of the Code of

Canon Law, for the Revision of the Code of Eastern Canon Law, and of the Cardinal Overseers of the Institute for Works of Religion, one of the major financial institutions of the Vatican.

But they were only titles at this time. They said nothing about the deep personal feelings he had for John Paul, for the loyalty and compassion and devotion that were part of his complex character.

There was a list of people that had to be informed of the Pope's death, the first two being the Dean of the Sacred College, Cardinal Carlo Confalonieri, and the Pope's Vicar for the city of Rome, Cardinal Ugo Poletti. Cardinal Confalonieri would, in turn, call a meeting of those cardinals in Rome. It would be held at eleven o'clock that morning.

The cardinals around the world would have to be summoned to Rome for the funeral and the conclave to elect the 264th successor to St Peter. The traditional novena of Masses for the dead Pontiff, the *novendiales*, beginning with the funeral Mass, *praesente cadavere*, would have to be organised. There were special medals to be struck, orders to be given to close the great, heavy bronze doors of St Peter's, a traditional symbol of the death of a Pope, and to suspend, as again tradition dictated, all the officials appointed by John Paul.

And the world had to be told. Little more than an hour had passed since the Pope's body was found, and later blessed by the Pope's Vicar for the Vatican City, Monsignor Canisio van Lierde, yet only those within the walls of the Apostolic Palace were aware of the drama taking place.

A carefully worded statement was prepared in that curiously stilted language that stamps official Vatican releases. It read: "This morning, 29 September 1978, about five thirty, the private secretary of the Pope, contrary to custom not having found the Holy Father in the chapel of his private apartment, looked for him in his room and found him dead in bed with the light on, like one who was intent on reading. The physician, Dr Renato Buzzonnetti, who hastened at once, verified the death as having presumably taken place around eleven o'clock yesterday evening through an acute coronary thrombosis".

The news was to be released through Vatican Radio but at seven thirty-one on Italian Radio channel Two, the noted broadcaster, Gustavo Selvo, cut short an important story on the Red Brigade to say: "We interrupt the broadcast to bring you grave news . . ."

At seven forty-two Vatican Radio made the official announcement.

Within hours all the cardinals of the world would know, within hours the radical Cardinal Paulo Arns, with the world's biggest diocese of six million people in Brazil, would be in mourning, as would the conservative Cardinal John Carberry, of the United States. Cardinal Stephen Kim, who had bravely stood up to the corrupt South Korean government, would hear the announcement in Seoul. It would be heard in Nigeria by Cardinal Dominic Ekandem, the first cardinal to be appointed in that West African country. They would hear the news and mourn and perhaps feel troubled within as they considered the effect of the Pope's death on the stability of the church.

The world leaders were informed and later sent their carefully prepared messages of sympathy, so many sounding as though they had come from a text book on foreign diplomacy and not from the heart. Said the President of the United States, Jimmy Carter: "He held out the promise of combining his predecessors' finest qualities, reaffirming what is enduring and strong in the Catholic tradition, while expanding the frontiers of the Church to cope with the needs of the modern world." From Buckingham Palace in London, Queen Elizabeth II said: "Although he was such a short time in the High Office to which he had been called, the humility and kindness shown by His Holiness will remain a lasting and inspiring memory." The President of Israel, Yitzhak Navon, referred to his "promising pontificate" and King Hussein I of Jordan mentioned "the noble objectives he aspired to".

And the ordinary people throughout the world, those who followed the teachings of the Church, who believed without question, were not ashamed to shed tears when they heard the announcement. Thirty people were attending Mass in John Paul's home village of Canale de Agardo when the parish priest, Father Aldrich, interrupted the service to announce the Pope's death. Then he rang the bells of his church to spread the unhappy news, and the village wept.

Soon the bells would also be tolling at St Peter's, the heart of the Catholic empire, and the people, many red-eyed from tears, would move quietly into the vast square and begin their vigil of death.

It was eight a.m. in the Metropolitan Curia of Krakow, an old building of high ceilings and creaking wooden parquet floors on Franciszkanska St, now busy with bustling little Polish-built Fiats and swaying tram cars. Cardinal Karol Wojtyla had been up since six a.m. and, after Mass in his private chapel, had gone for breakfast, arriving at the table a few minutes before eight o'clock.

At eight o'clock he was told that John Paul I had died. Pushing aside the eggs he was eating, he stood up, his face bleached of colour, his hands trembling. Then he walked quickly to his private chapel, closed the door behind him and knelt in solitary prayer. He asked for God's help in the days to come, help he needed to face the future because he was privy to a secret known only to a few. And with this knowledge he knew it was possible that never again would he be able to tramp and ski through his beloved Tatra Mountains or canoe across the cold and clear waters of the Mazurin Lakes.

It was possible he would never again see Poland.

CHAPTER TWO

Wadowice, a town of 14 000, is not a place where a tourist would bother to stop, unless he or she had become confused by the narrow roads and unfathomable direction signs and was lost. Fifty kilometres from the historically important city of Krakow, centre of intellectual thought, heartbeat of dissent, the town of Wadowice has little to attract the cameras of the tourist. It is built around a square, planted with fir and birch trees, surrounded by frowning old buildings painted in watery pastels, and smelling of good borstch, bad coffee and dampness.

Dominating the square, as they dominate even the meanest of villages in Poland, is a Catholic Church. For 650 years it has been a part of the town's life, the most vital part, and each Sunday morning the townspeople and those from the small landholdings surrounding Wadowice have come, well-scrubbed, squeezed into their best clothes, to worship. They would overflow the church as they listened, almost in awe, to the sermons.

St Mary's Church in Wadowice was, on Sunday, like every other church in this passionately religious country; packed tight with the faithful who resemble sardines in a can of disproportionate splendour.

But now the church in the square of Wadowice has taken on a new significance, a sudden sense of importance in the traditions and truth of the Catholic Church. People stand, some quietly, others chattering excitedly, before its gray facade, look up at the onion-topped tower with its clock chiming each quarter hour, gaze intensely as though expecting an immediate miracle or, at least, some small confirmation of their faith.

For this is the church where Pope John Paul II, when he was Karol Wojtyla, was first introduced to Catholic faith. Now it has become a place almost of adoration, attracting people from around the world. From a nun standing outside the church, trying to ignore the winter cold that lies like a solid block of ice from the ground to the leaden sky, they buy small colour portraits of John Paul II and some of the recklessly-coloured religious souvenirs that sell throughout the land. The manufacture of these must be Poland's biggest unheralded industry.

Then they walk a few yards to No. 7 Koscielna Street, the house where Wojtyla was born.

Three old ladies, their faces beneath their shawls lined by the years, cackle with excitement as they point the house to visitors and say: "That's where our Lolek lived". Lolek is a form of endearment reserved for those who grew up with Wojtyla, or have earned it by right of age.

Their help is unnecessary because Wojtyla's birthplace stands out in Wadowice like a travelling carnival after it sets up in a town. From the side of the building, flags in the red and white colours of Poland and the

St Mary's Church at Wadowice where Karol Wojtyla first received religious instruction.

yellow and white of the Vatican droop in the still, frozen air. A window on the ground floor has been dressed, in childish but earnest fashion, with twinkling lights, coloured ribbons, white carnations, a picture of John Paul II and a placard bearing the words:

OTO DOM
URODZENIA
KAROLA WOJTYLY
JANA PAWLA II

(This is the house of birth of Karol Wojtyla, John Paul II).

Over the doorway leading into a bare concrete courtyard are fir branches and red ribbons and a notice proclaiming: "In this house AD 1920 was born His Holiness John Paul II".

The house has recently been repainted in pale lemon and light fawn, a redecorating decision made after considerable soul-searching by the Wadowice city council. After all, the members of the council were good party members—in fact Wadowice has a surprisingly high number of party members, about 3000—and they were uncertain whether the atheistic State would take kindly to money being spent on the birthplace of the Vicar of Jesus Christ. But local pride, and the fact that Wadowice was immediately invaded by scores of journalists, prompted them to order the painters to do the job.

The outside has been painted, but inside the house is still peasant-poor and shabby. Mrs Jozefa Pindel, who lives there now, apologised for its appearance.

"The house does not look so good here in the courtyard," she said, pointing to bare concrete stairs leading up to the first floor apartment where the Wojtyla family once lived. "The city council should do something to make it more beautiful.

"There are people coming here now from all over the world. They have been coming ever since the great day when Lolek was elected. They arrive by car and by bus. Only last week some people from the Philippines came to see the house."

After studying the house, and possibly finding it no more inspirational than the other drab dwellings of Wadowice, the devout visitor can walk around the church to the parish office which proclaims its connections with John Paul II with photographs of the pontiff displayed in a glass case outside the front door. And if they are fortunate, if he is not swamped by letters from around the world, many from people who themselves were born in Wadowice, a prelate, Dr Edward Zachar, might show them the parish register which, in a few hand-written entries, covers the life and times of Karol Wojtyla: Born 18 May 1920; baptised 20 June 1920; ordained priest 1 November 1946; consecrated a bishop 28 September 1958; made an archbishop 30 December 1963; became a cardinal 9 May 1967, and elected Pope 16 October 1978.

In a few words, that is Wojtyla's history, a few strokes of the pen to record more than half a century of life, but in reality it is necessary to go back 1000 years to know the man. That is the Polish way. As an observer once said of Poland, whenever a Pole wants to explain some aspect of his work, or of the present situation, he starts, as a rule, by talking about Polish history.

The history of Christianity can be seen in the buildings that still stand in Poland; it speaks from old stone walls, yellow and stained by the ages, from ornately carved tombs, from the spiky monuments to never-forgotten martyrs, from the cold and beautiful marble beneath the feet, from such places as the Benedict Abbey of Tyniec, standing high on a hill in a little village half an hour's drive from Krakow. Excavations at the abbey in 1961 brought to light the remains of the abbots, one of whom held a paten of pure gold. The carving on it showed it dated from the 10th century.

The year, 966, is generally accepted as the date when the Slavic tribes of Poland accepted Christianity, their conversion following the marriage of Mieszko I, leader of the people living in the Vistula and Oder valleys, to a Czech Christian princess. The marriage was one of military convenience, not the first nor the last time that religion and politics have joined hands for the benefit of both.

Mieszko was not lacking in intelligence or cunning and knew that his best chance of survival in a warring Europe was to acknowledge the special position held in Christendom by Otto I as Emperor.

As Jerzy Dowiat emphasises in his work, *The Baptism of Poland*, Mieszko's main aim was to build up a separate Church organisation accountable only to the Pope in religious matters and himself in political matters.

"Following the conversion to Christianity of the Polish rulers, Poland joined the group of western and central European countries comprising the sphere of influence of the Roman Church. There was no room here for any country which refused to recognise Latin Christianity. Therefore for Mieszko too the choice was simple: either to become, sooner or later, the object of attack by powerful neighbours, or to take part himself in European politics. By accepting Christianity, he took the latter course, as this act brought him closer to such figures as the Pope and the Emperor, and gave him the surname 'The Emperor's Friend.' "

Born out of political expediency, the Church soon flourished with the people taking enthusiastically to the new religion, throwing out their old pagan gods, although keeping some traditions, and embracing the new God who, in those days, seemed to live entirely in Rome. Mieszko's successor in the Piast dynasty, Boleslaw the Lion-hearted, was just as wily and continued the trend. Missionaries travelled the land spreading the word which Boleslaw the Lion-hearted saw, quite reasonably, as a way of uniting his country, of dousing the fiery tribal arguments, and of serving the interests of the state.

Adam Piekarski, in his history, *The Church in Poland*, points out that in Poland, like other Christian countries, the main motive for baptism in those days was submission to the royal will.

"The baptised population nevertheless continued to live according to the old customs and to retain the old rites enriched only by the worship of Christ, who frequently replaced the old tribal gods. For this reason, the Piast state not only financed Church activity but also assisted it in enforcing Church regulations, particularly those regarding fasts, the observance of Sundays and holy days, penance, and the like".

There were some setbacks to the Christian religion in the beginning of the 11th century, mainly due to internal squabbling and a number of people who pined for the old gods and the old ways and weren't even sure where Rome was anyway. Nor could they comprehend the Pope.

Matters became even more difficult when in 1079 the Polish king, Boleslaw the Bold, had an argument with Stanislaw Szczepanowski, Bishop of Krakow, which he concluded by having the church leader chopped into small pieces. The bishop, a conservative man, had criticized the king's expansionist policies and had waved a disapproving finger at what he considered were the ruler's immoral ways.

This action by Boleslaw the Bold helped him not one whit in the business of public relations, as the early historian, Gallus Anonymous, noted: "This harmed him (Boleslaw) greatly, when he gave a sin for a sin, when for treason he sent the bishop to have his limbs chopped off. For we neither absolve the treachery of the bishop, nor approve of the king's taking vengeance so hideously".

The bishop's body was carried to a little church in Krakow, where once had stood a heathen temple. It is now called Skalka, the original structure having been replaced by a baroque church which contains the block on which Bishop Szczepanowski was dismembered. It is inscribed with the words: *Siste gradum divus tinxit me sanguine praesul.* (Stop, you passerby, the Saint bishop bespattered me with his blood.) Two hundred years later the bishop was proclaimed a saint, a patron of Poland, and at Skalka, at the memorial to St Stanislaw, the young Karol Wojtyla spent many hours in prayer.

The influence of the Church, no doubt helped by the martyrdom of Bishop Szczepanowski, spread and by the 12th century there were nearly 1000 churches in Poland, with a network of bishoprics covering the land. One hundred years later there were 21 dioceses within the borders of Poland. The entire country prospered, reaching in the 15th century what has been called its "Golden Age".

Professor M. K. Dziewanowski, in his book, *Poland in the 20th Century*, describes Poland as then attaining a high level of cultural development "stimulated in part by the new spirit of Renaissance humanism then penetrating from Italy, and by the intellectual ferment stemming from the Protestant Reformation. The royal capital of Krakow became a cultural and political centre of considerable importance. Throughout the 16th century the University of Krakow was overflowing with students, most of whom came from poor families. The sons of the wealthy were able to travel abroad to attend the famous universities of western Europe, especially those of Paris, Padua and Bologna. The University of Krakow, where the great astrologer Nicholas Copernicus studied, spread its influence over the whole of central and eastern Europe".

So progressive was the country that in 1523 Erasmus of Rotterdam felt compelled, albeit a trifle condescendingly, to write: "I congratulate this nation which used to have a bad reputation for its barbarity and which now, in sciences, jurisprudence, morals and religion, and all that separates us from barbarism, is so flourishing that it can rival the first and most glorious of nations".

But throughout Catholic Europe things were changing, the Church was under attack from those seeking reform, especially of papal power and corruption among some members of the hierarchy, and Martin Luther was soon to nail his Theses to the door of Wittenburg Cathedral. Already the influence of the reformist preacher, John Huss, had spread from Prague through Poland and the Taborites, a radical movement that broke away from the Hussites, gained a reasonable following among Poles, especially those of the peasant class. Monasteries were attacked and inquisitors assaulted, but the Taborites were finally beaten in the Battle of Lipany.

However, Poland remained Catholic overall, even staunchly so, and at the same time showed a remarkable degree of tolerance in a Europe where heretics died in flames at the stake or were torn apart on monstrous racks. The country became a haven for those who disagreed with the dogmas of Rome, and no person, no matter what his or her religious belief, was prosecuted, let alone persecuted. Freedom of religion, always accepted, became the law of the land in 1572.

"I would" said the then chancellor of the realm, Jan Zamoyski, "have half of my life if those who have abandoned the Roman Catholic Church would voluntarily return to its vale: but I would prefer giving all my life than to suffer anybody to be constrained to do it, for I would rather die than witness such an oppression".

Furthermore, in Poland non-Christians such as Jews were allowed the freedom they could not find in many other European countries. Thousands found a refuge there after they were driven out of Germany by persecution. King Casimir the Great, in fact, placed Jews under the special protection of the crown. It is an important point because in more recent Polish history there have been accusations of strong anti-semitism in Poland, some of it true, some based on the understandable paranoia developing after the horror of such hells as Auschwitz, some of it a part of Stalin's baneful influence, some of it false.

But later in the 17th century the overall attitude of tolerance changed, not the least reason being the help given by members of Protestant sects to the invading armies of Sweden. Many Poles came to believe that non-Catholic groups were untrustworthy, that only through the Catholic religion could there be national unity. And then after a series of wars the country was divided between Prussia, Russia and Austria. At this time there were many who believed that the Holy See in Rome virtually deserted Catholic Poland, that the country no longer counted as a political factor in the Vatican's plans. Also some of the higher clergy were only too willing to help Tsarist Russia, even though the invaders were of the Orthodox belief.

When General Tadeusz Kosciuszko, a national hero after whom the highest mountain in Australia has been named, lead a popular uprising in 1794 and declared the freedom of all peasants, the people of Warsaw condemned to death the bishops they believed had betrayed the national cause. Bishop Jozef Kossakowski and Bishop Ignacy Massalski were hanged at the gallows and the primate Michal Poniatowski, accused of spying, committed suicide. Understandably upset by the unseemly demise of some of its leaders in Poland, the Vatican issued a special papal epistle (breve) welcoming the collapse of the Kosciuszko insurrection and calling for allegiance to the Prussian king.

Adam Piekarski, in *The Church in Poland*, argues that Rome's friendly attitude to non-Catholic states at the expense of Catholic Poland resulted "from the fear of social revolution". It should be noted that Piekarski's history of the Church in Poland was published by an official organisation of the present Communist state.

He adds: "Notwithstanding Rome's conciliatory policies towards the partitioning powers, the latter proceeded to curtail Church activities or even abolish them altogether. In the Austrian-held territory religious orders began to be abolished and seminaries were put under government control.

"In the Prussian-held territory, Church property was taken and put under state administration, while dioceses were entrusted to subordinates of the Prussian king. The German language was introduced into Jesuit colleges, which were turned into government schools intended to train Catholic clergy committed to Prussia. Church services began to be delivered in German, but this met with the resistance of the Polish clergy as well as that of congregations and had little success.

"Catherine II forbade the promulgation of any Church ordinances without her consent, personally reorganised the bishoprics, and by various means of coercion restricted or totally abolished the operation of the Greek Orthodox and Uniate churches. Some members of the episcopate received a regular salary from the Empress."

In spite of the attitude of Rome, the people of Poland still remained faithful to the Catholic Church, as well as fiercely determined to regain their independence. Resistance to the Russian regime grew and the Church became the focal point of it. Churches were often packed with people singing patriotic songs and expressing sentiments not likely to amuse the leaders of Russia. In 1861 Russian troops entered several churches in Warsaw and beat the parishioners with rifle butts, as well as arresting them. There were more uprisings as the struggle for independence grew stronger, more violent, more bloody, ending in the doomed uprising of 1863–64...

The defeat of the Polish people in the uprising was, writes Professor Dziewanowski, a "milestone in Polish history, the dying gasp of the old Romantic Poland. Following the suppression of the revolt, the last remnant of autonomy that Russian Poland had enjoyed between 1832 and 1864 was abolished. The so-called committee of reconstruction set to work reshaping the administrative structure of the country, with civilian and military power united in the hands of a Russian governor general.

"Garrisons numbering up to 300 000 soldiers were quartered in a country of some seven million people. Russian was made the official language, and Polish law courts and schools were supplanted by the Russian system and staffed with officials from distant parts of the Tsarist empire. In 1869 the University of Warsaw was closed, and in 1886 the Polish bank was made into a branch of the St Petersburg State Bank. The very name of Poland was abolished and replaced by the new term, Vistula Land."

In the Prussian-controlled areas of Poland, the people were determined not to become mere citizens of German provinces. They formed their own farming co-operatives, their own banks, their own newspaper. These efforts at self-identity infuriated the German leader, Otto von Bismarck, and he began to pour more money into the country in an attempt to completely colonise it through economics. The Poles responded by displaying even more religious and national zeal.

But all that changed when the Serbian student, Gavrilo Princip, assassinated the Austrian archduke, Francis Ferdinand, and Europe was consumed by the flames of World War I. After the fires had burned out, the smoke cleared, the bodies counted, the dead mourned, the complex and bitter arguments over borders and territory at least partly resolved, President Woodrow Wilson of the United States was able to proclaim on 8 January 1918: "An independent Polish state should be erected, which would include the territories inhabited by indisputably Polish populations, which would be assured a free and easy access to the sea, and whose political and economic independence and territorial integrity should be guaranteed by international covenant".

Fine sounding words they were, but in some quarters they carried little weight. All western Poland was still controlled by Germany, and then the Bolshevik Army advanced on the east, taking a further slice of Polish territory. Poland was still searching for its proclaimed borders even as they were being smothered by invaders. Nor was the internal situation one that contributed towards stability.

Professor Dziewanowski described it thus: "The war had ruined Poland economically and left behind a sediment of bitterness and pent-up hatred. Many factories had been dismantled and sent to Germany. With the cessation of hostilities more industries were suddenly closed down, throwing large numbers of unemployed workers into the streets to demonstrate their wrath. Inflation, profiteering and black marketing were rampant. The prolonged

industrial unemployment resulted in appalling pauperisation and subsequent radicalisation of the working class. Moreover, a large part of the
Polish labour force was still abroad, evacuated to Russia in 1915 or forcibly
deported to Germany between 1916 and 1918. Some of the returning workers
were not only swelling the ranks of the unemployed but were preaching
the dictatorship of the proletariat. Consequently, the country was passing
through a period of economic chaos and social conflict, in some ways not
much less acute than that of Russia or Germany".

In other words Poland was ready for Communist revolution.

In 1920 the Red Army was advancing on Warsaw and there were many
observers in the West who had already consigned Poland to the rapidly swelling grab-bag of Communist nations. Stalin had his vision of a partly Communist Europe and writing to Lenin he said: "For the nations which
formerly belonged to old Russia our (Soviet) type of federation may and
ought to be considered as leading towards unity. The motives are obvious:
either these nations had no independent existence of their own, or they lost
it a long time ago; that is why they would be willing to accept without
much friction our Soviet (centralised) type of federation. The same cannot
be said of nations which did not make up part of the old Russia, which
existed as independent states. But if such states became Soviet states, they
would have to establish some sort of relations with Russia. I am speaking
of a future Soviet Germany, Poland and Hungary. It is doubtful whether
those people which have their own governments, their own armies, their
finances, would agree, even if they became Soviet states, to establish with
us a federal union of that type which links us now with the Bashkirs or
the Ukrainians . . . They would consider federation of our Soviet type as
diminishing their national and state independence . . . On the other hand,
I do not doubt that for those nations a confederation would be the most
acceptable form of relations with us".

But the Poles were not ready or willing to be taken over. Stalin would
have to wait for another world war before he saw his dream of a Communist
Poland turn into reality. The Poles, under the leadership of Jozef Pilsudski,
defeated the Red Army at Warsaw, the first Polish victory in more than
two and a half centuries.

The country was ravaged, the people were in a poor condition, in fact
described by a visiting British diplomat as being "ragged, thin and anaemic,
with sunken cheeks and great hollow eyes", and the land tired and battered
by war. But a great part of the country was now free; 123 years of foreign
rule had ended.

It was into this uncertain and troubled world, in the upstairs apartment
of 7 Koscielna Street, Wadowice, that Karol Wojtyla was born on 18 May
1920.

CHAPTER THREE

"They must build a monument to him in the place where he was born. For what has happened has been the greatest event in Poland for 100 years."

So spoke a man of Wadowice. In his enthusiasm over a Polish cardinal who had become Pope, he dismissed the historical events that have moulded Poland into what it is today, the two world wars that tore the heart out of the country, the revolutions, successful and otherwise, the suffering, the bloodshed in the streets, the various shades, both harsh and soft, of Communist rule. Only of importance was the fact that in Wadowice, a town graced by little that has been eventful, the man destined to be a pope was born on 18 May 1920.

Karol Wojtyla came into a poor family. His father, also Karol, was a retired lieutenant of the Corps of Supplies, first in the Imperial Austro-Hungarian Army, then the Polish Army. His pension did not allow for any luxuries for the young Wojtyla, his mother Emilia (nee Kaszorowska) or a much older brother, Edmund, who became a medical doctor. Edmund died when Wojtyla was still a boy, having caught scarlet fever from a patient.

Wojtyla's father was a cultured man—"a nice and good man", as he has been described—who was deeply religious. Their home, on the first floor of 7 Koscielna Street, lay within the shadow of St Mary's Church, then 600 years old, and Wojtyla's first memories were of the bells tolling for the Sunday Mass, the crowds pouring along the cobbled streets to the baroque front doors.

Wotjyla had but to cross the street to join the throng. He later became an altar boy at the church and Jozef Drewniak, a singer and actor now living in Australia, remembers him as organising the other boys in their duties. "He was four years older than I but I can recall him looking after the roster of altar boys, organising them to do the correct things. Even when he was young he had a very strong personality and all the other boys looked up to him as an example."

Sometimes his father would don his army uniform when he escorted his son to church, or when they strolled the streets together, which are the first memories the Chancellor of the Metropolitan Curia in Krakow, Mikolaj Kuczkowski, has of him. "I did not pay much attention to him as a boy but I remember him walking with his father who was in uniform. They always made a fine pair."

Wadowice was in those days a quiet place—as it remains today—a town of 8000, the centre of an agricultural district made up of a patch-work of pocket-sized farms, and inhabited by clerks, tradesmen and small business

Karol Wojtyla with his mother Emilia Wojtyla.

The birth registry in Wadowice showing the history of Karol Wojtyla from his birth to his election as Pope.

Karol Wojtyla with his father, Karol.

Karol Wojtyla as an altar boy (second from the left in the first row).

owners. School began at eight a.m. and those who were altar boys had to sprint from the church after the seven a.m. Mass to get to school on time. Each class was 55 minutes, with a five minute break between, and school lasted until four p.m. Then the children did their homework or were expected to help their mother in the house, or often their father in the fields or at his business.

After their duties, especially in the long summer twilights when the air was heavy with the scent of fir and birch, they played football or palant, a game in which a stick was bounced up into the air and hit by another stick. Wojtyla excelled at these games. In football he always played in the position of goal-keeper. Frequently the boys practised their footwork with the ball on the street beside the church, an activity that caused much irritation to the parish priest. When the ball slammed against the wall of the church, he would run, cassock flying, through the front door and shout: "Get off with you! Play somewhere else!" In summer they swam in the cool waters of the mountain-fed River Skawa, but it was the long winters, when Wadowice lay buried beneath snow, that Wojtyla loved most because he could go skiing in the hills around the town. His delight in skiing, his pleasure at feeling the snow swish beneath his feet, the cold air bite into his face, was one that never left him. There was something about the purity of snow that forever appealed to him.

At the age of nine Wojtyla's mother died. It was a blow to the boy, and according to Monsignor Kazimierz Figlewicz, at Wawel Cathedral in Krakow, who knew him from his earliest days, "one could look close at him and find traces of the experience". But the death brought Wojtyla closer to his father and they became more like friends than parent and child.

Because he was born when his parents were middle-aged, Wojtyla was always surrounded by old people and this tended to make him precocious, and pushed him towards an earlier maturity. But Lolek, as he was called by his friends, was not a spoilt brat. His father saw to that.

"It was another style before the war," recalls Boguslaw Banas, an old friend. "Fathers used their belts in those days. They didn't have to talk—just a look was enough. Lolek's father was a strict disciplinarian. We all used to walk like circus ponies."

After school Wojtyla would often go to the little basement cafe run by Banas' mother, and they would play together for a while before Karol went home for more studies and the dinner prepared by his father. And then, like a ritual, the two, the young boy and the old retired army officer, would stroll along the streets of Wadowice, a couple noticed and looked upon with fondness by many. Karol would go to bed early because each morning he was at church for the seven o'clock Mass. And he was never late.

While Wojtyla was discovering life, was enjoying the infinite pleasures of boyhood, his country was attempting to chart a course through the sometimes choppy seas of its new independence. The right wing parties, the National Democrats and the Christian Democrats, were seen by some as

The ancient Benedictine Monastery, one of the oldest buildings in Poland, at Tyniec, near Krakow.

*Children outside the Cloth Hall in Krakow's
main square.*

being too authoritarian. The leftist parties, lead by the Polish Socialist Party, were seeking reforms, especially in the agrarian sphere. The Church, trying to stay aloof, had been granted a privileged position in the Constitution of March 1921, which guaranteed equality and religious freedom to all, but stated specifically that the Roman Catholic Church would hold the "foremost" place among the religions. Four years later a concordat was signed between the Polish Republic and the Holy See in Rome. It was agreed to only after stormy scenes in Parliament where many deputies argued that the concordat would impose significant limitations on state laws. As well as guaranteeing the Catholic Church full freedom, it imposed limits on the taxation of Church property, allowed clergymen special legal protection and exemption from military service, and made the teaching of religion obligatory in schools below the university level.

It was a major boost for the Church in Poland. And it kept its position after the May 1926 coup d'etat of Marshal Jozef Pilsudski who, backed by left-leaning groups, and frustrated by the attempts of the rightist parties to keep him out of power, challenged the government by force of arms.

Pilsudski had hoped he could overthrow the government by appearing in Warsaw at the head of military units loyal to him. He believed the show of arms would be enough to force the government to capitulate, but it took a bloody, three-day struggle in the streets of the capital before he achieved victory.

The hierarchy of the Catholic Church stayed neutral as far as Pilsudski was concerned, although some of the more conservative members of the clergy accused the new government of being too radical and—greatest sin of all—having leanings towards the hated Masonic movement.

Also growing slowly in strength at that time, although by no means yet a danger to the Catholic Church, was the Communist Party of Poland. Unfortunately for the party, it had decided to follow the theories of Rosa Luxemburg which denied the existence of the Polish Republic and instead wanted the country merged with the USSR with some parts returned to Germany. Several deputies representing the Communist Party were elected to parliament but in 1926 the party was declared illegal. The Church would not have a major confrontation with Communism in Poland until after World War II.

By the time he was 11 and was attending secondary school, Wojtyla had emerged as possibly the brightest young intellect in Wadowice. "He was the best pupil at school", says Dr Edward Zachar, who taught him religious instruction, "his marks were not only very good, they were a mark higher. I would call him an ideal pupil. I used to do the notices for the pupils who were charged with bad behaviour. But not even once was Karol's name there".

As he grew up he became increasingly involved with the rituals and traditions of the Catholic Church in Poland, with the zeal the people displayed in their faith, the passion they showed when they became involved in important religious festivals. One such event attended by the young Wojtyla took place, as it had done for almost 400 years, in green hills not far from Krakow. It is the "new Jerusalem" of Poland, and became a part of Church lore on Good Friday, 1595, when a woman had a vision in which she saw Christ crucified between two thieves. Her husband conceived a plan in which the holy places of Jerusalem could be reconstructed in the area and so was founded Kalwaria Zedryzdowska.

Each Easter almost 100 000 people cram into the village, to see and take part in the Passion Play, putting up with atrocious conditions, housed in primitive fashion, eating only the most basic of food, for there is no other available, and cheerfully enduring rain, sometimes sleet and snow, and the cold and the mud that is soon churned into ankle-deep porridge. Unconcerned, joyous in their faith, they come from all parts of Poland, old ladies in black, the young from the mountains with their highly decorated white trousers, the ordinary peasants in the best clothes they can afford from the small returns of their meagre landholdings.

P. C. Matheson, lecturer in ecclesiastical history at Edinburgh University, and a Scottish Calvinist, describes the remarkable scenes he saw during an Easter visit to the area: "In the mornings the pilgrims move in their village or local groups from shrine to shrine along the Stations of the Cross or another of the four possible routes. They are led, not by priests or by the friars, but by their own lay leaders and precentors who, sometimes haltingly, sometimes with passionate eloquence, read out the ancient prayers and 'give the line' to the hymns. Some groups numbered hundreds and packed the chapels solid, standing, kneeling, lying flat on the floor, as the candles spluttered and the chants were intoned. In the distance the singing of other groups could be heard. There were only five in my favourite group: three teenage girls, a lass of about seven clutching flowers, and their leader, a young chap in sand-shoes. For all their laughter and informality, the seriousness of intent was unmistakable. They skipped off solemnly, singing their liturgy, savouring their religion. Not easy, one thought, to imagine a Scottish parallel.

"From our hillside vantage-point (I was there with an ethnologist friend) the whole countryside seemed alive—colourful groups of the most diverse accents on the move, singing, chanting, praying, climbing on hands and knees up the stairs to Pilate's place, kissing each step as they went (each harboured a relic), belting off to a local shop for a loaf and some mineral water for lunch, collapsing for a breather around a friendly tree. What was more remarkable, the naturalness or the supernaturalness of it all?

"In the course of the afternoon the groups gravitated back to the monastery's huge baroque church, whose onion towers loom high over the sprawling village in the valley. Inside, packed to suffocation with exhausted but ecstatic humanity, service after service took place, and the ways of elemental piety were relayed on loudspeakers to the corridors outside. Here, too, movement was almost impossible. Queues for confession mingled with crowds around a shop selling lurid pictures, statues and other religious trinketry, and the over-spill from the church. Near me one gnarled old man, his chin propped on the window ledge, staring into space, suddenly groaned his way to his knees and joined the surge of song. In the courtyard in front of the church, stalls and vendors innumerable sold most of the non-necessities of life, including candyfloss and badges of western pop groups.

"Towards dusk the Passion Play began, with local folk taking the part of Jesus and the others. The backdrop was the monastery's white wall. Spotlights and loudspeakers picked out the drama for the singing masses on the hillside—the intensity of a covenanting conventicle yoked to the spectacle of the Tattoo.

"On Thursday the Passion Play swept out into the countryside. In a Murrayfield-size crowd we churned through the mud, straining for a glimpse of the betrayal and arrest of Christ. A squad of soldiers rattled their way through the pilgrims to reach the 'Mount of Olives'; boys and girls, perched precariously in windy trees, saw the disciples running pell-mell down the hill. Jerusalem *was* in Poland. One was caught up in the immediacy of it all.

"On Good Friday we were up at 5.30. Not that we had slept much, for all through the night the singing had continued in the church. At six the rain was cascading down, the ground a quagmire, and throughout the day rain, snow and even hail continued. Faint hearts, we desperately hoped for a postponement. It was not to be. Blankets over their heads, gumbooted and patient in penance, old and young watched the final scenes before Pilate, listened to the sermons of the Franciscans after each event, hunched their way forward to the climax at 'Calvary' itself, a steep, stone hill. Up this the peasant Christ dragged his cross, the mob/congregation all around him. Two women rushed through a cordon to kiss his robe. No longer a play, this was the theatre of reality".

But although Wojtyla was a keen church-goer, was interested and fascinated by all its rituals, there was no indication that he would take Holy Orders. At least it did not reveal itself on the surface. What went on in the boy's mind was not known because, as Dr Zachar says, to make such a decision "is a very intimate part of a person's life. He never showed an inclination to be a priest ... but then a young boy is not keen to show such thoughts to his friends, to public opinion. Not until he is sure".

One day the Archbishop of Krakow, Cardinal Adam Sapieha, a prince not only of the Church but of the Polish nation, came to Wadowice to visit the parish and Wojtyla, as head boy of the high school, was asked to prepare a speech. It showed lines of intellectual thought and religious perception that impressed the cardinal.

"You seem to be a very clever young man," Cardinal Sapieha, said in thanking Wojtyla for the speech. "Are you going to be a priest?"

"No," Wojtyla said firmly. "I am going to university to study literature. And I'm also interested in the theatre".

It was the theatre that most fascinated Karol Wojtyla. He had become

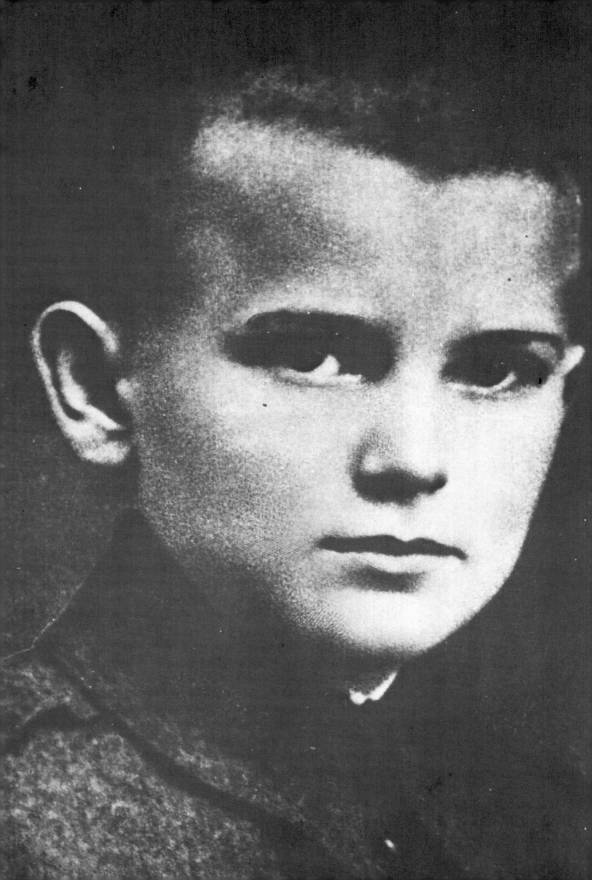

Karol Wojtyla aged 12.

friendly with Mieczyslaw Kotlarczyk, a theatre enthusiast who taught literature at a secondary school in Wadowice, although not the one attended by
Wojtyla. Kotlarczyk was later to become one of the prime movers behind
the Rhapsodic Theatre, which in the bleak years of World War II did much
to keep alive the free spirit of Polish thought.

Wojtyla revelled in the trappings, the intellectual side, the discipline of
the theatre. It opened up a new world to him, peopled by those who often
shared the same aspirations and dreamed the same dreams. His first theatrical performance was at high school where he played the juvenile lead in
Maidens' Vows, a classic comedy written by Aleksander Fredro in 1832. His
part was that of a somewhat frivolous but kind-hearted young man and by
all accounts he filled the role with ease.

Wojtyla reached the end of his school days in Wadowice as a teenage
boy admired and respected by all. How much of that admiration and respect
can be taken as gospel is uncertain because the truth has tended to become
obscured by the following events in his life. Was he the perfect boy at school?
Did he not lie, cheat, bully, which are the normal frailties of childhood?
Was he always the model son devoted to an aging parent, an attentive pupil,
a lad of religious intensity who fulfilled every obligation to the church? They
are questions which must remain unanswered because, in the thoughts of
those who know him, Karol Wojtyla already walks with the angels. So
shattering, so traumatic was the election of a Polish priest to the head of
the Roman Catholic Church that there are none in Poland who would speak
of the man except in the most reverent and cautious of tongues.

Chancellor Kuczkowski says: "He was the masterpiece of how a young
man should be and should behave. Saint Jacob said that, who in his
language is a proper person, then he is in fact a proper person. So it was
with Karol. He never said anything about people, always tried to find the
good side".

Dr Zachar thought long about the question when asked, then replied:
"Naturally, no one is perfect. But I cannot recall any penalty I had to give
him. It is quite possible he did wrong things like any other boy, but it was
nothing serious."

Monsignor Figlewicz said: "He was vivid, quick-minded and very good,
by nature an optimist. He was a good school boy".

A childhood friend, Wlodzimierz Piotrowski, said: "I can't remember his
ever getting a grade below 'very good'. He surpassed us all, but never tried
to impose his will on us". Kazimierz Forys, who taught Wojtyla Polish and
Latin at high school, remembers him as being a boy who was "extremely
solid and had an undoubted talent for humanism. He knew how to inspire

Karol Wojtyla at Wadowice Elementary
School (back row, left).

his colleagues in the theatrical work in which he was so interested. He was very religious and pious. Every day, before school and after it, he used to drop in at the church."

At least, as far as the education of Karol Wojtyla went, their memories remain true. It is proved by his report of his last year of school in Wadowice, which shows, almost with irritating smugness, although none was intended, that he was exceptionable in every subject: "Behaviour, very good. Religion, very good. Polish language, very good. Latin, very good. Greek, very good. German, very good. History, good. Physics and chemistry, good. Mathematics, very good. Philosophy, very good. Physical culture, very good". A note at the end of the report adds: "For the whole year he was not present for only six hours and for these he had a good excuse".

After graduating top of his class at 18, Karol moved with his father to Krakow where he enrolled at Jagiellonian University, an ancient and revered hall of learning. It was 1938 and Europe was moving inevitably towards war.

Hitler was already determined to occupy Poland. Totally ignoring the

Versailles Treaty, sneering at the weakness of European and British leaders, he had built up the Wehrmacht until it consisted of 36 divisions. His aim was to use countries such as Poland merely to give the German people "a wider living space". On 23 November 1937, he said in an address to the SS Political School at Sonthofen: "The German people has a right to control the whole of Europe and to transform it into the Teutonic Reich of the German people".

The theorist of the Nazi Party, Alfred Rosenberg, was even more straight-forward. "We cannot", he said, "have any consideration for Poles, Czechs ... they must be pushed eastwards, in order to make their lands available for the ploughs of German peasants."

Near the end of 1938, Hitler summoned the Polish ambassador in Berlin, Jozef Lipski, and demanded the return of Polish Pomerania and Danzig, a demand rejected twice by the Polish Government. After the second rejection, the German propaganda machine poured out a torrent of lies, abuse and threats, declaring that the German minority in Poland was to be "liberated" from Polish "oppression and persecution", just as the Sudeten Germans had been freed from the "Czech yoke".

Hitler spelled out his real intentions towards Poland later when he said: "Danzig is not by any means the main cause of the disagreement. The chief objective is to get new areas for Germany in the east and to control and safeguard new sources of food stuffs. The question of Poland being spared therefore does not arise".

The Catholic Church in Poland at this time, while looking anxiously at Hitler's aggressive moves, seemed more preoccupied by what it felt was the threat of Communism. It was a classic case of not being able to see the forest for the trees. In 1936, at the Plenary Synod held in Czestochowa, the Church warned Catholics they were "diligently to beware of communism, the most dangerous plague of the contemporary world".

Of course the Church was merely looking after its own welfare, its vast properties, because it feared these would be taken over under a Communist regime and Hitler had not yet displayed his murderous attitude towards the clergy. Just before the war, the Church owned more than a million acres of land, residential buildings, monasteries, presbyteries, administrative buildings, schools, hospitals and orphanages, as well as small industrial firms and handicraft enterprises.

It boasted more than 20 million members in 5100 parishes. There were 11 300 priests, and 16 700 nuns and sisters. There was an active political arm, Catholic Action, and Catholic youth organisations had more than 300 000 on their lists.

Such was the state of Poland in 1938 when Karol Wojtyla entered Jagiellonian University in Krakow. The country trembled while the Church, cocooned in its red robes, aloof and remote from reality, studied Communist Russia with a powerful telescope while it peered myopically in the direction of Nazi Germany.

CHAPTER FOUR

When Karol Wojtyla, fresh, eager and burning with enthusiasm, walked into the Jagiellonian University to study Polish literature at the arts faculty, he was walking into history. He was soon surrounded by it, could feel it in the old stone buildings, some going back 500 years, could see it in the university museum's collection of 15th century astronomical instruments and globes and in the library's priceless medieval manuscripts and books printed in the 16th century.

Perhaps he could, in his imagination, hear the voices of such great former scholars as Nicolaus Copernicus, the astronomer, who attended the university in the 15th century, hear him question the theories of the two official astronomical systems, Aristotelian and Ptolemaic. It was in the field of astronomy that the university excelled in those days, prompting the Nuremberg doctor and humanist, H. Schedel, to write: "In all Germany there is in the field of astronomy at least, no university more famed". Perhaps he could see the ghosts of Marian Smoluchowski, the creator of the kinetic theory of matter and the greatest Polish physicist after Madame Curie; of Leon Marchlewski, who discovered chlorophyll in 1896; of Odon Bujwid, the pioneer of bacteriology. Perhaps he could feel the influences of scholars from Hungary, Switzerland, Italy, Spain, from lands that exist now only in history books such as Slovakia, Croatia, Saxony, Prussia, Bavaria, Lusatia, Wittenberg.

The university Wojtyla was entering had its origins in the old cathedral school of Wawel in Krakow. The university itself was established in 1364 by a royal charter which declared that it should "produce men in the maturity of their council excellent, through the adornment of virtue perfect, and in various skills cunning". It has continued to this day: reaching the heights in learning as it did at the time of Copernicus; struggling for its existence when Sweden occupied Krakow in the 17th and 18th century; followed by the invasions of Prussia and Austria. It was almost wiped out by the Nazis who reacted against Polish intellectual thought like barbaric savages.

Wojtyla shared with his father a semi-basement apartment at 10 Tyniecka Street, in the district of Debniki, close to the Vistula River which sweeps in a great figure U through the heart of Krakow. It was not an easy life. They had only the military pension of Wojtyla's father on which to live.

At university he became friendly with Juliusz Kydrynski, now a noted writer and translator, who was one year younger than Wojtyla. Their friendship grew out of the poetry they both loved.

"He wrote poetry and I did and it was the thing that made us close friends," says Kydrynski. "We met not only at the university but at the public poetry readings they held in those days."

Unlike many students at Jagiellonian University who often spent the nights drinking in the cafes, arguing over matters that hold no arugment, trying to bed the young women of the city, Wojtyla kept to his studies. He had no regular girlfriend. He sometimes visited the cafes, for they were the centre of much intellectual discussion as well as frivolity. He talked passionately about literature to his fellow students who included such future well-known writers as Wojciech Zukrowski, Tadeusz Holuj and Marian Pankowski. Also encouraging him in literature were his professors, eminent scholars such as Stanislaw Pigon, Stefan Kolaczkowski and Kazimierz Wyka.

"He was a very serious thinking young man," says Kydrynski, "but he was by no means what could be called gloomy. He had a good sense of humour, a man like most of us. But, you know, even at that time there was a kind of aura around him, something he created. I suppose you would call it a special kind of seriousness. You would be quite at ease with him, but at the same time you would not go beyond certain limits of frivolity. I did not notice that he had any special leanings towards the religious life in those days. He was always a pious, religious man, but by no means a bigot. He was a practising Catholic, would go to church, of course, but I would call him liberal thinking. Religion was not his main interest in those days."

Literature and the theatre were. He was soon helping to arrange public poetry readings and at that time was writing folkloristic ballads in the style of the then popular writer, Emil Zegadlowicz. He attended every new theatre premiere he could, allowing for his limited money and the studies of the Polish language he was undertaking at university.

Wojtyla's interest in the theatre brought him into contact with the newly-established Krakow Theatre Fraternity, later to be renamed Dramatic Studio 39. It was a private venture for amateurs and among its members were not only students but people of all classes, including young workers. Wojtyla's great desire to be an actor was fulfilled when he was given a part in the staging of the dramatic poem, *The Knight of the Moon*, written by Marian Nizynski with music by K. Mikuszewski. It was a Faustian legend, although the man who is now Pope did not play the part of the devil. It tells in a light-hearted way the story of Pan Twardowski, a nobleman who sold his soul to the devil, but when being carried off to hell at the end of their contract, uttered a prayer, was let go and landed on the moon.

It was a memorable moment in Wojtyla's life when in the summer of 1939, the turmoil of Europe being a distant rumble from behind far-off borders, he stepped on to the stage. All else was forgotten. He was a part of the Polish theatre he loved with such passion.

The play was staged, as part of the Krakow Days Festival, in the courtyard of the old university. The characters in the play represented constellations and signs of the Zodiac. Wojtyla was, appropriately enough, Taurus for that was the sign under which he was born. So into the courtyard, surrounded

Poster for the play Knight of the Moon *which featured Karol Wojtyla.*

Karol Wojtyla, arrowed, in the production of Knight of the Moon.

by magnificent gothic porticos, across the stone pavement, where so many great men had walked before him over the centuries, strolled Wojtyla wearing a curiously mixed garb of sports attire, shorts, boxing gloves and on his head a Taurean mask which he would take off at various points during the play. The text he spoke may have been trivial, but it is said he made an impact with his delivery and appearance. Especially his appearance.

Apart from the theatre, Wojtyla would spend hours revelling in the ancient city of Krakow, peering into the churches that years later would come under his protection, studying the monuments, exploring the castles, the ruins, the monasteries.

Krakow's history goes back to the Slavic tribes who lived isolated behind the natural fortifications of the Carpathian Mountains and therefore escaped the marauding Roman legions. Sacked by Czech troops in 1031, it later became the capital of Poland and by the middle of the 13th century it was a prosperous city. Little huts crowded the narrow streets, while, surrounding the stone monasteries built by the Benedictines, the Cistercians, the Dominicans and the Minorites, stood the grand houses of the knights.

The people of the town were safe behind the walls of the monasteries, as the Tartar hordes found twice when they invaded the city. By the 14th century, Krakow was an important centre of art, science and finance, packed with merchants, scholars, craftsmen, weavers and goldsmiths, builders and stonecutters. The great age of Krakow lasted until the end of the 16th century; a time of wealth, new art forms and magnificent churches. Then a decline set in and, after a fire in the Wawel Castle, the king moved to Warsaw taking with him the privileges he had so readily spread among the nobility of Krakow. This was followed by wars, civil disturbances and the plague, reducing a once great city almost to ruins. The town became dilapidated with a slum-like atmosphere that gave it an abandoned look. It revived again in the second half of the 19th century when new suburbs were added and the green belt, called Planty, was laid out over the ruins of ancient fortifications.

Karol Wojtyla spent many hours in prayer and meditation in the Church of Our Lady, which stands in one corner of the Market Place, one of the largest squares in Central Europe. He would gaze with a mixture of awe and admiration at the vast altar piece of the high altar, a masterpiece carved by Wit Stwosz between 1477 and 1487. As one observer of it says: "The lyric and dramatic expressions of the whole scene, the dynamism yet precision of the carving, the charm of the Virgin Mary and the realistic figures of the Apostles surrounding her, all these contribute to the merited fame of the altar-piece which has justly been considered the most valuable work of wood carving north of the Alps".

Wojtyla was not to know, of course, that he would be looking at the altar piece for the last time in several years. It was taken down in 1939 and hidden in Sandomierz, but the Germans, ever eager to fill their museums and satisfy Goering's vanity with looted treasures, found it and took it to Nuremberg.

It was returned in 1945, but it took 64 000 working hours before it was restored to its former glory. ,

Wojtyla would wander past the Barbican, built in 1498 and, oddly for this part of Europe, modelled on Arab military art, and gaze up at the 115 ft (35 metre) St Florian's gate, a medieval fortification built at the end of the 13th century.

But more than all other places he would linger at Wawel Castle, built on a bluff overlooking the Vistula River. He would wander through the central courtyard of the castle, one of the masterpieces of the Renaissance in Northern Europe, where once the knights held tournaments. Then he would walk into Wawel Cathedral, a mixture of romanesque, gothic, baroque and Renaissance art. And here also lay a part of the often violent history of Poland, the tombs of kings and leaders and great writers.

He would sometimes walk down the steep stone stairs to St Leonard's Crypt, which was carved out in the 12th century. He would stop at the tombs of 14 kings of Poland, their wives and children and such national heroes as Jozef Poniatowski, Tadeusz Kosciuszko who led the people in revolt against the combined armed might of Russia, Austria and Prussia and was one of the heroes of the American War of Independence, and Marshal Jozef Pilsudski who created a nation out of the wreckage of World War I.

Perhaps he lingered at the tomb of Julius Slowacki, the 19th century romantic poet, who dreamed of then impossible things. One of his dreams, *During Unrest The Lord Will Strike*, predicted the election of a Slavic Pope.

He would not only look at the treasures of Wawel Cathedral, soak himself in its history, marvel at the heroism of those whose bones crumbled there, but he would visit his old friend from Wadowice, Kazimierz Figlewicz, who had been appointed a vicar at the cathedral. He kept in regular contact on a social basis and on the first Friday of each month helped serve Mass.

Wojtyla never, as Figlewicz recalls, failed to turn up to fulfil his duties. He did not fail on 1 September 1939, when war came to Poland and for the first time the sirens howled over the old city of Krakow.

CHAPTER FIVE

On 25 March 1939, Hitler announced to his generals, at a secret meeting, with meglomaniacal arrogance: "Poland should be totally subjected. This country shall not be taken into consideration as a political factor for whole decades".

Six days later, the document-waving, vacillating British Prime Minister, Neville Chamberlain, committed his government with the words "in the event of any action which clearly threatened Polish independence, and which the Polish government accordingly considered it vital to resist with their national forces . . ., to lend the Polish government all support in their power". The words failed to impress Hitler. He was already working on his plan to attack Poland, code-named Fall Weiss, and six months later, at four forty-five a.m. on 1 September 1939, without a formal declaration of war, the Nazi armies smashed through the border. They did it in classic Blitzkrieg style, throwing 75 crack divisions with 2400 tanks and 2000 aircraft against the Polish forces. Warsaw fell 28 days later. And in London, the British government backed its guarantee of support for Poland by ordering the RAF Bomber Command to drop leaflets on Frankfurt, Munich and Stuttgart saying it was wrong for the German government to do such things. No wonder Hitler laughed at the world.

Hitler's attitude to Poland was made clear immediately the defending armies were crushed. The Poles, he said, were to be nothing more than "a reservation, a vast Polish labour camp. Poles will never be raised to a higher level". Dr Hans Frank, the Governor of Krakow, added: "From now on the political role of the Polish nation is ended. It is our aim that the very concept *Polak* be erased for centuries to come. Neither the Republic, nor any other form of Polish state will ever be reborn. Poland will be treated as a colony and Poles will become slaves in the German empire".

The country was carved up like a turkey. Pomerania, Posnania and Upper Silesia were made a part of the Greater German Reich. The rest of Poland was made a Government General, with Dr Frank as the Governor and Krakow as the capital. The Royal Castle at Wawel became Frank's residence and other major buildings were taken over by the SS, the army, the police and various German government agencies.

And, of course, the Jagiellonian University, where Karol Wojtyla had begun his higher education only a year before, was closed. The university was preparing for its 575th academic year when the Germans occupied Krakow on 6 September 1939. The Germans were determined to wipe out all Polish intellectual thought because they saw Poles only as slaves and there was no room in the plans of the Reich for those who studied, debated and questioned.

On 6 November the Nazis put into full force their plan to grind Polish culture to dust. In the great hall of the university they arrested 138 professors and lecturers.

But Wojtyla and other students were equally determined to continue their education and early in 1940 they established an underground university. Secret meetings were arranged in private lodgings, not an easy task with German police and troops on every corner, with informers listening to private conversations.

One place where they met was the home of Juliusz Kydrynski at 10 Felic-janek Street in the heart of old Krakow. One by one so they would not be noticed by the ever-alert Gestapo, the students slipped through the front door and climbed the ill-lit concrete stairs, nervous at the dark shadows on the landings, until they reached the apartment on the third floor. And there they would talk among themselves, listen to lecturers who had escaped arrest, tense and fearful that at any moment there could be a pounding on the door. Such was the thirst for knowledge and the determination not to be crushed by the Germans that by 1942 the underground university was organised into five secret faculties. In the three years from 1942 until the end of the war, 136 lecturers risked their lives to teach more than 800 students.

There were times when Wojtyla and his fellow students were close to arrest. "One of the meetings we had arranged was due to take place in about an hour" recalls Juliusz Kydrynski. "The chairs were all arranged in the room for about 30 people. Then the Gestapo arrived. They were asking for somebody whom we probably knew and they saw all the chairs. My mother said we were preparing for a party. This seemed to satisfy them and they left. But that was a very close thing because there were often people sitting around waiting for a meeting to start. If the Gestapo had arrived when there were people there they would have thought we were plotting against them. But fortunately the Gestapo never arrived while we were having a meeting otherwise I would not be speaking today. They were dangerous times for all of us".

Just how dangerous they were is shown by the fact that 30 eminent academics from the university died as a result of the cold, disease-ridden brutality of concentration camps. The Germans systematically went about destroying the university, pillaging the departments and destroying books and equipment. Of the 139 departments, institutes and clinics in the famed old university, with its impressive parade of scholars over the centuries, 12 were completely destroyed, 47 suffered serious damage, 70 were partly damaged and only 10 could commence work without difficulty after the end of the war.

Like all students at the underground university, Wojtyla lived on two levels. He studied and went to secret classes in the evening and during the day worked as a labourer. This was necessary so he could obtain an *Arbeitskarte* (work certificate). Without it he would have been transported

*The limestone quarry where Karol Wojtyla
worked during the war.*

*The Solvay factory where Karol Wojtyla
worked after leaving the quarry.*

to Germany as a forced labourer which, in the eyes of the Germans, was the rightful task of all Poles.

Wojtyla found work in a limestone quarry belonging to the Solvay chemical works, on the outskirts of Krakow. It was not a pleasant place in which to toil—cold almost beyond endurance in the snows of winter, the air filled with fine, choking rock powder in the hot winds of summer.

Juliusz Kydrynski, who worked with him at the quarry, describes life in those bleak war years in his book of memoirs, *Tapima*, published in 1969.

"The work was carried on, of course, in the open air, but at the bottom of a limestone valley, so it was bearable. In the winter I managed with Wojtek and Karol (Wojtyla) to step, every now and then, into a small hut heated with an iron stove. It was a shelter where we were allowed to spend no more than quarter of an hour a day, during our breakfast break. Those breakfasts were not given to the workers, of course. We brought them with us from home: slices of low quality rye bread with jam, and black 'ersatz' coffee in tin flasks. We warmed the coffee on that iron stove. In practice we stayed there for more than a quarter of an hour, and repeated the experience every two or three hours.

"In charge of the quarry was an old Solvay worker by the name of Krause—a good Pole, in spite of his German name—who was extremely friendly to Karol, Wojtek and myself, a feeling we reciprocated heartily. Soon we were friends with all the quarrymen; they were wonderful people, who knew very well our peculiar situation, quite common in those days, of university students being forced to undertake unusual tasks to obtain the *Arbeitskarte*, and often serving as cover for quite different activities. The older and genuine quarrymen tried to make it easier for us, particularly in the winter, with its severe frosts. We were indebted to them and were most grateful.

"The quarry was situated in the fields of Zakrzowek, a village between Debniki and Borek Falecki, where the actual Solvay factory stood. Tracks of narrow-gauged railway led to the individual work sites, and on them stood tip-waggons, once red but for a long time white with the limestone dust. A quarry man had to fill one such waggon with stones each day. It was very hard work . . .

"We, 'amateurs', in the early days of our work were unable to fulfil the daily norm. For this reason, we were used for ancillary work, which was not easy either. It consisted of carrying on wheel-barrows the soil from under the stone, thus clearing up the work places. Sometimes we would pump out the water gathering there, with the help of an archaic manual pump. It was then that we came to know with great understanding the fatigue sailors must have felt in the old days when, using the same method, they spent long hours pumping water out of sinking ships.

"A few months later, however, we too were ordered to work with the stone. After a few months' training with the spade and the pump, we were not afraid of the stone-hammer. Soon we learned how to manoeuvre it, that

The old courtyard at Krakow University where Karol Wojtyla studied.

Karol Wojtyla's first church at Niegowic.

Karol Wojtyla lived in the top floor of this house in Felcianek Street, Krakow, for a short time during the Second World War.

The house at Tyniecka Street, Krakow, where Karol Wojtyla lived on the bottom floor.

Karol Wojtyla and other priests worked, ate and slept in this room at the Archbishop's Palace, Krakow during the last year of the war.

is, to hit the 'head' of the stone, having learnt to estimate properly where that 'head' was situated. One had to hit the stone in such a way that the chips would not wound the face or the eyes. The thing was to hit the stone—no matter what its size, sometimes really big—so that it would break into smaller pieces after as few hits as possible. Then one had to load the smaller stones with forks, their spikes tipped with little balls, into the waggons.

"Among the many waggons, a small, old-fashioned railway engine would move on the tracks, steaming copiously and noisily. It reminded us of a fast, glistening, black cockroach, but even so we liked it. Its appearance broke the monotony of our work, because the engine took away the full waggons and brought new, empty ones. And then, in the winter, one could warm oneself, though briefly, by its squat boiler.

"One summer Wojtek and I were left working with the stone, while Karol was given a somewhat different task. There was in the quarry a shot-firer by the name of Labus, a picturesque and popular character. A stooping old man with a moustache, hobbling up and down the slopes, with a box full of ammonite cartridges and a long stick with which he placed the cartridges in openings made in the rock by means of a pneumatic drill, he was well known as an indispensable part of the quarry landscape. On Krause's order Karol was made Labus' assistant. They divided their duties in such a way that Karol placed the cartridges and fuses in position, while Labus watched these actions and then personally lit the fuses. They would then both run to a safe distance. After a while an explosion would rip large blocks away from the rock face. When the dust settled, a rhythmic sound of hammers could be heard again.

"I must confess that, together with Wojtek, I envied Karol a little his 'advancement' which enabled him now to spend the best part of the day in the hut where, chatting to old Labus, he would wait for a suitable time for another 'shot'. That advancement put him apart somewhat from the common quarry folk. But I suppose Karol was made to stand out from the crowd. After all, some twenty odd years later he became the Archbishop of Krakow, then a Cardinal".

Conditions became more brutal at the quarry after Wojtyla left in 1944. The Germans put a unit of Ukrainian soldiers in charge. Hated by the Poles and despised by the Germans, the Ukrainians would retaliate by getting drunk. One day they rounded up the workers at the quarry, ordered them to lie on the ground and informed them they were to be shot. The Ukrainians accused the workers of being members of the Polish resistance. They were setting up machine guns when the driver of the steam engine, which had come upon the scene, blew out a vast cloud of steam, obscuring the workers and confusing the drunken Ukrainians. A German officer was contacted and he ordered the Ukrainians back to their barracks.

The years spent in the quarry had a deep effect on Wojtyla. In 1956 he was to write a poem called *The Quarry*, a powerful and emotional work which

was published in the monthy magazine, *Znak*, in June 1957. Part of the poem is dedicated "to the memory of a fellow worker" and vividly describes his death—"a stone smashed his temples, and cut through his heart's chamber". He portrays the funeral—"they took his body, walked in a silent row"— and concludes:
"Should his anger now flow into the anger of others?
It was maturing in him through its own truth and love,
Should he be used by those that come after, deprived of substance, unique and deeply his own?"

When Wojtyla wrote the poem, Poland was going through a period of bloody turmoil. In June 1956, the workers of Poznan took to the streets and demanded more "bread and freedom". They also shouted for independence from the heavy hand of Russia. The Polish government, under Soviet pressures, did not hesitate and ordered the army to suppress any demonstrations. Tanks rolled into the streets of Poznan and 54 people were killed and several hundred injured.

Boleslaw Taborski, a Polish poet and translator now based in London who has made a considerable study of Wojtyla's writings, says that the events in Poznan may have prompted Wojtyla's poem. He used his own memories of the wartime experiences in the quarry to oppose the iron dogma of Stalinism—that the present generation of workers must sacrifice all for the good of future generations. The Christian view is that every man is a unique person and must not be so deprived.

"But it would be wrong to consider *The Quarry* as a political poem," argues Taborski. "It is above all a hymn in praise of human work, its value and importance."

Wojtyla describes in some detail the actual work in the quarry, showing how man's energy cuts and shapes the stone for human use and declaring that "the greatness of work is inside man". Even though man used electricity to help him,
"yet can the current unbind their full strength?
it is he who carries that strength in his hands: the worker".

Wojtyla's poem is rich with images of great beauty: To quote a few lines:
"Hands are the heart's landscape. They split sometimes
like ravines into which an undefined force rolls.
The very same hands which man only opens
when his palms have had their fill of toil
Now he sees: because of him alone others can walk in peace".

Taborski sees the four parts of the poem—"Material", "Inspiration", "Participation", "In memory of a fellow worker"—as forming an impressive artistic entity. "They are also evidence" says Taborski, "of how meaningful and fruitful in the human sense it was for the author when he had to engage in heavy physical work during the war through dire necessity. He had the strength and the ability to participate in it fully, as in so many other occupations he engaged in during his life".

The tough physical work in the quarry gave Wojtyla the right to say:
"There is silence again between heart, stone and tree.
Whoever enters Him keeps his own self.
He who does not, has no past in the business of this world.
Despite all appearances".

After the work at the quarry, which began early in the morning and ended at around three p.m., especially in the winter when night comes early in Krakow, he would carry back to the city what he could scrounge during the day, a sack of cabbages, or peas, or coal, and store it in the cellar of his home at 10 Tyniecka Street. The meagre wage he earned at the quarry was the only money coming into the home, his father's army pension having been stopped after the German occupation. One day in 1941 he returned home at lunchtime to find his father dead.

The death deeply shocked Wjotyla. Since the death of his mother when he was nine, he had been practically inseparable from his father. After the funeral, aged 21 and feeling alone in a brutal, ravaged world, he moved into the apartment where his friend Juliusz Kydrynski lived. And about the same time, unknown to his friends, he began quietly to study theology.

"After the death of his father he leaned much more to religious affairs and to spiritual matters," says Kydrynski. "But even though he was living with us, I had no idea he was studying theology. He kept it a secret to himself."

Another friend, Mrs Zofia Pozniakowa, said she was also unaware of Wojtyla's secret studies of theology. "Here in this parish before the war there existed a Catholic association of young men. During the war they got together again, but kept it a secret because of the dangers. Karol also met a tailor who lived in this area called Jan Tyranowski. He was a remarkable man, a spiritual teacher, who influenced Karol very much. Later they used to come to our house where Tyranowski would read the scriptures and other religious writings and they would all discuss it later. But you have to remember that in those days you kept things secret. It was the best way for survival."

So secret, in fact, that one day Mikolaj Kuczkowski, then a vicar at Wawel Cathedral, looked at the virtues of Wojtyla, his close connection with the Church, his firm, stated belief in God, and decided he had the potential to make a good priest. With another friend from Wadowice, Adam Biela, he went to Wojtyla's home to put forward the proposition.

Wojtyla smiled. "You are too late. I am already studying theology on a private basis."

Meanwhile Poland was being torn apart. The whole country was the target of persecution, mass arrest, torture and murder. In fact Governor Frank boasted that "all the forests in Poland would not suffice to produce the necessary quantities of paper" needed to print notices of execution. And not far from Krakow, within the diocese of the city, there was established the Auschwitz-Birkenau complex of concentration camps. The first prisoners, Poles, were taken to the camp on 14 June 1940. Soon the trains with their choked waggons of humanity were arriving at the camp from all over Europe, a scene described by the camp commandant Rudolf Hoess in his autobiography: "The vans were unloaded one after the other. After depositing their baggage, the Jews had to pass individually in front of an SS doctor, who decided on their physical fitness as they marched past him. Those considered capable of employment were immediately taken into the camp in small groups. Taking an average of all the transports, between 25 and 30 per cent were found fit for work, but this figure fluctuated considerably. The figure for Greek Jews, for example was only 15 per cent."

Hoess soon discovered that bullets, disease, hunger, beatings, the cold and punishingly hard work were not enough to keep up with the Nazi plan of extermination. On 3 September 1941, Cyclon B gas was introduced as a much more economical way to fulfill the daily quota of death. Soon the stench of burning flesh from the crematoriums spread over the land around Auschwitz and the fires from the pyres were so bright at night that the German air defence complained they could be visible to hostile aircraft.

Hoess wrote: "Towards the end of summer (1942) we started to burn bodies at first on wood pyres bearing some 2000 corpses, and later in pits, together with bodies previously buried. In the early days oil refuse was poured on the bodies, but later methanol was used. Bodies were burned in pits day and night, continuously. By the end of November 1942, all mass graves had been emptied. The number of corpses in the mass graves amounted to 107 000".

There were other ways to kill. The deadly routine of the camp, even such inoffensive-sounding duties as the roll-call, exterminated prisoners like animals in a slaughter house. Seweryna Szmaglewska, a prisoner in the women's camp, described a roll-call: "After having counted the prisoners in front of their barrack, the room seniors began to escort women, weakened by fever or the after-effects of dysentery, and placed them on stools or on the ground. Finally dying women were carried out and were laid upon the ground to be counted. Inert human figures, stretched out on the wet, muddy ground and covered with blankets, dirtied with the mud, arrested the eye of the healthy prisoners, newcomers to the camp. It is impossible to avert one's eye—everywhere in front of the barracks similar sights are to be seen. Somebody whispers, as if speaking to himself: 'Just as well that Auschwitz is kept under seals of secrecy, that children do not know how their mothers die.' "

Many of the prisoners were forced to work in the camp for a time before being exterminated, providing, of course, they survived the brutal conditions under which they slaved. "We kept running with the sods," recalled a former prisoner, Jozef Kret, "trying with all our might to be quick, in spite of the weight we had to carry, endeavouring to avoid the beatings, not that it helped, however . . . the *capo* would hit every running man with his long stick anyway. Our strength was ebbing fast; we could not stand the killing tempo much longer. The blows and the horrible pain made us exert ourselves to the utmost. Moll (*SS-Hauptscharfuhrer*) watched the realisation of his order as he stood on the dyke. His face expressed his satisfaction."

And so they came to this nightmare place, Poles, Czechs, Russians, Hungarians, Belgians, Yugoslavs, Bulgarians, Austrians, Jews and Christians. Men, women and children. A prisoner who was forced to empty the gas chambers and burn the corpses, a fearful task that also meant death because such foul things were marked top secret and those who knew must die, wrote and then buried a note in a glass jar which was found after the camp was liberated. "The children were so pretty," the note said, "so well made, that it was striking, when compared with the rags they were covered with ... The children had noticed the smoke from the chimney and they realised they were being led to their death. They began running hither and thither in the yard in a dead fright, clutching their heads in despair ..."

The Nazis were as methodical as ever in dealing with children in the camp, as was witnessed by one prisoner: "During the selection of children, the SS men placed a rod at the height of 1.20 metres. Children who passed under the rod would be gassed. Small children, knowing only too well what was awaiting them, tried hard to push out their necks when passing under the rod, in the hope of escaping gassing."

Rumours of Auschwitz were heard in Krakow but the stories seemed so monstrous, so beyond human comprehension, that they could not be believed. Life in Krakow was difficult enough without being assailed by tales from a nightmare.

Wojtyla and his friends continued their own form of resistance and, determined that Polish culture would not die, they began to gather in secret to read plays, then founded an amateur underground theatre. Later they were joined by two well-known professional actors, Wladyslaw Woznik and Zdzislaw Mrozewski.

One day Wojtyla was browsing through a second-hand bookshop in the company of Juliusz Kydrynski, when they met the great Polish actor Juliusz Osterwa, a man who had considerable influence on the Polish theatre in both the prewar and postwar periods.

Kydrynski introduced Wojtyla and explained their ambitions and dreams for an underground theatre which would continue to work under the very noses of the Nazis. Osterwa was delighted at the scheme. He agreed to help them in their first productions.

Producing plays in this clandestine fashion was dangerous for all concerned. Kydrynski has no doubts that they would have been shot or sent to a concentration camp if they had been caught. They were defying the Nazis by taking part in an operation that was expressly forbidden. Polish intellectuals and those who dared keep alive the culture were treated almost as cruelly as were the Jews. The Nazis took quite literally the words of Nietzsche: "Blood and cruelty are the foundation of all things".

The members of the underground theatre moved from house to house, always arriving or leaving singly or in pairs. They had to ensure they were at their own homes before curfew, which in the autumn and winter months was often as early as seven p.m. They had to be careful of informers, although, as Kydrynski says, "we invited only those people we knew and with whom we could be quite open. Karol remained calm through all this, keeping a good sense of humour. But he was aware of the risk. Everybody was".

Wojtyla was writing poetry at this stage, and also began to write plays on Biblical subjects, among them a drama on Job, which still remains unpublished.

Guided by Osterwa, the amateur group produced their first play in Kydrynski's third floor apartment at 10 Felicjanek Street. It was Act II of *The Quail* by the Polish writer Stefan Zeromski (1864–1925), a social drama of love having to be sacrificed for duty. Wojtyla played the part of an earthy country teacher, Smugon, whose wife, played by Danuta Michalowska, was loved by the idealist Przelecki with Kydrynski in the role.

It was a great moment for the group. Even though only a handful of people saw the production, they were keeping alive the spirit of Polish culture. Outside on the narrow streets the grey-clad forces of the Third Reich patrolled and issued their demands for identification and passes and in the ancient citadel of Wawel Castle, where once the kings of Poland had lived, sat Governor Hans Frank, signing documents that sent hundreds to their death. The Gestapo raided houses, tanks clanked over the expanse of the Market Place. But in the apartment above Felicjanek Street such things no longer existed as the actors entered another world.

Soon after the first production, Mieczyslaw Kotlarczyk, who was an old friend of Wojtyla, came to Krakow to live. He was the man who in Wadowice had introduced Wojtyla to the theatre, had fanned the sparks of interest the boy had shown in the great writings of the Polish stage. They both moved into the apartment in Tyniecka Street where Wojtyla had once lived with his father.

Wojtyla also put the amateur group, which had so proudly produced Act II of *The Quail*, at Kotlarczyk's disposal. "Kotlarczyk immediately suggested that they should stage works of epic poetry", says the actress Danuta Michalowska. "A group of five actors made up the company. There was Kotlarczyk and Karol Wojtyla and three actresses—myself, Krystyna Debowska-Ostaszewska and Halina Krolikiewicz-Kwiatkowska, who had acted with Karol in the school performance of *Maidens' Vows*. Her husband, a sculptor, was the stage designer. They took long narrative poems and arranged them theatrically, selecting their texts with precision and logical structure. Visually the performances were rather static and were based on strictly observed conventions which were modelled on medieval theatre. That is, an actor's position on stage was always significant. On the right of the stage stood the positive characters, on the left of the stage the negative ones and in the middle of the stage the indifferent ones. Performances took place, of course, at private houses and they were attended by small groups of between 15 and 20 people."

On the night of 1 November 1941, against a black back-cloth, in a small room, the Rhapsodic Theatre was born. The first production was *King Spirit*, based on a visionary poem by the great 19th century romantic poet, Juluisz Slowacki.

Using the always popular theme of re-incarnation, the poem deals with the eternal struggle between rebellious spirits and those divinely inspired for power. Part of the poem concerns the struggle of the 11th century king of Poland, Boleslaw the Bold, with the Bishop of Krakow, Stanislaw Szczepanowski. The bishop was killed and dismembered on the orders of the king and was later canonised and became the patron saint of Poland. The king, abandoned by his subjects, left the country and died as a monk at Ossiak in Austria.

Wojtyla's part was to narrate the beginning of the poem and the entire story of the clash of wills between the king and the bishop. His first performances were powerfully dramatic but were changed later to a more muted and subdued treatment as if they were a confession of many centuries ago.

The experience of taking part in the play had a deep effect on Wojtyla, one that was to stay with him in later years when he followed in the footsteps of Stanislaw Szczepanowski and became the Bishop of Krakow. On his way back from Rome, after being made cardinal, Wojtyla went to Austria and stopped at Ossiak at the tomb of Boleslaw the Bold, the man who had murdered his long-ago predecessor, and there he celebrated Mass. He was also deeply involved in preparing for the celebrations to mark the 900th anniversary of the death of St Stanislaw—8 May 1979—when he was elected Pope.

Slowacki's works were selected for the second production of the Rhapsodic Theatre. This time it was a more light-hearted work, the poem *Beniowski*, about an 18th century Polish-Hungarian nobleman who became Emperor of Madagascar. It abounds in satire and digressions on the lines of Byron's classic *Don Juan*.

The third production was based on *Hymns*, a cycle of poems written by Jan Kasprowicz (1860-1926), a poet associated with the Young Poland movement at the turn of the century.

Out of the Young Poland movement came many fine artists and possibly the greatest of these was the writer and painter, Stanislaw Wyspianski, who lived from 1869 to 1907, and was closely associated with Krakow. Wojtyla and the theatre group chose for their fourth production his best-known play, *The Wedding*, a shattering comment on Polish society. Fragments of the important third act were performed, with stage directions also recited, an innovation since adopted by other directors. Wojtyla played the part of a young peasant, Jasiek, who was entrusted with a symbolic golden horn with which to sound a call to arms, but unfortunately lost it.

Wojtyla revelled in these productions. He did not mind the long hours spent in rehearsals, even though he was involved in hard work at the quarry and was forced, like all Poles, to live on meagre rations—small quantities of bread and jam, cabbage, potatoes and occasionally tiny pieces of meat. He was also by now immersed in his theological studies. He knew the importance of the underground theatre, its ability to keep alive the culture threatened by the Nazis and years later would write that the "company, totally cut off from the normal basis of theatre production . . . confirmed its conviction, that the essential element of dramatic art is the live human word".

At this stage Wojtyla's life almost ended. He was struck by a car near the quarry and was found unconscious on the road by fellow workers. He spent some weeks in hospital and at the home of a friend, Mrs Zofia Pozniakowa, recovering from head and other injuries.

The fifth production of the Rhapsodic Theatre was *Norwid's Hour*, based on the writings of Cyprian Kamil Norwid, a great post-romantic philosophical poet who lived from 1821 to 1883, a writer neglected in his lifetime, but who has been growing in stature ever since.

The sixth production was based on the epic poem *Pan Tadeusz*, by the great romantic poet Adam Mickiewicz (1798–1855), and the seventh was the last in which Karol Wojtyla took part. Again the company chose the works of Slowacki, this time the drama *Samuel Zborowski*, a tale of a rebellious Polish nobleman executed in the 16th century. Slowacki saw the rebellion of the nobleman as the opposition of thinking people against the conventional and soulless established order that then existed—a philosophy that was to have its echo later during the oppressive Stalinist period. Wojtyla played the title role in the seven performances of the play.

"It was obvious by then that his mind was on other things", says Danuta Michalowska. "By then he had given up his studies in Polish philology for theological studies and was a seminarist, even though he continued working at Solvay. He honoured his commitment to the production of *Samuel Zborowski* but seemed more and more distant as time went on. His thoughts were elsewhere."

One of the performances of *Samuel Zborowski* was given at 10 Szwedzka Street in the apartment of Mrs Zofia Pozniakowa, who lived there with her unmarried sister, Helena Szkocka. "We were all in great danger but it didn't seem to matter", says Mrs Pozniakowa. "The production of the theatre was all that was important." Wojtyla was a great friend of the family and had visited the house since the days when he first arrived in Krakow in 1938. It was from a lodger in the house, Jadwiga Lewaj, that he took lessons in French. He would also spend hours listening to Mrs Pozniakowa playing Bach and Chopin on the piano. They would discuss the great poets of Poland and the theatre. And in his own house, not far away, he wrote another play about Adam Chmielowski, a talented painter born in 1846 who gave up art and, taking the name Brother Albert, founded a religious order catering for the poor.

Even though he gave up active participation with the Rhapsodic Theatre,

Wojtyla never lost interest in the group. As the poet Taborski writes: "He remained on friendly terms with its members and cherished the ideas propounded by its other founder, Mieczyslaw Kotlarczyk. The Rhapsodic Theatre emerged from underground at the end of the war and continued its activities, but was forced to close during the period of Stalinist repression in 1953. It was reopened after the Gomulka 'thaw' in 1956, although not without difficulties.

"On 7 April 1957, *Tygodnik Powszechny*, the weekly Catholic newspaper published in Krakow under the auspices of the archbishop, carried a series of statements on the necessity of restoring the theatre to its old venue. Among them was an article entitled *Drama of Word and Gesture*, signed Andrzej Jawien, the pseudonym used by Karol Wojtyla. Unlike the other statements, Wojtyla does not enter into polemics, does not even mention the topical issues involved, except for his concluding statement: 'Mieczyslaw Kotlarczyk needs a suitable workshop for his work—and that is why the Rhapsodic Theatre ought to exist'. For the rest, Wojtyla describes the essential characteristics of this type of theatre.

"His article shows Wojtyla to be an interesting theoritician of a theatre based on the word appropriately used with the minimum of decor, props or action, in order to stimulate thought. These ideas are expounded further in another article by Wojtyla published in *Tygodnik Powszechny* on 19 January 1958, entitled *Rhapsodies of a Millenium*. It refers to a production of Slowacki's *King Spirit*, inaugurating the renewed activity of the Rhapsodic Theatre 16 years after the original production of the same poem had inaugurated the work of the underground company of which Wojtyla had been a member. It is not a review, though, but a restatement of the Theatre's aims, using the example of this particular production.

" 'This theatre,' Wojtyla says, 'in which there is so much *word* and relatively little *acting* safeguards young actors against the destructive development of individualism, because it will not let them impose on the text anything of their own; it gives the actors an inner discipline . . . A group of people, collectively, unanimously, somehow subordinated to the great poetic word, evoke associations of ethical nature: it reveals and stresses particularly strongly that piety which is the point of departure for the rhapsodists' work, and the secret of their style' ".

Taborski concludes: "These words read both like a reaffirmation of loyalty and a farewell by a founder member now in pastures new to a company which, though renewed, was already nearing the end of its existence. Obviously the need for physical theatre, which in a few years would find its culmination in the experiments of Grotowski, was making the Rhapsodic Theatre obsolete, although Wojtyla's words about the need for thought-serving words have not lost their validity".

By 1944 Germany had all but transformed Poland into a nation of slaves, using starvation, torture and murder to break the will of the people. Then came 1 August 1944. A day of unexcelled courage and a day of massive treachery and monstrous cynicism. The Red Army had been advancing on Warsaw and by the end of July was only 40 miles from the capital. On 29 July a Moscow-based radio sent out a message to Poland: "Poles! The time of liberation is at hand! Poles to arms! ... Every Polish homestead must become a stronghold in the struggle against the invaders ... There is not a moment to lose."

The Poles, believing the Russian army would soon be at their side, rose up against the Germans on 1 August. But nothing more was heard from Moscow as the Poles, with pitiful arms, fought the might of the German army in the ancient streets of Warsaw. In fact, the Russian army was given definite orders not to advance over the 40 miles that separated it from the capital. The Poles, handicapped by a lack of food and ammunition, fought on for 63 days before capitulating. As a revenge, Hitler, in an insane rage, ordered that the historical and cultural monuments of Warsaw be blown to pieces. The uprising cost the country 200 000 lives, while the Russians, with their massive numbers of aircraft, armour and men, stood cynically by.

It was, of course, a coldly calculated move on the part of Moscow as M. K. Dziewanowski emphasises in his book, *Poland in the 20th Century*. "The Soviet stand during the Warsaw struggle was motivated largely by political and not military considerations. It was, simply, an effort to destroy the most active elements among the non-Communist resistance ... George F. Kennan has described Stalin's behaviour at the gates of Warsaw as 'the most arrogant and unmistakable demonstration of the Soviet determination to control Eastern Europe in the postwar period'."

The Warsaw uprising infuriated the Germans and they fell savagely on the people. In Krakow on the Sunday following, a day now known as Black Sunday, the Nazis went amok, shooting people in the street, smashing in doors of houses to drag people outside to murder them in public. Miraculously, the Germans did not enter 10 Tyniecka Street, even though the door was unlocked. Inside was Wojtyla kneeling in prayer.

With the Germans bent on revenge and not caring who were the victims, the Archbishop of Krakow, later to become Cardinal, Adam Sapieha, decided that several young seminarians would have to be placed under his protection. Sapieha was in an awkward position. As a leader of the Catholic Church he was expected to follow the Vatican's example and remain neutral in the struggle that was destroying Europe. As a Pole he could not. It was a shaky tightrope, strung between duty and patriotism, on which he walked throughout the war. He treated the German occupiers of his city with disdain. To him, with his lineage going back to the 14th century, a prince of both the Church and the nation, the Germans were no better than barbarians. Governor Frank frequently tried to inveigle Sapieha into inviting him to the archbishop's palace, but the cardinal ignored all requests. Finally Frank placed Sapieha in a position where he could no longer refuse. The German arrived at the palace for tea and was shown into the apartments.

Then Sapieha ordered the meal to be brought. Served on exquisite porcelain covered in gold, a valuable antique owned by the Sapieha family, the meal consisted of sparse slices of black bread spread thinly with jam—the food the Poles lived on daily and about the only sustenance available in the shops to anyone but Germans.

On the Monday following Black Sunday, Sapieha sent Mikolaj Kuczkowski to tell Wojtyla to come immediately to live within the walls of the palace and continue his studies towards priesthood. Escorted by two men, one at the front and one at the back for protection, Wojtyla was taken to the palace where he joined a handful of other students at the secret seminary. Of course, Wojtyla's absence from Solvay was soon detected by the German *Arbeitsamt* (employment office), he was proclaimed an absent worker and the police began searching for him. But at Sapieha's secret request, his name was removed from the list of workers at Solvay and, as an identity, he disappeared from the face of the earth.

At the palace the students lived and worked in one room. Their meals were sent to them. They never stepped outside. And there they stayed until the end of the war. There is no doubt that Wojtyla and the other students would have been arrested and probably executed had they been caught by the Germans. The invaders were no respecters of men and women who entered the service of the Church. As far back as 1939 the Race and Resettlement Head Office of the Nazi Party had drawn up detailed instructions for the destruction of the Church in Poland, which included the abolition of religious worship in the Polish language and the observance of Polish Catholic holy days, with the Poles being allowed to observe only those holidays approved by the German state.

There were widespread arrests of priests and nuns. A total of 3646 priests were imprisoned in concentration camps and 2647 were murdered. A total of 1117 nuns were imprisoned, with 238 exterminated and 25 dying from other causes. The concentration camps in Poland held priests of other nationalities as well. In Dachau, besides 1473 Poles, there were 448 Germans, 159 Frenchmen, 106 Czechs, 63 Dutch, 46 Belgians, 28 Slovenians and 173 of other nationalities. Many Polish clergymen, about 120 it has been estimated, were subjected to criminal medical experiments such as those performed by Dr Carl Clauberg at Auschwitz.

The book, *The Church in Poland*, by Adam Piekarski, gives a detailed rundown on the way the Church was persecuted by the Germans: "The ordeal of the Polish population in Pomerania during the occupation began with the tragedy of the diocesan clergy. As early as the beginning of October, 1939, two hundred and thirty priests from the diocese of Chelmno were shot dead along with members of the chapter and professors of the Higher Seminary. In all, 303 clergymen of the diocese of Chelmno, or 47.8 per cent of the total in the diocese, were killed in the closing months of that year.

"In 1939 most churches in Pomerania were closed down and converted to theatre halls, offices and warehouses. The German authorities ordered the removal of Polish inscriptions on gravestones. It was forbidden either to give confessions or to deliver sermons in the Polish language. Throughout the diocese 3070 small chapels and wayside crosses were barbarically destroyed. As a result of the extermination policy pursued by the occupation authorities, a mere four priests in the diocese of Chelmno escaped death. Monasteries and convents also suffered annihilation.

"In the first stage of the campaign against the Church in Silesia, all Polish church organisations and religious associations were disbanded and all Catholic publications and religious institutions suspended. A ban was issued on the building of new churches and chapels and on the erection of holy images. The Higher Seminary in Silesia was forbidden to admit new students. Following the removal of Silesian bishops from their posts, an order was issued banning the observance of high holy days and the organisation of processions. By order of the president of the Katowice Regency, children were not allowed to be instructed in Polish for the first Holy Communion. During the five years of terror, the diocese of Katowice suffered serious losses. Of the total of 489 priests, 80 were sent to concentration camps and 30 to prisons; six were killed at their posts and 43 died in concentration camps; 29 were expelled from the diocese and 12 banned from performing their pastoral duties.

"In the archdiocese of Poznan and Gniezno, as in Pomerania, the Nazi authorities were ruthless in putting into effect their plan for the destruction of Catholic churches. As early as the first month of the occupation, Arthur Greiser, the *gauletier* of the so-called *Warthegau* (Warta region), made a fundamental division of the population into Germans and Poles in an effort to establish at all costs two Churches, Polish and German. To this end the occupation authorities restricted all pastoral, charitable and cultural activities of the Church. The first wave of arrests in November 1939 was followed by three successive large-scale round-ups of clergymen, in February and August 1940 and October 1941. In Poznan nearly all the priests were arrested and put in concentration camps. The only bishop remaining in the *Warthegau* was the Vicar-General of the Poznan diocese, Walenty Dymek. He too was forbidden any contact with the priests and the faithful; he was under permanent house arrest supervised by the Gestapo. From 1941 the Polish Catholic population of Poznan could make use of only two churches, and even there the Germans controlled every aspect of religious and church life. Over the whole *Warthegau* the German administration ordered the clergy to announce from the pulpit an order by which all prayerbooks containing the "subversive songs" *Boze cos Polske* (O, God who has Poland saved), *Serdeczna Matko* (Gracious Mother) and *Z tej biednej ziemi* (From this Poor Land), were to be turned over to the police. In litanies it was forbidden to mention Polish saints or to invoke the Queen of the Polish Crown.

"In the archdiocese of Gniezno, the oldest bishopric in Poland, the Metropolitan Chapter was the first to be forbidden any activity. Subsequently all curias were closed and priests ordered not to leave their parishes without permission. To intimidate the clergy and the faithful, the former were falsely charged with the preparation of an uprising and collaboration with organisations of the resistance movement. Dozens of priests were deported to concentration camps as early as 1939. By the end of 1940 nearly all churches, convents and monasteries were closed. Sisters and religious alike were expelled. Sermons in Polish and traditional Polish hymns were banned from the entire archdiocese.

"The diocese of Plock also suffered severe losses due to the occupying power's ruthless enforcement of its plan to Germanise the so-called Incorporated Territories. In the first months of the war alone, a large group of the priests of the diocese were arrested; together with their bishops, they later perished in the Dzialdowo concentration camp. Throughout the entire war the diocese lacked a leadership, half the parishes lacked priests, and the clergy were sent to concentration camps, and shot by firing squads.

"In the first months of the war alone, 110 priests from the diocese of Plock perished in concentration camps and prisons.

"A similar reign of terror held sway in the diocese of Wloclawek, in which church life almost completely ceased after the deportation of Bishop Kozal and a group of clergymen. By the end of the war personnel losses had reduced it to nearly half of its prewar size.

"In the diocese of Lodz, after the removal of the bishops, a campaign of annihilation was directed against nearly all the rest of the clergy. Of the total of 347 priests at the start of the war, 150 were murdered in camps and prisons. As a result of arrests and deportations to camps, more than half of the priests were deprived of the possibility of performing their pastoral duties.

"Although in the so-called General Government the occupying power applied different methods than in the incorporated territories, nevertheless it acted ruthlessly and did not stop short of atrocities.

"The administration of the General Government issued numerous orders obstructing the performance of religious practices by the Polish population. First and foremost, all prayers, litanies and hymns reminiscent of Poland were ordered to be removed from missals, prayer-books, and other books.

"Lists of all Jews converted before the war were demanded of parish offices, and at the same time the administration of baptism to Jews without the permission of the police authorities was forbidden. Mixed marriages were banned. Round-ups of people emerging from churches were a daily occurrence.

"The Church also suffered grievous losses in the Galicia District incorporated into the General Government in 1941. In March 1944 twenty-one clergymen were murdered. The German and Ukrainian reign of terror in the area forced 39 priests to abandon their posts. A climate of terror and persecutions also reigned in Warmia and Mazuria. Most of the 40 Catholic priests who identified themselves as Poles and spoke Polish were arrested and sent to concentration camps. Many of them were later murdered.

"The massive repressive measures against clergy in the archdiocese of Warsaw and in the dioceses of Lubli and Czestochowa led in many decanates to a complete standstill in religious life.

Nor did the terror spare the Catholic hierarchy in Poland. In 1939, after the murder of nearly all the members of the Chelmno Chapter, Bishop Konstanty Dominik was removed to Gdansk. Bishop Michal Kozal of Wloclawek perished in Dachau in 1943. Archbishop Antoni Nowowiejski and Bishop Leon Wetmanski of the diocese of Plock perished in Dzialdowo in 1941. Wlodzimierz Jasinski, Bishop of Lodz, was arrested on 6 May 1940 and deported to Biecz toegther with his coadjutor Father Tomczak. The Bishops Stanislaw Adamski and Juluisz Bienick of Katowice were removed to Krakow on 28 February 1941, and Romuald Jalbrzykowski, Archbishop of Vilna, was arrested on 22 March 1942. On 17 November 1939 the Lublin Bishops Marian Fulman and Wladyslaw Goral were arrested. The former was interned in Nowy Sacz from February 1940 to 1944; the latter stayed in the concentration camp at Oranienburg before dying in a Berlin prison.

"A patriotic stand was taken by Archbishop Adam Sapieha, Metropolitan of Krakow, who repeatedly protested to the Nazis against the persecution of Poles. Cardinal August Hlond, chairman of the Polish episcopate, who had left the country at the beginning of the war (for which he often reproached himself), frequently alerted Pope Pius XII to the tragic situation of the Polish people under the German occupation and to the persecution of the Roman Catholic Church. His protests were without the slightest result, however".

There were many among the clergy who showed outstanding bravery in the face of German brutality. One such man was Father Maksymilian Kolbe, who became prisoner 16670 in Block 11 at Auschwitz. This building of thick brick walls and shuttered windows was the camp prison and was known as the Block of Death. Court sessions were held there, travesties of justice with 200 death sentences being passed in a session lasting two or three hours. After sentencing, the prisoners were made to undress and then were taken to a courtyard beside the block, placed against a wall and shot in the back of the neck. Some were not allowed even that small dignity in dying. They were executed in the lavatory. Conditions for those awaiting death, for they knew that was inevitable, were attrocious, as one prisoner describes: "At nine o'clock, after supper, I went towards Block 11. There were the so-called bunkers in its cellars. Together with 38 fellow-prisoners we reported to the block senior of the penal block; we had to spend three nights there as punishment. The block senior reported the actual number of prisoners to the *Block-fuhrer* on duty and they both led us to the cellars where we were locked in cell No. 20. Before people are locked in the cells they are usually searched thoroughly, but this was omitted that night. As a result of the omission some *capos* had with them cigarettes, matches, a candle and some reading matter. At 10 o'clock the *capos* lit the candle, read and smoked. There was less and less air in the cell. The temperature rose higher and higher, so that we took

The sculpture in the Nowa Huta Church, Krakow, of Father Maksymilian Kolbe who was murdered at Auschwitz.

Krakow's main square with the Town Hall, Clock and Cloth Hall.

The interior of St Mary's Church, Wadowice.

off our coats and trousers, finally our underwear too. Soon it was impossible to stand. Men began knocking into one another, fidgeting and swearing; they tried to break in the door but it did not give in. The lack of air was insupportable, the odors emitted by gasping men were unbearable; those physically weak collapsed, those who were stronger fought to get nearer to the door where there was some air. After some time all the prisoners lost consciousness and in the morning, when the door was opened at five o'clock, we had to be dragged into the corridor and were laid there. We were stark naked. From among the 39 persons locked into cell No. 20, only 19 had survived. Six persons out of the 19 had to be carried immediately to the hospital where four of them died".

The death of Father Kolbe, who was then in Block 14, followed the escape of a prisoner who was never recaptured. The German officer in charge of the block, Fritch, charged all prisoners in Block 14 with collective responsibility for the escape. They were to die of starvation in the infamous underground cells of Block 11.

Ten men were selected to die. Kolbe was not one of the chosen prisoners but stepped up to Fritch and asked to be taken in place of another man, Franciszek Galowiczek, who was married with a large family. Fritch, somewhat astonished, asked Kolbe who he was.

"I am a Catholic priest", Kolbe replied.

Kolbe was shut in Block 11 without food or water and 14 days later was executed by an injection of phenol. His body was tossed with hundreds of others into the crematorium.

On 17 October 1971, Father Kolbe was beatified. In making the move Pope Paul VI said: "Alas, world history will not be able to erase these tragic pages". On the first anniversary of the beatification, held at Auschwitz, Cardinal John Joseph Krol, at that time Archbishop of Philadelphia, told the thousands who attended the ceremony: "In Maksymilian Kolbe we see the thousands of Polish priests who were ill-treated and down-trodden. We see the thousands of Catholics and thousands of Jews, Protestants, Czechs, Russians, Hungarians and gypsies, the thousands of victims of different nationalities".

At the end of the war Poland counted its dead and its material losses. They were enormous, one of the greatest disasters ever to befall a country. More than six million Polish citizens died during the six years of the Nazi occupation. Of these, 5.3 million died as a result of various forms of terror and 600 000 died through direct hostilities.

Auschwitz told the full story of the horror of Nazi rule. The Germans tried to wipe out traces of their methods of mass extermination, blowing

The death block at Auschwitz.

up the crematoriums in the Birkenau complex. But there were still mountains of evidence to stun the Soviet troops when they entered the camp on
27 January 1945. Everywhere they encountered gallows and mass graves.
They recognised the human ashes and charred bones scattered across the
soil at Brikenau. In six barracks they found 348 000 men's suits and 38 000
pairs of men's shoes, 836 500 women's dresses and 5200 pairs of women's
shoes. Huge piles of human hair were discovered in store rooms.

The International Military Tribunal in Nuremberg later chilled the world
with the statement "more than four million persons perished in
Auschwitz".

The Auschwitz and Birkenau camps have been left intact as monuments
to the massive cruelty of the Nazi years. Wojtyla made frequent pilgrimages
to the camps as a bishop and a cardinal. Auschwitz was in his diocese and
at one Mass he celebrated, 400 000 people came to pay tribute, to stand
in prayer before the plaques which in 20 languages state: "Four million
people suffered and died here at the hands of the Nazi murderers between
the years 1940 and 1945".

CHAPTER SIX

After the war, as Poland struggled to rise from the devastation of blitzkrieg, starvation, torture, murder and genocide, Karol Wojtyla continued his studies towards priesthood. The country was in a desperate state. Food was short. People were homeless and lost and torn apart from families. But the city of Krakow had emerged relatively unharmed from the holocaust. Warsaw had been levelled but Krakow had escaped the destruction of bombardment, of street fighting and of Hitler's madness.

On 1 November 1946, Wojtyla was ordained by Cardinal Sapieha in the cardinal's private chapel within the walls that had hidden the young priest during the last year of the war. His first mass was held in Wawel Cathedral, in the crypt of St Leonard by the tombs of kings and heroes of Poland. A few days later he returned to his home town of Wadowice to celebrate solemn Mass.

Recognising that Wojtyla was no ordinary priest but a man of intellect, one who should go far in the Church, Cardinal Sapieha sent him to Rome and several locations in Europe for further study. In fact Wojtyla spent considerable time ministering to Polish refugees in Belgium, Holland and France, working in the field with them, trying to understand their peculiar and tragic problems.

During that time he kept in constant contact with his friends in Krakow, writing them lengthy letters that at times were tinged with sadness, at times filled with an innocent wonder at the direction in which his new path was taking him.

From France he wrote: "The last weeks of the academic year were a time of very intensive work and preparation for this so-called licenciate which is an examination covering the whole field of theology. Thank God, the examination went quite well and I have time to think about other things now. For a change I am writing this letter from Paris which I managed to reach on my way through Marseilles and Lourdes. The Prince Archbishop (Sapieha) told me that I should use the holiday months to see France, Belgium, perhaps also Holland and study the pastoral methods which are being applied there. Pastoral methods are a thing which is very difficult to describe and assess. What one can achieve depends on the grace of God and on one's own awareness under the influence of the grace of God. But I am concerned not only with pastoral methods but also with various historical places and buildings which can be seen here. For instance northern France with its Gothic architecture . . ."

From Rome he wrote: "Please believe me that time flies incredibly quick. I don't know how the one and a half years of my studies have passed. Studies, observations, thinking—all this is like a spur to a horse. Every day is absolutely packed. This gives me the feeling that I am serving God according to my possibilities and in accordance with his will underlying which I am to follow by the will of my superiors. I am always in spiritual touch with Poland. I am always thinking about my country. I pray for her, read about her, although I know very little about those who are close to me. Of some I do not know anything . . ."

In another letter from Rome, he wrote about his studies and the news he had just received that his old wartime friend and religious teacher, Jan Tyranowski, had died. "This system under which I am learning is not only tremendously wise, but is also beautiful. And at the same time it speaks with such simplicity. It turns out that the Thought and the Depth never need many words. Perhaps the deeper the Thought, the more it needs no words . . . It is still difficult to write about my experiences. There are so many levels, so many aspects. Deo gratias! If God permits, one day we will have a close talk about this . . . I extend my cordial thanks for the news concerning Jan . . . Yes, yes, it so often happens: God takes away those who have voluntarily offered themselves to him . . ."

Wojtyla's studies in Rome, which so delighted him in the way they honed his brain and sharpened his thirst for knowledge in the field of philosophy, took place at the Pontifical Angelicum University under the French Dominican, Reginald Garrigou-Lagrange, who was noted as an uncompromising traditionalist. It is said that the influence of Garrigou-Lagrange has always remained with Wojtyla and is displayed today in his theological conservatism.

Wojtyla obtained a doctorate in theology for his work on St John of the Cross, the Spanish poet and mystic who lived from 1542 to 1591. A Carmelite friar, St John tried to spread a message of reformation through the Carmelite order, but was imprisoned at Toledo and there suffered under harsh and brutal treatment. He wrote his first poems in jail and escaped nine months later to continue his work among reformed friars. After further disputes between the reformists and the traditionalists, John was sent to a remote friary where he fell ill and was again treated badly by superiors. It was only after his death that he received recognition for his work. His poems, including *The Dark Night of the Soul, The Spiritual Canticle* and *The Living Flame of Love*, came from the depths of his own experiences and have a literary beauty all their own. He has been called "one of the most attractive of Christian mystics". He certainly proved attractive to Wojtyla, not only for his philosophy but for the structure and wording of his poetry.

Wojtyla returned to Poland in 1948. It was now a politically different country from the one that he had left. A dubious election in 1947 put the government in the hands of the communists, although at first it was a relatively benign regime that tolerated ownership of small parcels of land and allowed minor businesses to operate without interference. The Catholic Church was left alone to a great extent, with even some party leaders joining in religious ceremonies. There was freedom to work where one pleased, freedom to move, freedom to listen to foreign radio broadcasts, freedom to criticise—but only if that criticism was done in private.

Even so, Polish bishops were unhappy about the way their country was heading. In 1946, an episcopate pastoral letter said: "The supreme order of this historical moment is to consolidate a new Polish life in the Christian spirit, the source of which is the Gospel and the interpretation of it taught by the Church ... Poland should be a modern, just and happy country enriched by the achievements of knowledge and technology, cultured and wisely organised. But Poland cannot be godless. Poland cannot be communist. Poland must remain Catholic."

Pope Pius XII praised the bishops for their stand, saying in a letter: "You have been guided by a vigilant pastoral conscientiousness when on the question of political elections you have given directions to the faithful befitting the needs of the hour."

The government headed by Wladyslaw Gomulka was trying to find its own form of socialism, was trying to walk an independent path free from Russian influence. But it did not take kindly to what it considered was the gross interference by the Polish Church and the Vatican in the affairs of the country. And when Gomulka was later suspended from his post as Secretary-General after being found guilty of "nationalist deviation", the hardline communists did not forget the Church's earlier role.

In 1950 the Sejm (Parliament) had its revenge when it nationalised the Church's vast estates. Some 500 000 acres were taken over by the State, but at the same time a fund was established to help those parishes that were short of money.

An agreement was also signed between the Church and the government in which the State pledged it would not limit the scope of religious teaching in schools and that the work of clerical teachers would be treated on an equal basis with that of other teachers. It also guaranteed the right of the Church to engage in charitable activity, the publication of books and periodicals and freedom in religious practices and traditional pilgrimages.

In return some of the obligations of the Church were expressed as follows:

"The Episcopate will appeal to the clergy in order that in their pastoral work the latter may instruct the faithful in accordance with the teachings of the Church, to respect the law and the State authority.

"The Episcopate will appeal to the clergy in order that in its pastoral activity the latter may exhort the faithful to intensified effort in rebuilding the country and increasing the prosperity of the nation.

"The principle whereby the Pope represents the highest authority of the Church applies to matters of faith, morality and church jurisdiction, whereas in other matters the Episcopate is guided by the Polish *raison d'etat*.

"On the assumption that the mission of the Church can be realised in various socio-economic systems established by the secular authority, the Episcopate will explain to the clergy that it should not oppose the extension

*Karol Wojtyla photographed soon after he
was made a priest in 1946.*

*St Florian's Church, Krakow...the second
church where Karol Wojtyla worked.*

of the cooperative movement in rural areas, since any cooperative system
is in essence based on the ethical assumption that human nature aspires to
voluntary social solidarity which has as its goal the public welfare.

"In keeping with its principles, the Church, while denouncing all anti-state
pronouncements, will in particular oppose the misuse of religious sentiments
for anti-state aims.

"While denouncing all crimes, in keeping with its principles, the Catholic
Church will also combat the criminal activity of underground bands and
will condemn and punish clergymen guilty of participation in any form of
underground and anti-state activity.

"In keeping with the teachings of the Church, the Episcopate will support
all efforts aiming at the consolidation of peace and will oppose, insofar as
possible, any plans to provoke a war."

On paper it sounded fine. The government hailed the agreement as a
precedent, the first act of its kind among the communist nations. But in
truth it curtailed the freedom of the Church, forced its leaders to keep quiet
on subjects they felt should be raised. And later, as Stalin's iron claw gripped
Poland, the government interpreted the agreement any way it felt necessary.
Too often the fine-sounding words were twisted into a mockery of
themselves.

It was in this period of suspicion and tension that Karol Wojtyla was
assigned as auxiliary priest to the village of Niegowic, 35 kilometres from
Krakow. It was a small parish on a river flat, centred around a red brick
pile of a church with an old wooden bell tower in front.

Although he was there only a year, the villagers today proudly com-
memorate his time. The house opposite the church displays banners and
photographs of John Paul II in its windows, and when a stranger stops people
come out of their houses to tell half-remembered stories of Father Wojtyla.

"He was always wanting to do things for you," said one old man. "Nothing
was too much trouble at any time of the day or night. But even then we
could see he would not be long with us. He was obviously going to be a
very important man."

In 1949 he was assigned as auxiliary priest to the parish of St Florian
in Krakow, a move which enabled him to continue his theological studies
at the Jagiellonian University. The church stands near the massive Grunwald
memorial, a celebration of the victory of King Wladislaw Jagiello over the
German order of the Knights of the Cross in 1410. It was destroyed by the
Germans during World War II, but was patiently rebuilt by the Poles exactly
as it had been before the war.

St. Florian's Church also proudly displays its connections with John Paul
II. A placard on the notice board says that while he was there he baptised
229 children and conducted 160 marriages inside the old baroque
building.

Besides the everyday work in the parish, Wojtyla became more and more
involved in philosophy. He held frequent evenings of discussion with friends
from the university and the Church and he was seen as a man who was
an original thinker and whose capacity to learn, to absorb knowledge on
a wide scale, bordered on the remarkable.

CHAPTER SEVEN

Father Bernard Witkowski was astonished. An American priest of Polish extraction, he had been delegated to look after Karol Wojtyla when the then cardinal was visiting the United Stated in 1976. In the days that followed, he had become more and more impressed by Wojtyla's intellect, his capacity to absorb and remember, but what amazed him was the night the Polish church leader sat down with cardinals from Italy, Germany and France. "So that they could all be brought into the conversation," recalls Witkowski, "Cardinal Wojtyla just flipped from one language to the other with no difficulty at all. He explained everything that was going on in all languages so that nobody would feel left out. I was amazed."

Wojtyla has frequently flabbergasted—and delighted—people with his powerful mind. He does not use it merely to impress, as a kind of intellectual party trick. He is a genuine thinker, with his own philosophies, his own methods of trying to solve some of the mysteries of life. Above all he loves to share his thoughts in long hours of discussions with friends of equal intellectual capacity. Professor Henryk Wereszycki, a teacher of history at Krakow, remembers: "Due to Wojtyla's initiative, some very distinguished Krakow professors of physics and chemistry and myself, the only humanist in the group, met regularly at his private apartments to discuss general philosophical and social problems. At the beginning we talked about private problems. He was always interested in concrete, human matters. Then one of us would deliver a short, introductory speech on the appointed theme. The cardinal as a rule began to talk only when the discussion was fully developed. We always looked forward to this moment with the keenest interest. What he said was always thought out, composed, balanced and to the point. We knew some of his views but this did not prevent us from contradicting him. But though he was never authoritative we always recognised his authority. He used factual arguments and always tried to soften rather than sharpen contradictory points of view. But these were not the final words of our discussion. The cardinal usually left us about eleven o'clock at night and we talked until early in the morning. The impulse given by the cardinal did not die. The impression after these high-level intellectual meetings was unforgettable."

Wojtyla has expressed his thoughts in five books he has written. He has also found time to write around 500 essays, articles, poems and plays during his years as priest, bishop, archbishop and cardinal. It is an impressive tally because his works are not the lightweight scribblings of instant thought, but frequently complex and sometimes abstruse.

When he returned to the Jagiellonian University, Wojtyla continued to study ethics, the subject dearest to his heart. As Marian Jaworski, a Polish professor of theology, says: "He was always interested in ethics. He attempted to plumb the mysteries of a human person to find some norm for human behaviour. His explorations were always creative and bold. He was led by a love of truth".

At Jagiellonian University, he received his second doctorate for his thesis *On The Possibility of Constructing Catholic Ethics on the Basis of the System of Max Scheler*. It was an important work because it attempted to bring together the Thomist and phenomenological aproaches to philosophy. Thomist philosophy, which owes its origins to St Thomas Aquinas (c. 1225–74) expresses its approach to truth in terms of cause and effect and combines the revelation of God with the use of human reason. The causal concept, where, for example, all moving things are seen as the effect deriving from an unmovable first cause, was the approach that Aquinas chose to explain the existence of God. But it was his introduction of reason that was to prove more radical an influence on the development of philosophy in the West. It was to lead over many hundreds of years to a secular rationalism—not that Aquinas would have wished it so.

It was against this later secular rationalism that phenomenology waged its campaign. Phenomenology focusses on the experience and consciousness of the self and tries to provide recognition for realities which cannot be acknowledged by reason alone. In the view of Max Scheler, one of the proponents of phenomenology, love, of which God is the source, is the great principle of human relationships. Now, love is an idea, an experience, an activity which is difficult to treat in a rationalistic way, hence it was against the rather cold, almost mathematical approach to truth, towards which rationalism had moved, that phenomenological philosophy found its feet.

For Wojtyla, grounded in the Thomist approach of cause and effect, with a strong rationalistic element (albeit Christian), there appeared to be a weakness in the approach of Scheler, and yet there was a fresh and attractive emphasis on love, both of God and man, and upon human relationships. Personhood, Scheler argued, cannot be defined as the basis of continued existence because that would not distinguish man from things. The person is constituted by values. He is a continual activity. It is not so much that persons "are" but that they "become" as they concretely realise values.

These ideas seemed attractive to Wojtyla and in his thesis he sought to integrate Scheler's philosophy with that of his Thomist background.

In 1953, while Wojtyla was working at St Florian's Church, he was noticed by the philosophy professor of the Catholic University of Lublin, Stefan Swierzawski. The university's rector, Mieczyslaw Krapiec, takes up the story: "Dr Wojtyla was known as a good talker, thinker and a great friend of academic youth. The Dean of our philosophical department, Jerzy Kalinowski, invited him to come to Lublin and deliver a lecture. The lecture made a very good impression and the young doctor's zeal radiated on the audience. So we invited him to have regular lectures to our students. In 1955 he became holder of the ethics chair at the university".

The Catholic University of Lublin—Katolicki Uniwersytet Lebelski, commonly known as KUL—is yet another paradox of Poland. It is the only university in the Communist world that is not controlled by the State and has become the centre of an intellectual alternative to Marxism. It was established in 1918 in Lublin after a Polish priest and professor, Father Idzi Radziszewski, personally visited Lenin in Russia. Father Radziszewski had been rector of the small Polish Academy of Catholic Theology in Petrograd and he badly wanted to transfer the college to Polish soil. Previous to that there had been a theology faculty at the University of Wilno, but the students had been a troublesome lot. The Russian government decided to detach the theological faculty and transfer it to Petrograd, formerly St Petersburg, where an eye could be kept on the turbulent Polish seminarians. Now Poland wanted it back.

Lenin gave Radziszewski permission to take back the faculty's library and equipment to Poland and Lublin was chosen as the city in which to establish the university.

It was expanded into a liberal arts college with four faculties: theology, philosophy, canon law and humanities, which also includes departments of Polish literature, French literature, history and art history. There are also various institutes at KUL, including the Institute of Church Musicology, the Institute of Historical Geography of the Church in Poland and the recently-opened Institute of the Pastorate of Polish Migration which, among other things, conducts an annual summer school for people of Polish extraction abroad.

KUL was a local university for the Lublin area until it received its national charter in 1938, although some faculties were previously recognised by the State. Without the charter, KUL would not have survived. Even so it has had a difficult time, especially in the Stalinist period of the early fifties when its departments of civil law and economics were abolished because their view of the world did not agree with the Marxist vision. In the mix-sixties the departments of English and German were closed by the government, apparently because they represented links with expatriate Poles. Curiously the French department was allowed to remain. Also in 1953 the faculties of theology at Warsaw and Krakow were abolished, leaving KUL with the only theology faculty in Poland, although an academy of Catholic theology was later established in Warsaw.

The State tried to counter the influence of KUL when it set up an alternative university, a rival school of learning, almost next door. This is the Maria Curie-Sklodowska University, named after the discoverer of radium who was herself, ironically, a practising Catholic. It is a large university, dwarfing KUL and is the State university for south-eastern Poland.

The professors at the two universities have a good relationship. The atmosphere at KUL, students insist, is noticeably freer than at the State university next door. Its very presence is a powerful symbol, but its threat is potential, and therefore much more difficult to counter. Its role is behind the trenches,

not in the front line. It is not even engaged directly in ideological contro-
versy: dialogue with Marxists has been attempted, but it was the worried
communist authorities who stopped it. KUL's professors view this with wry
amusement.

The effect of the Stalinist sanctions of the 1950s was to throw KUL into
sharper focus as the main centre of Christian culture in the communist
world, standing almost as an affront so close to the border of Russia, the
Marxist Promised Land. It thus has a significance out of all proportion to
its size.

KUL's opposition to the official State ideology is implicit rather than explicit, discreet rather than overt. It eschews a direct confrontation with contemporary Polish Marxism, a course of action with consequences the Church
would think twice about before risking. But the pressure of the State apparatus is always there and Father Krapiec has to use all his considerable political skill to keep KUL going in the face of bureaucratic obstacles and
obstruction. As KUL's Professor of Ecumenical Theology, Dr W.
Hryniewicz, observed: "We always live either in the frying pan or in the
fire".

Wojtyla was soon a popular figure at KUL. His lectures were the "box
office hits" of the university, drawing big crowds whenever he spoke. Jerzy
Galkowski, now assistant at the Department of Ethics, remembers: "I went
to his lectures as a first year student. There were always crowds of people
to hear him. I recall words that a friend of mine, a priest, told me when
he explained the reasons for the big crowds. He said the lectures contained
perfect material for sermons. Professor Wojtyla was the perfect lecturer. He
was not a dry theoretician but was always showing problems in the context
of life's experiences. In him theory and practice melted together".

Wojtyla's early days at KUL were at a time when it was dangerous for
a priest to hold and preach views that were not in accord with those of
the State. The heavy hand of Stalinism was across the land, imposing a
grey conformity on independent institutions and cultural activities. Relations
between the State and the Church worsened, reaching their lowest ebb in
1953 when the Primate of Poland, Cardinal Stefan Wyszynski, was placed
under house arrest in an isolated monastery in the Bieszczady Mountains
in the south of Poland. The move to silence the primate was politically foolish and caused more unrest among Church leaders. The following year nine
bishops and 800 priests were put in prison. It is interesting to note the wording of an official government history of religion in Poland which dismisses
the arrest of Wyszynski with these words: "From 24 September 1953 Stefan
Cardinal Wyszynski, chairman of the Episcopate, ceased to perform Church
duties . . ."

The ears of the secret police were everywhere. Arrests were commonplace.
Hundreds were liquidated, including many of those who had fought bravely
against the Germans during the war. The Polish Government grew further
and further away from the people, prompting a joke: "Question: 'What is

Cardinal Wyszynski and Karol Wojtyla at the opening of the Academic Year of the Catholic University, Lublin.

now the best way of committing suicide?' Answer: 'It is very simple. Just jump into the gap separating the nation from the Party.' "

It was not until two years after Stalin's death, in March 1953, that there was some easing of the tension that had stretched Poland almost to breaking point.

Even after Wojtyla was appointed auxiliary bishop of Krakow in 1958, he continued to hold his professorship of ethics (moral philosophy) at KUL. His students travelled the 110 miles from Lublin to Krakow for seminars which were held in crowded conditions in his small flat at 21 Kanoniczna Street, an old building with a crumbling 16th century facade in the shadow of Wawel Castle. Sometimes the seminars would last from three p.m. until midnight, when the students would make the journey back to Lublin by train or bus. But as time went by he became more involved in the business of running the Church in Krakow and was frequently absent on visits to Rome.

His close associate at KUL, Professor Tadeusz Styczen, who ran the philosophy department on a day-to-day basis in Wojtyla's absence, recalls that the burden of work on Wojtyla became almost unbearable. But Wojtyla was reluctant to give up his work with students. He loved the academic side of his life.

So he devised a plan where he could mix the two, that of academic and of Church leader. He took his students on excursions to the Wolski woods near Krakow or into the Tatra Mountains. And there in the countryside, in the fresh air that pumped new life into his sometimes tired body, Professor Wojtyla would sit on a log and lecture to the students sprawled out on the grass before him.

Although he is now head of the Roman Catholic Church, Wojtyla is still a professor at the university. He has said that his pupils will now have to travel to the Vatican for seminars. And in all the years he has been professor, he has never collected his salary. He asked instead that it be used to provide scholarships for poor pupils.

Wojtyla's expertise as an educator sometimes backfired on him, giving him problems in recruiting lecturers for his faculty at KUL. On one occasion he made a special request to the Ursuline order to allow one of his students who had received a PhD, Sister Miriam Szymeczko, to be released to join the academic staff at Lublin. This prompted the Ursulines to take another look at Sister Miriam. If Professor Wojtyla wanted her, she must have a lot of potential so she was immediately appointed to an important post in her order. The same happened to another student who gained a PhD, Sister Karolina Kasperkiewicz, of the Sacred Heart order. As soon as Wojtyla showed interest in her as a lecturer, she was given important work to do and eventually became a Mother Superior-General.

All his life, Wojtyla's pen was never still. His insatiable curiosity as to why human beings are on this earth, the very purpose of their existence, kept him fully occupied producing books, newspaper and magazine articles and lectures. His thesis, *On The Possibility of Constructing Catholic Ethics on the Basis of the System of Max Scheler*, was published by KUL in 1959.

In 1960 KUL published Wojtyla's *Love and Responsibility*, which was later revised by the publishers of Znak, in Krakow, in 1962. It has also been translated into Italian, Spanish and English. This work, said to have indirectly influenced Pope Paul VI's important encyclical, *Humanae Vitae*, is a pioneering study of sexual ethics from a current Catholic viewpoint. Subtitled "An Ethical Study", it is based on a wide specialised reading, and stresses the importance of responsible and personal love as opposed to impersonal and indiscriminate sex.

*Karol Wojtyla camping with students from
the Catholic University at lakes near Krakow.*

In an article for the official Vatican newspaper, *L'Osservatore Romano*, he expanded on the thoughts he had expressed in *Love and Responsibility*: "A correct and penetrating analysis of conjugal love presupposes an exact idea of marriage itself. It is not the 'product of evolution of unconscious natural forces', but a 'communion of persons', based on the reciprocal gift of self. And for that reason a correct judgment on the concept of responsible parenthood presupposes 'an integral vision of man and of his vocation'. To acquire such a judgment, 'partial perspectives, whether of the biological or psychological, demographic or sociological orders', are not at all sufficient. None of these perspectives can constitute the basis for an adequate and correct answer to the questions formulated above. Any answer that comes from partial perspectives cannot but be partial. To find an adequate answer, it is necessary to keep in mind a correct view of man as a person, since marriage establishes a communion of persons, which comes into being and is realised through the reciprocal gift of self."

After clarifying the essence of conjugal love which finds its source in God who *"is Love"*, and the principles on the basis of which "an exact judgment of responsible parenthood should be formulated", Wojtyla affirmed that the "encyclical *Humanae Vitae* contains not only clear and explicit norms concerning married life, responsible parenthood and the correct regulation of births, but through these norms it also indicates the values. It confirms their correct meaning and warns us of the false one. It expresses the deep concern to safeguard man from the danger of distorting the most fundamental values . . .

"The Vicar of Christ reminds modern men, restless and impatient, and at the same time threatened in the area of the most fundamental values and principles, of the laws that govern this area. And since they are not patient and seek simplifications and apparent facilitations, he reminds them what must be the price for true values, and what patience and effort are required to reach these values. It seems that through all the argumentations and appeals of the encyclical, full, moreover, of a dramatic tension, there reach us the Master's words: 'By your endurance you will gain your lives.' For it is a question just of this, when all is said and done."

Person and Action, published by the Polish Theological Society in Krakow in 1969, concerns problems of ethics, not just sexual but also social. "Every man has to be accorded the fundamental right to act," wrote Wojtyla in *Person and Action*, "that is to say the freedom of action; and in fulfilling that action a person fulfills himself. The sense of that right and that freedom consists in the conviction about the personalist value of human action. On the basis of that value, and because of it, man is entitled to utter freedom of action."

And later he said: "Individualism would safeguard the good of the individual above the common good; totalitarianism—as can be confirmed from various experiences in history—would safeguard some common good above the good of the individual. But in both these tendencies, in both systems of thinking and behaviour, we find basically an identical way of thinking about man. One can describe that way as a- or anti-personalist, while for the personalist way of thinking what is significant is the conviction about the ability of the human person to participate. Of course, that ability has to be actualised, shaped and cultivated so that it would grow to maturity."

In 1975 Wojtyla's fourth book was published, an impressive work called *The Foundations of Renewal: A Study of the Implementation of Vaticanum II*. As the title suggests, it is about the work of the second Vatican Council. Here again Wojtyla stresses the importance of developing the dignity of human personality, as directly based on the teachings of the Gospels. He also sets out his view of the participation of the Church in the Development of the world's affairs.

In 1976 Wojtyla was invited by Pope Paul VI to deliver the lectures at the Lenten retreat of the Pope and his household. They were published later that year under the title *Segno di Contradizione*. In them he touched in a moving, profound, at times poetic way on some of the problems besetting the modern world. One of the problems he dealt with was the difficulty of fulfilling the aspirations of the human spirit in direct contact with God. He wrote: "An expression of the transcendence of the human spirit is found in prayer, but it can also be found in silence. That silence which sometimes seems to divide man from God is also a peculiar act of uniting the human spirit with Him."

But in the Lenten lectures Wojtyla did not shrink from pinpointing the evils resulting from anti-love dominating the modern world—the anti-love which lies at the root of all kinds of abuses committed by man against man. These are "his abuse by production, by consumption, by the state in various totalitarian and crypto-totalitarian countries under various regimes that start with lofty humane declarations and end by violating elementary human rights. It is anti-love that divides the communists into classes, that incites nations and peoples to fratricidal clashes, and splits the globe into opposing 'worlds'." Wojtyla concludes that the way to combat these dangerous evils is to restore love to its rightful place in both private and public life.

The denial of God is, of course, one of the principles on which Marxism is built. Wojtyla proceeded to tear apart that principle.

"If it is desired to grasp the problem of the denial of God at its roots, it is necessary to set out from an analysis of the first denial that is not superficial. We must, then, go back, so to speak, beyond the reality of man: we must go back to the reality of Satan. It is obvious that contemporary anthropocentrism, in even the Christian and theological field, keeps it at a distance and almost denies it. We all know that there were protests when the Holy Father merely recalled the elementary truths of ecclesial doctrine just on this matter. They were also recalled by the Sacred Congregation for the Doctrine of the Faith in the study *Christian faith and the doctrine on Satan.*

"Satan, the spirit of evil, appears in Genesis as a reality that now exists, 'ready', so to speak, already operating in the world. The description of the creation of the universe refers only to visible reality, to the 'land' and the 'sky', as the elements of the empirical cosmos. The biblical description itself is silent, on the contrary, with regard to the non-empirical reality. However, even if Genesis does not explain to us the origins of Satan, of the evil spirit, we can identify him at once at the moment of his first appearance, without any difficulty.

" 'The serpent was more subtle than any other wild creature that the Lord God had made.' (Gen 3:1) We begin, therefore, at the level of nature, in the framework of the description of the empirical world. Immediately afterwards, however, comes the sentence which takes us beyond this level, out of the empirical world: 'He said to the woman', the Bible goes on, ' "Did God say You shall not eat of any tree of the garden?" And the woman said to the serpent, "We may eat of the fruit of the trees of the garden; but God said, 'You shall not eat of the fruit of the tree which is in the midst of the garden, neither shall you touch it, lest you die'." But the serpent said to the woman, "You will not die. For God knows that when you eat of it your eyes will be opened, and you will be like God, knowing good and evil." ' (Gen 3:1–5)

Grunwald Statue, Krakow, with St Florian's Church in the background.

Skalka Church, one of the most revered
religious sites in Krakow. The men in front
are playing cards.

"Man is amazed by these words. The evil spirit can be recognized and identified not through any definition of his being, but exclusively by the content of his words. So in the third chapter of Genesis, that is, at the beginning of the Bible, it becomes clear that the history of man, and with it the history of the world with which man is united by means of the work of divine Creation, will be subject to the dominion of the Word and of the anti-Word, of the Gospel and of the anti-Gospel. Up to now we have heard the Word which had manifested itself in the simple affirmation of the whole of creation, the work of God, and in the first place in the affirmation of man created in the image of God. Let us now see along what paths the anti-Word moves.

"We begin with the first lie: it might still be recognized as an error of information; it would even be possible to recognize in it a certain appearance of the search for correct information. The woman corrects the wrong information easily and spontaneously, perhaps without having a presentiment that it is only a beginning, a prelude to what the 'Father of lies' will tell her. And look at what follows: first, he questions God's truthfulness: 'you will not die!'; then, he strikes at the very nature of the Covenant. The God of the Covenant is presented to the woman as a sovereign jealous of the mystery of his rule, as an adversary of man who must be opposed, against whom one must rebel. Finally, Satan formulates the temptation, which he draws from the very core of his own rebellion and denial: 'When you eat of it your eyes will be opened, and you will be like God, knowing good and evil.' (Gen 3:4–5)

"The Father of lies does not present himself to man as denying the existence of God: he does not deny his existence and omnipotence, which are expressed in creation; he aims directly at the God of the Covenant.

"The unreserved denial of God is impossible, because his existence in the created universe, in man, . . . even in Satan himself, is too obvious. The Apostle wrote: 'Even the demons believe—and shudder' (James 2:19), thus proving that they, too, are not capable of denying the existence of God and his sovereign power over every being. On the contrary, the destruction of the truth concerning the God of the Covenant, the God who creates from love, who offers humanity the covenant in Adam in love, who out of love puts before man requirements which touch the very truth of his created being, the destruction of this truth is complete, in Satan's words.

"This is what I mean by anti-Word. But at the same time this anti-Word is put into close connection with the Word. Well, did not the Word say that man and woman were created in the image of God? And Satan affirms: 'You will be like God, knowing good and evil.' It is almost as if he drew the conclusion, at least one probable conclusion, from the Word: if you were created in the image of God, does this fact not include also knowledge of good and evil, like God? But Satan is not only the author of the incorrect conclusion. He wishes to impose his own position, his own attitude to God. He does not care at all about man's 'divinity'. He is anxious only to communicate, to transmit to man his rebellion, that is, that attitude, with which he—Satan—defined himself and with which, consequently, he put himself outside the truth. This means: outside the law of dependence on the Creator. That is the content of his 'non serviam' which is the real antithesis of another self-definition: 'Michael—Who like God'. And the subject of this 'non serviam'—according to Tradition—became the greatest created intelligence: the 'Day Star'.

"Thus in the few sentences taken from Genesis the evil one manifested himself and expressed his nature. Satan's temptation at this point goes considerably beyond what is actually accepted by the first man, female and male. But even what was accepted was sufficient to trace the direction of the further development of man's temptation.

"What strikes us in the third chapter is the ontological and psychological precision of the biblical description. The woman does not wholly accept the content of the temptation: she accepts it only in the limits of her human conscience and freedom. Nevertheless, what she accepted was, unfortunately, sufficient. Let us listen to the Bible text: 'So when the woman saw that the tree was good for food, and that it was a delight to the eyes, and that the tree was to be desired to make one wise, she took of its fruit and ate; and she also gave some to her husband, and he ate. Then the eyes of both were opened, and they knew that they were naked.' (Gen 3:6–7.)"

It was not the kind of philosophy likely to endear him to the communist rulers of Poland. They would much prefer the man held his tongue and locked away his typewriter. But his passion for truth would not allow him to remain an aloof and silent person, for he saw the work of the Church as more than merely looking after the spiritual needs of its followers. He continued his theme in articles written for the Krakow weekly Catholic newspaper, *Tygodnik Powszechny*, and *Znak*, a monthly magazine, and in speeches on various important occasions. He also wrote many specialised works in the fields of theology, philosophy, ethics and sociology for learned periodicals published by the Catholic University in Lublin. His writings have appeared in Scientific Journals of KUL, Philosophical Annuals, Theological-Canonical Annuals and Annuals of Social Sciences.

Truth and freedom were the subjects he held dear. He wrote a series of articles for *Tygodnik Powszechny* under the general heading of "Ethical Primer" and in 1958 he had this to say: "Christian ethics, in its conflict with empiricism and positivism, behind which inevitably ethical utilitarianism is lurking, defends not only the same social virtues which are so previous a heritage of revelation, but it defends the very foundations of those virtues in man, their *raison d'etre* in a person. A person is a free being, but his freedom does not mean independence from society; a person is a free being within the framework of social life. A person uses his freedom well when, on the natural basis of his tendency to social life, he develops real social virtues. Those virtues at the same time determine the implementation of common good. A human person cannot develop and perfect himself apart from it."

In 1964, after the Jagiellonian University, celebrating its 600th anniversary, had excluded theology from its courses and was now a totally lay institution, Wojtyla again spoke on truth: "Aiming at truth, as a basis of human culture, remains closely connected with aiming at good, with moral law and the feeling of justice . . . The human spirit, seeking for truth, seeks also for an expression of that truth in the order of action, in practical life. The truth consists in the deep morality, as far as man's inner life is concerned, and in relations between people as well as relations between nations and socieites . . . Today, when we celebrate the 600th anniversary of Krakow University, I wish her, our Alma Mater, that, just as over the past 600 years, so over the decades, centuries and millenia that will follow—man should be present in there in all his truth; man who is born to learn truth, fight for it, offer sacrifices for it and perish in concentration camps. I wish this Alma Mater of ours, whom I love like my own mother, to embrace the whole man, to be ready to undertake the effort of learning the whole truth, the truth about all reality, the visible, sensory, natural reality, as well as the super-sensory, invisible, supernatural . . . I wish her to go on serving truth, the culture of our nation, and mankind."

The same year he told the club of Catholic Intelligentsia in Krakow: "Every man lives a life of culture in some way, and finds himself in the orbit of the culture of his time. In a sense, the greatest work of culture is man himself—not any of his works or products, but himself . . . Human action and its results remain closely connected with who the man himself is, and with what he surrounds himself in life. Works of human culture are the fruits of that work of culture that is man himself . . . Creating works of Christian culture can be not only a confession of faith, that is to say giving a testimony, but an apostolate. But because of that we must carefully think out under what conditions we can effectively wish for others to participate in the same truth which, thanks to Christ and the Church, is our share. Truth is the foundation of culture—and that foundation we must keep like the apple of our eye."

In 1978, at the inauguration of the academic year in Krakow, Wojtyla was straight to the point on his favourite theme: "The Church does not wish anything more than to bring up the complete man who, guided by truth, is also a truly mature member of society . . . Education in spirit and in truth, education leading to the true freedom, has been a particular expression of the Church's service of our country. We want to go on fulfilling that service."

Such was the way Wojtyla expressed his thoughts to the public—to the Polish people who were Catholics and also to members of the Party and the government who were opposed to many of the Church's beliefs. But there was another way in which Wojtyla expressed himself and that was through his poetry. The very nature of poetry gives the writer an opportunity to portray deep inner feelings and these feelings were an essential part of the poetry of Karol Wojtyla.

CHAPTER EIGHT

In 1950 a young priest, a man of stocky stature with penetrating blue eyes, walked up the steep stairs to the cramped, untidy warren of editorial offices where the weekly newspaper, *Tygodnik Powszechny* (Catholic Weekly) was compiled in conditions of almost Dickensian squalor. He handed a collection of poems to the editor, Jerzy Turowicz, asking that if they were acceptable they should be published under the pseudonym Andrzej Jawien. They were acceptable. Turowicz immediately recognised the poems as works of considerable merit, the sort of intellectual material on a religious theme his newspaper had been searching for and trying to cultivate among young writers since it was established after the war.

Andrzej Jawien was the pseudonym chosen by Karol Wojtyla. He had taken the name from the hero of a small prewar novel, *Heaven in Flames*, by Jan Parandowski, the story of a man who loses his faith but eventually comes to regain it. There is no evidence to suggest that the religious turmoil which the hero underwent had any special significance for Wojtyla. But Wojtyla, like many men of his generation, must have read the novel and the name lingered in his mind. Later he signed a couple of poems with the initials "A.J.". His last published poem, which appeared in 1975 when he was a cardinal, was signed Stanislaw Andrzej Gruda in an attempt to regain some anonymity, for the real name of Andrzej Jawien was already well known in literary and Catholic circles in Krakow.

The one gap in his published works was between 1953 and 1956, the period when *Tygodnik Powszechny* was taken over by the Communist-sponsored Pax Organisation. Its sister publication, the monthly magazine *Znak*, was forced temporarily out of business. All regular contributors during those years turned their backs on *Tygodnick Powszechny*, under its new management, refusing to write for it.

The Pax Organisation was, like much that occurred in Poland after World War II, a paradox. It was a fascist group encouraged by Stalin who had become alarmed at the way Poland was marching towards its own form of socialism, especially after the revolt by Yugoslavia. The Secretary-General of the Polish Communist Party, Wladyslaw Gomulka, was forced to undergo the humiliation of publicly confessing his sins against socialism and was removed from his post, later to be placed under house arrest. Stalin imposed his will across the land, backing it by threats and by the use of such groups as the Pax Organisation, which was specifically aimed at the Catholic Church.

The founder of Pax was Boleslaw Piasecki, a leader of the prewar fascist Falanga Party, some of whose members openly boasted they had killed communists, socialists and Jews. Piasecki admired Hitler, especially for the ruthless way in which he crushed minority groups, but his admiration turned sour when war broke out. For Piasecki was, above all, a Pole, a patriot, a man to whom his country meant more than all the philosophies devised by twisted minds. Opposing the German occupation, he was arrested by the Gestapo and would have been shot but for the intervention of Mussolini. Then came one of those curious sidelights of history where the real and unreal combine. Piasecki, in 1943, led a group of fascist guerilla fighters who were opposed to almost everyone in the war-ravaged country—the Germans, the Russians and even the Polish Home Army under the authority of General Wladyslaw Sikorski's government in London. Only Poland mattered to Piasecki.

When the Russians occupied Poland at the end of the war, Piasecki was in jail and was on the short list of those whom Moscow had ordered to be liquidated. But with the agility of an eel, Piasecki slipped out of that predicament by offering his support to the Russians. He was not only released from prison and given a well-paid job in publishing, but taken under the protection of General Serov, the chief of the Russian secret police. It soon made Piasecki one of the wealthiest and most powerful men in Poland. His Pax Organisation was given a newspaper and publishing monopoly, which later took over *Tygodnik Powszechny*, and he was given sole rights for the production of religious medallions, rosaries and the highly-coloured pictures of Mary and Jesus which sell in Poland like reproductions of beach sunsets in Western countries. It was a lucrative monopoly and one to which the Pax Organisation later added sections of the chemical industry.

Piasecki displayed his wealth, at one time being the only Polish owner of a Jaguar car. "It is very difficult," writes British journalist Richard West, "for a foreigner to understand that the sort of people who enjoy much wealth and power here, the kind of people associated with Pax, are disliked much more by genuine communists than what one might call the right wing. I have heard the most poisonous abuse of Piasecki and his hangers-on from the Poles I know who are communists. He is disliked for his sucking-up to the Russians, although anti-Russian feeling is not nearly as strong here today as it used to be. He is disliked for his anti-Semitic past and perhaps most of all, from the Roman Catholics, because both as a fascist and a communist, he had tried to subordinate the church to the politicians."

Tygodnik Powszechny was returned to its owners in 1956 and they have continued publishing the newspaper since, although not without difficulties. The regime has placed obstacles in their path, such as a strict limitation on the amount of newsprint they can purchase. "When Cardinal Wojtyla became the Holy Father, we could have published thousands more copies of the paper than we did," said a present member of the staff. "But we had to restrict the number of copies because of the lack of paper. They just wouldn't give us any more. Within a few days the paper was changing hands at several times the usual price."

Wojtyla's poetry attracted considerable attention when it was published exclusively in *Tygodnik Powszechny* and *Znak*. His work developed strongly over the years until, in the words of fellow poet, Boleslaw Taborski, Wojtyla emerged as "among the major religious poets of our time".

An insight into Wojtyla's thoughts on the connection between poetry and religious vocation can be found in a work published by the London-based Poets' and Painters' Press in 1971. Called *Words in the Wilderness* and edited by Father Bonifacy Miazek, it is an anthology of poetry written by priests. Wojtyla supplied the book's introduction, although no poems of his were included. Wojtyla said the poems had only one thing in common . . . they were all written by priests, but they could be read independently of the fact that the authors had taken religious vows.

Said Wojtyla: "Poetry has its own significance, its own aesthetic value and criteria of appreciation which belongs to its proper order. And that is what the authors included here are concerned about. But doubtless they are also concerned with making a point about their religious vocation. And very many of those who will read these poems may ask themselves questions regarding the mutual relationship of priesthood and poetry writing. Priesthood is a sacrament and vocation, while writing poetry is the function of talent; but it is talent too that determines the vocation."

Boleslaw Taborski, himself a respected poet, who lived in Krakow for some time during the war, has made a study of Wojtyla's works and has searched through newspapers and archives in an effort to trace the writings published under so many pseudonyms. He has compiled the remainder of this chapter, with translations of the poems by Jerzy Peterkiewicz.

One may call all Wojtyla's poems religious poetry, in its deepest, innermost sense and message. But the phraseology and imagery used is by no means devotional or superficially "religious". On the contrary, it is intensely personal, though it deals mainly with inner life and experiences. It shows a relevance to the problems of modern man. One has the impression, though, that on becoming a priest, Karol Wojtyla continued writing poetry because it was still a natural means of expression for an important aspect of his personality. But in time he came to regard it more and more as an instrument to express thoughts rather than emotions—thoughts, let us add, connected with his religious work.

It should be remembered that Wojtyla's poetry spans three decades, from the mid-1940s to 1975, and as time went by it reflected with a single-mindedness his main task of a concerned and committed pastor. Wojtyla's poetry has always been one of ideas rather than images, notwithstanding the striking imagery of some, or parts, of his poems. It can be said that in time he transcended poetry, as it were, in the sense that only some formal aspects, like rhythm or line pattern, remained. His poetry became philosophical and religious reflections, in the form of poetry.

In his early published poems Wojtyla carried his ideas forward through images, but they were still tied to the underlying religious thought. It has recently come to light that his first published poem was published anonymously in the monthly *Glos Karmelu* (Voice of the Carmel), issued by the Carmelite order in Krakow. Entitled *A Song of the Hidden God* it was a cycle of 17 shorter poems and appeared in print in March 1946 (poems 9–17) and March 1947 (poems 1–6). Poems 7–8 remain unpublished. However, his first more widely known poem and the first to be published under the Andrzej Jawien pseudonym was *Song of the Brightness of Water*, which appeared in *Tygodnik Powszechny* on 7 May 1950. A cycle of eight shorter poems, it retells the story of Christ and the Samaritan woman, using the Gospel quotation from John 4.13: "Jesus said to her, 'Everyone who drinks of this water will thirst again, but whoever drinks of the water that I shall give him will never thirst again.' " The first two poems in the cycle—*Looking into the Well at Sichar* and *When You Open Your Eyes in the Depth of the Wave*—are the poet's description of the water at which he is looking. The water in the well becomes the water of life in which human faces are reflected. If a man can look beyond the surface, can look in a way that is different from the everyday looking at things, he will be able to visualise the memory of a past event.

The event comes into focus and the Samaritan woman takes over the narration, speaking now in the first person until the end of the poem. *Words Spoken by the Woman at the Well, Departing* and the fourth poem, *Later Memories of the Meeting*, recall the event of her meeting with Christ and its significance for her. The fifth poem, *Conversations in Her between Him and the Men of the Wall of the Evening*, carries on the dialogue, within her between Christ and men, concerning the blood sacrifice offered by Him:

"He:
   I have come to tip the balance with blood."

The last three poems, *The Samaritan Woman, The Samaritan Woman Meditates* and *Song of the Brightness of Water*, conclude the reminiscences of the Samaritan woman, ending with her song of inner happiness.

Wojtyla's next published poem was inspired by the announcement by Pope Pius XII on 1 November 1950 of the dogma of Assumption of the Virgin Mary. In Krakow the celebrations connected with this event took place on 8 December on the Feast of the Immaculate Conception. Two days later *Tygodnik Powszechny* published Wojtyla's poem, *Mother*.

It was a major work, taking up the entire front page of the newspaper. And it can be considered evidence of how deeply the poet was involved emotionally in the problem of Our Lady's motherhood, both divine and human. The poem has a complex structure, which will become a frequent feature of Wojtyla's writings, in that it is divided into three parts. Each part then divides into shorter, titled poems. Parts One and Three are spoken in the first person by Mary. Part Two is spoken in the first person by the Apostle John who addresses her.

In Part One, Mary, after Christ's Ascension and before her Assumption, looks back on the childhood of Christ in a series of poetically beautiful images, recalling "the stillness of faraway little streets, arrested in space like

A funeral service of a member of the
Archbrotherhood of the Sufferings of the Lord.
The Order was founded in 1595 by the Bishop
of Krakow and now has twelve members who
meet mainly for charitable purposes.

glass" and the "child's voice" of her son. She recalls the moment of Annunciation and expresses her great, unceasing astonishment over the child which was her own, but also the child of God. He was the fruit of her life and body, but the light and radiance in Him did not come from her ("Astonishment at her only child"). She then reflects on how the realisation of her Son's divinity and the Mystery grew in her gradually ("Mature concentration."). In the second part of the poem, the Apostle John, addressing Mary, describes the moment of his calling:

"I am John the fisherman. There isn't much in me to love.

I am still on that lake shore, gravel crunching under my foot—

and, suddenly—Him."

At Christ's behest, John had called her mother, so she can now be the mother of all men. Christ, though now far away, can be regained through Communion, and Christ's body, taken through bread, is for Mary a recollection of the living little child hugging her. In the third and final part of the poem, Mary realises how, from a woman and a mother, she grows to be the Mother of God. At the end of the poem she reflects on her death here on earth, which for her, will be the union with her son and the passing to a new time. Her thoughts, as in the former poem, turn into song, where she will praise the birth of man in God and of God in man.

On 19 October 1952 *Tygodnik Powszechny* published a poem by Wojtyla under his favourite nom-de-plume, Andrzej Jawien, called *Thought—Strange Space*. It is perhaps the most philosophically complex of Wojtyla's works, an intricate weaving of thought divided into four parts which also subdivide into shorter titled poems. Even so it has a unity of theme. In Part One he considers the problem that sometimes occurs when we confront truths,

". . . and lack the words,

have no gesture, no sign;

and yet we feel—no work, no gesture or sign

would convey the whole image."

As Jacob did, we have to grapple with the image alone. But our deeds will not be able to embrace all the profound truths we have to think out. Humans suffer most, Wojtyla says, from that lack of "seeing", so they have to grapple with words instead, but words resist thoughts.

In Part Three of the poem, the author transposes his arguments into an image depicting the biblical Jacob, a shepherd who was so at one with the earth's forces, that, unlike modern man, he was not alienated from nature; he had the power of vision. Even though he was not articulate and lacked words, he understood his thoughts. And when he sent away his animals, children and wives, he felt in his loneliness that someone was embracing

him and would not let him go. That someone "opened his awareness".

Part three of *Thought—Strange Space* begins with the image of drops of rain which "gather in themselves the whole greenness of spring leaves" so that they transcend their own limits. In the astonishment at the sight, one must not divide one's thoughts from the brightness of objects. The poet goes on to consider the fallacy that thought can embrace all things.

In Part Four, Wojtyla concludes that to find the place where Jacob had wrestled with the angel, one need not go to the Arabian desert, but descend within oneself in stillness and solitude. And finally the truth will be revealed when appearances fall away.

After the publication of *Thought—Strange Space*, almost five years passed before another of Wojtyla's poems was seen in print. The main reason was the suspension in publication of *Tygodnik Powszechny* and *Znak* following the takeover by the Pax Organisation. But the break somehow contributed to a new phase in Wojtyla's poetry. His new poems were not so much concerned with philosophical speculations, but were closer to immediate human problems. His poem, *The Quarry*, was printed by *Znak* in June 1957, a poem in praise of human work, packed with images of great beauty. Then in 1957 he wrote another remarkable poem which appeared in *Tygodnik Powszechny* of 30 March 1958. It was the last poem he would have published in that newspaper.

Called *Profiles of a Cyrenean*, it tells how Simon happened to be passing by when he was forced, albeit reluctantly, to carry the cross of Christ on the last road to Golgotha. The story seemed to Wojtyla to be especially apt for our time. He says in effect that we are all Simons as we all must carry crosses we do not wish to be burdened with, and we all rebel against it.

The three-part poem begins with the poet's reflections on the different profiles—outlines—of men, and comes to the conclusion that it is the profile of Simon of Cyrene which he knows best. He then opposes the serenity of nature, where "insects dull the greenery, swaying the stream of the sun", to the human world, and then turns his thought to:

"in the artisans' hands, in the fingers of women
   typing eight hours a day
   black letters hang from reddened eyelids".
It is then that "He comes, he lays his yoke, on your back".

The middle part of the poem consists of shorter poems where he presents the different types of Simons of Cyrene of our time, and the crosses some people have to bear. He gives some of the poems the titles of the crosses—*Melancholic, Schizoid, The Blind Man, Actor, Girl Disappointed in Love, Children, The Car Factory Worker, The Armaments Factory Worker, Magdalene, Man of Emotion, Man of Intellect, Man of Will*. Some of these crosses are obvious enough. We would gladly help the blind who suffer a natural disability. Terrible too are the diseases of the mind, such as the one suffered by the schizoid. One can understand also the predicament of the worker in an arms factory who justifies himself by saying, "Though what I create is all wrong;

the world's evil is none of my doing." But the poet also has understanding for children too, who

"growing unawares through love, of a sudden they've grown up,
and hand in hand wander in crowds
their hearts caught like birds . . ."

There is understanding for the girl who has been disappointed in love, or for the actor who gives birth to so many people in himself and through himself, and in the end has to admit that the man "who survives in me, can he ever look at himself without fear?"

Even positive qualities such as intellect and will can become burdens, or crosses, as the Man of Will complains:

"No place for heart and thought,
only the moment exploding
in me, the cross."

Part Three of Simon of Cyrene has Simon speaking the poet's conclusions. "I want to be fair, so I bargain with you," he says. Then he contrasts his own little world with that other man's big world. Crowds pass by, all of them groping somewhere on the borderline of God. "Justice calls for rebellion—rebellion against whom?" is the question in the last line of the poem. Like no other of Wojtyla's works, his Simon of Cyrene touches on the dilemmas of the modern man who has lost his way, and for whom the good and the bad are so inextricably intertwined.

The name Andrzej Jawien disappeared from published works for nearly three years then reappeared in a spectacular way in the December 1960 issue of Znak. This time Wojtyla had written a play, The Goldsmith's Shop, or as he subtitled it, "Meditations on the sacrament of marriage", which at times takes the form of a play. In fact, it is both a meditation and a poetic drama in free blank verse of changing rhythms and numbers of syllables, with other scenes in prose. There are also excerpts from letters and a chorus appears several times. At first glance one can discern the easy "conversational" style which marked T. S. Eliot's later plays. In the opening lines, for instance, Wojtyla writes:

"Andrzej has chosen me and asked for my hand,
It happened today between five and six in the afternoon.
I can't remember exactly, I had no time to look at my watch,
or see the time on the tower of the old town hall.
In such moments one does not check the hour,
such moments grow in a person above time.
But even if I remembered to look at the town hall clock,
I could not have done it, for I would have to
look above Andrzej's head.
We were walking on the right side of the market square just
then, when Andrzej turned round and said
do you want to be my life's companion?
That's what he said. He didn't say: do you want to be my wife,

but: my life's companion.
What he intended to say must have been thought out before.
He said this looking in front of him, as if afraid just then
to read in my eyes, and at the same time as if to signify
that in front of us was a road, whose end could not be seen
—there was, or at least could be, if to his request
I replied 'yes'."

(Excerpts translated by B. Taborski who is preparing an edition of Wojtyla's plays.)

Apart from a couple of short scenes, the play is composed of monologues spoken by people seemingly standing together but not talking to each other. It is somewhat similar to Pinter when he was going through his 'Landscape and Silence' phase except that, unlike Pinter, Wojtyla's play is not about the inability to communicate; the monologues of the characters are directly connected.

Obviously this is not a play for the conventional stage, unless for a production by the Rhapsodic Theatre where characters, arranged statically, speak their lines to convey the meaning of the text rather than a visual presentation. Wojtyla probably had the Rhapsodic Theatre, where he once worked, in mind when he wrote the play because he was trying to preserve the conventions of that theatre. But now, after the avant-garde experiments of the last decade, this play could be performed in other ways as it has been on Italian radio.

The play is divided into three acts. Act One is called "Signals"—the context makes it clear it means "signs"—and deals with Andrzej and Teresa reflecting and reminiscing on the birth, growth, development and changing nature of their love for each other. Because they were thinking of marriage, they stop in front of a jeweller's shop. Looking at wedding rings, they ponder the symbolic meaning of them. They also remember the letters they sent each other years ago. They go into the shop, the jeweller measures their fingers, wraps up their rings "and looked into our eyes, as if he wanted to sound our hearts". While there, they have a vision of their wedding day with a chorus, presumably of wedding guests, commenting on their life together.

Act Two, called "The Bridegroom", brings in another couple. Anna is worried by the coldness of her husband, Stefan, and the apparent end of his love for her. But she is ready to forgive him and is determined to fight for her love. She often passes the jeweller's shop on her way home from work. She had not thought about it before, but the wedding rings on display give her the idea that she could sell hers.

"The jeweller looked at the workmanship, weighed the ring
for a long time in his fingers and looked
into my eyes. For a while he was reading
the date of our wedding
engraved inside the ring.

*The wierdly-cloaked members of the
Archbrotherhood of the Sufferings of
the Lord (also known as the Archbrotherhood
of Good Death).*

Again he looked into my eyes, put the ring on the scales . . .
then said: 'this ring does not weigh anything,
the needle points always to zero . . .
Your husband must be alive—
and your ring, or his ring, weighed separately
does not weigh anything—only both together.' "
The jeweller refuses to buy the ring. Anna tries to meet other men and
forget Stefan. A stranger, called Adam, persuades her never to forget Stefan
and, pointing to some girls passing by, recalls the Biblical story of the wise

and foolish virgins. Then he fortells the coming of the Bridegroom. "He still waits. He lives in expectation. Only this is, as it were, on the other side of all those loves without which man cannot live . . . How can I prove to you, Anna, that on the other side of all those loves which fill our lives—there *is Love!*" The Bridegroom she then sees has Stefan's face. The chorus recalls the story of the virgins again and Anna is given hope.

Act Three, called "Children", takes place much later. It concerns the love of Monika, who is the daughter of Anna and Stefan, and Krzysztof, who is the son of Andrzej and Teresa. Andrzej was killed during the war and Teresa brought up Krzysztof by herself. Now the young lovers ponder over their budding love, while Teresa and Anna reflect on the heritage of their problems passed on to the personalities of their children. The young ones also get their wedding rings from the old jeweller. On their wedding day, Adam, who has befriended young Krzysztof, takes the part of the boy's father in the marriage ceremony. The leading characters reflect on the meaning of their past histories. Anna considers herself one of the foolish virgins. Stefan still does not understand anything except, as he tells Anna, "how much have we lost because for so many years we did not feel as the children do". And Adam presents the author's view of love and what men do with it: "Love carries people away like an absolute, although it lacks absolute dimensions. But acting under an illusion, they do not try to connect that love with Love which has such dimensions . . . They lack humility towards what love must be in its true essence. The more aware they are of it, the smaller the danger that love will not stand the pressure of reality . . . Every person has at his or her disposal an existence, and a love. The problem is: how to build a sensible structure out of it? This structure must never be inward looking. It must be open in such a way that, on the one hand it embraces other people, on the other, reflects the absolute Existence and Love in some way, at all times."

After the play, Wojtyla's poetry entered what could be called the pastoral phase. He was already a bishop, and was soon to become archbishop, then cardinal. In the November 1963 issue of *Znak* he had published, under the initials A.J., a poem called *The Church*. It is divided into two parts, of which the first, *Pastors and Sources*, is really a cycle of nine shorter poems of six to ten lines each. The subtitle makes it clear that the poems are the result of Bishop Wojtyla's stay in Rome where he took part in the work of the Vatican Council. It is subtitled: "St Peter's Basilica, autumn 1962: 11 October–8 December." The imagery of the poems is inspired by the basilica itself and by the work of the Council. In spite of their complexity, the poems have a moving directness.

In *The Wall*, the very wall of the basilica leads him to thoughts about human destiny, as does the poem called *Abyss*. The basilica's floor, in the poem *The Marble Floor*, reminds him of St Peter whom he addresses directly:

"Peter, you are the floor, that others

may walk over you (not knowing
where they go), you guide their steps . . .
The rock is a gigantic temple floor,
the cross a pasture."
In a poem called *The Negro*, Wojtyla discovers the unity of thought with
people coming from distant lands:
"My dear brother, it's you, an immense land I feel
where rivers dry up suddenly—and the sun burns the body as the furnace
    burns ore
I feel your thoughts like mine."
In *Synodus*, he reflects on the work of the Council which will leave its
participants
"poor and naked, we will be transparent as glass.
that both cuts and reflects.
Lashed by conscience, this vast temple its setting,
the split world must grow whole!"
In *Gospel*, he reflects on truth "which must be hurtful and hide", but
which "supports man" when man cannot lift himself. The second part of
the poem, entitled *Birth of the Confessors*, is divided into two sections dealing
with the same theme as seen from two angles. The titles of the sections are
self-explanatory. One is "A Bishop's thoughts on giving the sacrament of
Confirmation in a mountain village" and the other is "A Man's thoughts
on taking the Sacrament of Confirmation in a mountain village". The
Bishop reflects:
"I am a giver, I touch forces that expand the mind;
sometimes the memory of a starless night
is all that remains."
The man thinks:
"How am I to be born?
saying: dry, dry, dry is the river bed . . .
Must I ask for a spring? If I have truth in me, it will break out one day.
I cannot regret it; my own self I'd regret!"
In May 1964, another poem by Wojtyla appeared under the initial A.J.
called *Reflection on Fatherhood*, possibly a fragment from his play *Mystery of
Fatherhood*, as yet unpublished. It is written in a kind of heightened prose
which can legitimately be called a prose poem. It is a monologue of a man
called Adam, but he seems to be the alter ego of the author. "For so many
years I have been living like a man exiled from his deeper personality, and
at the same time condemned to sound it deeply." His reflections touch on
the dichotomy between self-love and Love in a very personal way. "Loneliness is opposed to love. But on the borderline of loneliness, love usually
becomes suffering. Your Son suffered. He suffered because in all of us there
is the common denominator of untransformed loneliness." And later he says:
"To take in oneself the radiation of parenthood does not only mean 'to become a father'; it means 'to become a child' (become a son). Being the father

Life in Poland's villages has not changed.
The woman still carries her water as the
women have done for centuries.

of many, many people, I must be a child: the more a father, the more a child." Looking at what happened later to Wojtyla, it is difficult to read these words without being moved.

Wojtyla concludes the work with these words: "It can happen in the end that you will push this world of ours aside. You will let it crumble around us, and above all, in us. And then it will turn out that YOU remain whole only in the Son and He in You—and whole with him in YOUR LOVE. The Father and the Bridegroom. And everything else will then become unimportant and unessential, except this one thing; except the father, the child and love. And then also, looking at the simplest things, all of us will say: couldn't we have learned all this long ago? Was not all that always embedded at the bottom of everything that is?" (Excerpts translated by B. Taborski.)

Two years later, still using the initial A.J., a long poem in seven parts was published in the April 1966 edition of *Znak*. Wojtyla titled his work *Easter Vigil 1966*. Part one, called *Invocation*, has four sections. The first section is "A conversation with oneself begins" and the second section "A conversation with God begins".

"The human body in history dies more often and earlier than the tree.
   Man endures beyond the doors of death, in catacombs and crypts.
   Man who departs endures in those who follow,
   Man who follows endures in those departed.
   Man endures beyond all coming and going in himself in you."

These reflections are continued in the third and fourth sections in which the poet, tracing the meaning of man embedded in history, aims at finding the deeper meaning of man beyond history: man in God.

This was the last poem printed under the pseudonym of Andrzej Jawien or A.J. But nine years later, in 1975, *Znak* published a poem, signed Stanislaw Andrzej Gruda and called *Reflection on Death*. It follows the pattern of Wojtyla's previous poetry by being divided into several parts.

In Part One Wojtyla reflects on the autumn of human life, and then he turns to a contemplation on *mysterium paschale*—the mystery of passing "in which the order of passing is reversed" because at the end of death there is life, the mystery of resurrection. From Part Three on, the poet addresses God directly, and the reflections become a prayer.

Those were Wojtyla's major works. He was never keen on publishing his writings, regarding it as a sideline to his main activities as churchman and pastor. There are probably other works which have never been published that will come to light in the future. They will confirm that he is among the major religious poets of our time.

The controversial church at Nowa Huta,
Krakow, which Karol Wojtyla fought to build.

CHAPTER NINE

Sunday in Nowa Huta. From the Church of St Mary the great electric bells boom over this suburb of Krakow, over this melancholy place of sombre solid apartment blocks, remarkable only for the dreariness of their design. Many were built in the depressing days of Stalin and reflect the cold practicality of socialist realism, although a few newer blocks are built in the brighter colours of Scandinavian architecture.

Only the church shows real imagination and a sense of freedom, a great soaring shape of concrete and stone, topped by a roof in the form of a mighty ark floating now in the bleached blue of a winter sky.

The bells boom and from the apartment blocks the people begin pouring into the streets, laughing, chattering, as they flow along the footpaths in the thin sunshine. Their numbers swell as they get closer to the church, and soon they are a vast tide, thousands of people, shoulder to shoulder as they sweep towards the front courtyard of the church. Then they are jostling, pushing, squeezing to get inside the church, and one is reminded of a football stadium with the fans anxious to be in a good position before kick-off.

It is a few minutes before the eleven a.m. Mass. It has been the same for every Mass held that morning and the crowds will be no less for every other Mass held each hour during the day. How churches in other countries, often half empty on a Sunday, must look with envy at the way the faithful in Poland turn out to worship! Attending Mass here on a Sunday is not merely a duty, not only a communion with God. It is a religious fiesta.

Hundreds cannot get inside the church. They stand outside on the steps, in courtyards, on the street, to hear the Mass over loudspeakers, kneeling where they stand.

Along the street outside the church are the stalls of the carnival. They sell statuettes, crosses, junk jewellery, toys—sometimes tawdry plastic guns lie next to cheap metal crosses—toffees, cakes and religious pictures in impossible colours. But the biggest selling items of all are photographs of Pope John Paul II, pictures in black and white and in colour, framed and unframed, small prints and large prints, each one a reminder that in Nowa Huta the name of Karol Wojtyla is revered.

Wojtyla helped the people build their church. He did it in the face of Government opposition, for when Nowa Huta was designed for workers at the mammoth Lenin steel plant, the bureaucrats made no allowance for places of worship. They were considered unnecessary in the atheistic socialist state, a decadent symbol of old superstitious beliefs. Furthermore, the Government reasoned, Krakow already had around 200 churches which were more than adequate for the population.

But the people of Nowa Huta insisted. At first they worshipped in an old building, but then they demanded more, something that would become the centre of their life and their beliefs. There were minor riots in Nowa Huta over the issue. People marched in the streets in protest, not an especially wise move in a country where street protests are looked upon as being akin to armed insurrection. The people of Poznan had marched in the streets in 1956, and tanks had been brought in to crush them.

But the Government finally relented. In 1967 a permit was issued to build a church, although no help was given by way of money or materials. However the people of Nowa Huta—as well as people from many parts of the world—supplied what was needed and in 1977, before a crowd of 50 000, the church was dedicated by the then Cardinal Wojtyla.

After his spell at the Catholic University in Lublin, Wojtyla had been nominated as an auxiliary bishop on 4 July 1958, his consecration taking place at Wawel Cathedral on 28 September of the same year. He was then the youngest member of the Polish Episcopate. Less than four years later, on the death of Archbishop Eugeniusz Baziak, he was elected acting bishop and on 30 December 1963, he was appointed by Pope Paul VI as the Metropolitan Archbishop of Krakow.

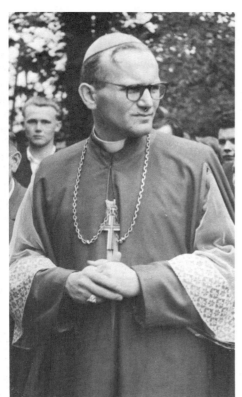

Crowds flock to the Nowa Huta church, Krakow for Sunday Mass.

Karol Wojtyla as a Bishop in 1965.

It was inevitable he would soon receive the red hat of cardinal. As Gary MacEoin and the Committee for the Responsible Election of the Pope point out in their book, *The Inner Elite: Dossiers of Papal Candidates*, there are various ways in which Church leaders can become cardinals. "Normally, the honour is conferred as a result of success in one of two fields, or perhaps in both. One is a lifetime of service in the Curia, and within the Curia the most promising career is as a member of the Vatican's diplomatic service. Practically every successful nuncio is in due course recalled to Rome and rewarded with a red hat. The other is by becoming the bishop of a diocese that is identified by reason of size and importance as entitling its head to be named a cardinal . . . The primatial see in any country with a substantial Catholic population is almost sure to carry the cardinalitial dignity . . . There is an element of luck in the process, being in the right place, knowing the right people; or alternatively, committing a gaffe and losing an opportunity. An occasional cardinal may have made the grade by political acumen or the ability to pull strings. But by and large, it is clear that those who succeed are men of superior ability, hardworking, clear-thinking, good executives and politically sophisticated . . ."

Wojtyla was made a cardinal on 29 May 1967.

By now there was an easing in the previously strained relations between Church and State. The Stalin era, with its persecution and blinkered leadership, was but a bad memory. Cardinal Wyszynski was released from house arrest in 1956 and Wladyslaw Gomulka was back as leader of the country.

But the easing in the relationship was relative. Whereas the State had previously beaten the Church with a heavy cudgel, it now used a supple cane. Both sides realised and understood their positions. The State knew that 85 to 90 per cent of the population were Catholics, most of them devout, regular church-goers. It also recognised the fact, albeit with some reluctance, that the Church was the major ideological force in the country. The Church, on the other hand, knew it could not push the government too far or else there could be Soviet intervention as happened in Czechoslovakia and Hungary. As one Government official said: "You can choose your friends, but you can't choose your neighbours". And the neighbour, Russia, has always peered closely over the fence, with heavy supplies of troops and armour near the border.

The collision course on which the Church and the State often sailed was seen in 1976 when the official communist group, the Polish United Workers Party, tried to have its role set out in the new constitution as "the leading political force". But after protests this was changed to the less autocratic "guiding political force in the construction of socialism".

A large part of that protest came from the Catholic Church. A pastoral letter from the Polish bishops said it was their duty to express their views because the majority of the community, who would be subject to the new constitution, were members of the Church. The Episcopate pointed out that for the communist party to be accorded the "leading" role would result in a dangerous division of citizens into two categories and would subject the "whole of our life to the materialistic outlook which would be unacceptable to believers". They said the rights and responsibilities of citizens should not be limited by a single ideological outlook and philosophical system.

They were also very critical of a proposed provision on citizens' rights which said that "the rights of citizens are inseparably linked with honest fulfilment of their duties towards their motherland". The wording was altered to "the citizens of the Polish People's Republic should honestly fulfil their duties towards the motherland and contribute to its development".

Of even greater significance was the proposed provision in the constitution which would have given the USSR the absolute right to intervene in Polish affairs. The Sejm (Parliament) was told that "confirmed in the constitution should be the principle of Poland's foreign policy: its participation in the world socialist system, its unshakeable fraternal bond with the Soviet Union". This would have brought Poland into line with many other East European countries and would have legalised Poland's lack of total sovereignty because of its dependence on a foreign power.

The bishops pointed out that the Church was "cojoined with the nation by a common history". It said that it must be remembered that the rights of the nation were bought at the cost of a century's toil and struggle in the cultural field and on the battle field. The upshot of the bishops' protests was that the vow of an "unshakeable fraternal bond" was amended to a statement that the Polish People's Republic "strengthens its friendship and co-operation with the USSR and other socialist countries".

In these confrontations, and others before and after, it was Cardinal Wyszynski who argued on behalf of the Church. The Episcopate believed that the Church should have but one voice and that voice should belong to the Primate of Poland. But Wojtyla did not take a silent back seat. On all documents attacking the Government, the name of Wyszynski came first, followed by that of Wojtyla, and then the other prelates of the Polish Church.

However Wojtyla often personally spoke out against the regime. For instance, during his 1976 visit to the United States he said: "The laws of human freedom are formulated more fully in the constitutions of new nations, but are these principles really respected everywhere? Do we not find people who are underprivileged because of their religious convictions? May we not even speak today of actual persecutions of Christians and others who profess their religion?"

Later, during the same visit, he mentioned how hardship had helped to reinforce Polish Catholicism. "The atheist character of the government forces people to consciously affirm their beliefs." In 1977 he presented a report by the Polish Bishops' Doctrinal Commission which severely criticised Polish attempts to impose materialism and secularism on Polish culture. It also criticised the Government's policy towards labour, saying that workers had been pushed beyond their physical limits thereby affecting their duties to their families and their religion.

In October 1978, a provocative letter from the Polish bishops was read out in churches. The man behind this letter was Wojtyla. It said: ". . . the spirit of freedom is the proper climate for the full development of a person. Without freedom a person is dwarfed, and all progress dies. Not allowing people with a different social and political ideology to speak, as is the practice of the State, is unjust".

Depending on various circumstances, such as the popularity of party leaders at the time, the relationship between the State and the Church went up and down, like mercury, between tepid and freezing. It was particularly chilly in 1966 when the Church was celebrating its millennium in Poland. The State and the Church held separate celebrations, with the State made to look foolish when few people bothered with its programme of events and instead attended in millions those organised by the Church.

At the same time the Polish bishops wrote a letter to the German bishops offering and begging forgiveness in an attempt to heal the deep scars of World War II. The letter angered the Government because it was also involved in delicate negotiations with the Germans over disputed territory. An official government publication says of the letter: "This gave rise to a nationwide campaign against the political overtones of the message. Leading

Karol Wojtyla then a Cardinal, stops to
admire a child in the streets of Krakow.

representatives of the highest State authorities appeared at mass rallies and sharply criticised the political line taken by the leadership of the Episcopate. The criticism met with the full agreement of the majority of the people. The Polish people felt that the wrongs of war criminals could not be forgiven and forgotten, nor could an equal sign be put between the guilt of the hench-man and the guilt of his victim. The wrongs of the Nazis who committed mass crimes against Poles and the citizens of so many other nations could not be forgotten".

Gomulka was deposed in 1970 after bloody riots in the Baltic coastal cities of Gdansk, Gdynia, Sopot and Szczecin. Workers appeared on the street after the Gomulka government put up food prices by as much as 25 per cent. Gomulka was replaced as party boss by Edward Gierek, and again there was a thaw in Church-State relations.

Gierek's first conciliatory gesture was the promise to return about 7000 buildings once belonging to the Church, although this promise was never fully kept. He also allowed more churches to be built, one of the things Cardinal Wyszynski had fought hard for over the years. In return the Church finally recognised the new western boundaries of Poland, appointing six Pol-ish bishops to the dioceses in the land acquired from Germany. This removed a long-standing irritant between the Vatican and Warsaw. There were visits between top Polish government officials and those of the Vatican in an attempt to normalise relations between the two states, but Wyszynski insisted that there could only be normalisation if full freedom was given to the Church. The Polish Government would not go as far as that.

In 1973 there was a confrontation between the Church and the State over the question of religious education. Two official reports, one on the current state of education, the other on the duties of the State with regard to the upbringing of young people, were published. Both documents stressed the need for a unified educational system designed to prepare its recipients for life in a "socialist" Poland. The school timetable was to be rearranged in such a way that it would be physically impossible to receive religious instruc-tion in a church.

The bishops of Poland angrily denounced the move, saying that "such intentions could deny a person his fundamental rights to freedom of con-science and religion which are guaranteed in the Polish constitution. State laws cannot be contrary to God's laws otherwise they are not binding".

More riots in 1976 over steep rises in the price of food led to another freeze in the relations between Church and State. Church leaders, such as Wojtyla, argued publicly that the people had a right to protest, and in his rolling cadences Wyszynski spoke out on the way the Church had cham-

Thousands of people follow Karol Wojtyla
through the streets of Krakow during a
religious procession.

pioned the cause of the workers: "... let no one think that the bishops embarked on a struggle against the system. No, they only recalled the Rights of Man, the family and the citizens in their country. These are the only objectives that guide us. We cannot accept comments appearing, in particular, in the foreign press, which scent political motives in everything we do. We are concerned with life, with the life of man, the nation, the family in the spirit of God's peace. These are the true motives guiding the Polish bishops and priests in their toil. We do everything in our power that our country may be calmer, better, quieter, so that weeping shall not be heard, so that no one shall be beaten up, persecuted or ill-treated, so that police truncheons may be returned to their cupboards, so that everyone may feel secure, peaceful and respected in his native home. This requires much good-will and co-operation of us all ...".

It was a courageous speech, typical of Wyszynski. In another speech in 1976 supporting workers who had been jailed, the aging primate said: "We wish our country to have as few prisons as possible. It is in the churches that freedom of the nation is tended and kept safe. Prisons should be the exception, not the rule for government".

The Polish bishops also took up the theme of freedom, especially that of religion, in a pastoral letter in 1976. They pointed out that the State was using the people's taxes to propagate atheism in a country overwhelmingly Catholic. They said: "In our country the great majority of citizens are believers and are members of the Catholic church. If, then, State officials make war on religion, they are guilty of abuse towards the citizens whose taxes pay for their services. The fight against religion is paid for with funds to which the practising Catholic must contribute. Who can fail to see the extraordinary contradiction behind this sad state of affairs".

Wyszynski has been the leader in the Church's battle against the State, although the primate once, without blushing, said: "The Church does not combat the regime in Poland". He added: "Bishops and priests ask neither privileges, nor appointments, nor rewards, nor decorations. We ask only one thing: that in our homeland Christ has His place, the Church being respected in its mission and vocation".

While Wyszynski often raged against the State, Wojtyla would take a more conciliatory line. For instance, during the Second Vatican Council (1962–65), Wojtyla and other bishops from Eastern Europe insisted on a strong statement on religious freedom in communist countries. But Wojtyla also stressed that the statement should not be so strong as to be counterproductive. Referring to a preliminary draft of the statement, he said: "It is not the Church's place to teach unbelievers ... let us avoid any spirit of monopolising and moralising. One of the major faults of this draft is that the Church appears authoritarian in it".

Wojtyla was at times involved in public disputes with Wyszynski, the most renowned occasion being when a Polish intellectual and Catholic, Jerzy Turowicz, wrote an article saying that it was time the Church leaders faced up to the fact that there was a crisis in the Church. Turowicz was the leader of the Catholic liberals in Krakow who pubished *Tygodnik Powszechny* and *Znak*. Publicly criticised by Wyszynski, it was feared by many intellectuals that Turowicz and the *Znak* group might no longer have the support of the Church. But Wojtyla defended Turowicz and managed to make peace between him and Wyszynski, as well as persuading Pope Paul to allow *Znak* to continue its work in Poland.

But above all Wojtyla recognised the fact that Marxism and Christianity were incompatible. His feelings were summed up on the day a top communist official telephoned him over a matter of some importance. Before hanging up the phone, Wojtyla said: "Until you officially recognise us, I don't see how we can talk to each other".

Karol Wojtyla is now surrounded by the rich trappings of the Vatican, by treasures that are beyond price, by elaborate ceremonies and ornate rituals. But as a Church leader in Krakow he cared nothing for the rewards of high office, even for the ordinary comforts of life. He would probably sympathise with a letter written to a Rome newspaper by a Jesuit priest, Piero Brugnoli, soon after he (Wojtyla) was elected Pope.

"Dear John Paul II, brother in Christ . . . For me, a poor Christian who earns his living day after day in a work which counts for little, cheek by jowl with men and women who are without faith, there are many questions in my mind and heart, even in these days of your papacy, and I should like to speak out about them. Some of them seem to be questions of substance—to begin with, I wonder about the mustering of all those worldwide audiovisual resources which brought your inauguration, with its cordons, its troops, it ceremony, into the homes of people all over the world, with you as centre of the spectacle.

"I am not alone in my questioning. The first question that occurs to many folks like myself concerns this enormous machine which has been deployed about the papacy from the death of Paul VI on. It makes us doubly hope that your papacy will be a long one, because there are many of us who wonder what image of the church emerges from this gigantic apparatus of lights, golden baubles, ceremonies, sabres, ambassadors and heads of state from all over the world—from all of this folklore, so to speak. Is it a festival centred about our 'common father'?

"But what shall we say if this whole circus has nothing to do with the 'evangelical form', that is, with the life of Jesus of Nazareth and His Gospel? What shall we say if this exaggerated piling up of seductive images of sacralisation and power, of prestige and display and wealth, of triumphalism, prevents the man in the street from seeing and understanding that the

THE PEOPLE'S POPE 119

church is the church of the poor, of God's people on the march in the context of the suffering and the struggle of the poorest? How can I explain to my comrades at work that you have nothing to do with all that, that the Council is something to be implemented gradually, and that one cannot wipe decades and centuries of worldliness out with a simple wipe of the sponge?

"Perhaps I'm a 'different' Christian. Perhaps because every morning and evening I am squashed in the bus like a sardine, and my contact with people makes me different. In any case, all of this disturbs me, and I fervently hope, if what we have been told about your past is true, that it also disturbed you to be enclosed by a scaffolding which the Council has long wanted to dismantle. There are many of us who wonder if the Gospel doesn't begin someplace outside all this pomp and ceremony. How can I explain to my fellow workers that Christ stands outside it? Or that this collective madness, pumped out in the columns of the *Osservatore Romano* no less than by the lay press and TV, is wholly transitory? Or that, if you were born into it the day you were reborn as Bishop of Rome, you will be able to free yourself from it? Or perhaps my difference is simply one of 'evangelical extremism', and *this* church, the only official face of Christianity, really needs all this tinsel to survive itself and the world, to strengthen itself and ensure its prestige as 'mother and teacher of peoples'? . . .

"If the Gospels are to make sense, certain radical choices must be made. If they are to make sense ecclesiastically, these choices must involve all bishops, beginning with yourself. You are well aware that the key words are poverty, sharing, brotherhood, hunger and thirst for justice, words which must be experienced within the life and struggles of the poor . . .

"For such was the life of Jesus of Nazareth, which I have ventured to propose as an example. It will not be a little matter if your example can serve as an indication for us.

"If you succeed, history will proclaim your success, based on your fundamental choices. I beseech you only, as you yourself have seemed to suggest, not to be afraid of a new departure, that is, of that Spirit which is the creator of new things and which lies at the heart of history and its every evolution. It will surely be a test. But 'Are you the one who was foretold to us, or must we wait for another?' "

Wojtyla so disdained worldly goods that when he was made a bishop he was reluctant to move into the official apartments at the Metropolitan Curia. He was quite content to stay in his cramped lodgings at 21 Kanoniczna Street, could see no reason why he should move into more luxurious quarters.

Those who ran the Curia thought otherwise. They were aghast that Wojtyla should want to stay in what they considered were rather mean lodgings, at least lodgings not good enough for a leader of the Church. But Wojtyla ignored their pleadings. Then when he was out of Krakow for a few days, they saw their chance. They went to his lodgings, removed his books and his few articles of clothing and placed them in the Archbishop's Palace.

*Wawel Castle from Kanoniczna Street where
Karol Wojtyla lived.*

Wojtyla was far from pleased when he returned home. He said nothing at the time, but later called those responsible into his office and gave them a stern reprimand.

The Archbishop's Palace in Krakow is a building with spacious rooms lined with paintings, including priceless 13th century works painted on wood, which are among some of the oldest pieces of art in Poland. Antique clocks tick on shelves and renaissance chairs are grouped around tables. Some of the furniture once belonged to the kings of Poland.

Wojtyla was offered a huge bedroom packed with valuable antique furniture, but he took one look at it then went searching for a smaller room more suited to his spartan tastes.

He was forever causing concern to his staff by his disregard for dressing in what was considered a proper manner. The staff continually brought him new clothes after first hiding the old, frayed garments he insisted on wearing. Even his car driver was moved to say: "I feel ashamed of the cardinal. He is always so shabbily dressed. Look at his shoes, shirts—they are worn out".

Nor did he care about food. It has been said that if the bishops of Poland have one sin, it is that of gluttony. They would sit down at tables laden with pates of game and fowl, with rolls of smoked goose, with roast hare in cream sauce and with beetroot puree, with tripe seasoned with pepper, marjoram and paprika and garnished with Parmesan sauce, with noodles garnished with plums and dusted with sugar.

But not Wojtyla. He purposely refrained from eating the things he liked, and always fasted before certain religious days. So little did he care about eating, in fact, that he used to upset the other priests with whom he was scheduled to lunch each day at one thirty p.m. As Mikolaj Kuczkowski, Chancellor of the Curia, recalls: "The cardinal was not punctual. He would set off for lunch but would be waylaid by people wanting to talk to him. They knew they could always get hold of him as he walked down the corridors to the dining room. And he never refused anyone who wanted to talk.

"So instead of getting to lunch at one thirty, he would be there at two o'clock or two fifteen. Of course, the soup was getting cold by this time. But we would always tell the younger priests who were getting agitated: 'The cardinal arrived for lunch at half past one. It is not true what your watch says'."

Wojtyla never stopped working. He transformed the back seat of his car—a Volga—into a miniature office by installing a table and a reading lamp. If people were accompanying him in the car, he would, after a short chat,

say: "Well, let us start working. The time is catching up on us". One day
there was a fault in the car's electrical system and the driver suggested the
lamp should be switched off because the car might not reach Krakow. "As
long as it shines, we will permit it to shine," Wojtyla said. They eventually
reached Krakow. At another time they left without the lamp and Wojtyla
was horrified to find he faced four hours in which he could not read. He
immediately ordered the car to return so that the lamp could be fitted.

Expecting others to work as hard as he did, Wojtyla would not listen
to their complaints that they could not do their allotted tasks. He asked
that in certain matters his assistants advise him on what to do, not tell him
what they thought he wanted to hear. He believed in preciseness and the
use of time in the most economical way possible.

This did not mean he was a harsh taskmaster, nor a man who did not
think of others. On the contrary, as his friends frequently point out, he was
especially considerate of other people. A few years ago a reception was
organised in Krakow for Father Bukowinski, who had been transported to
Russia during the war and had spent 13 years in Soviet labour camps. After
being freed, he had stayed on in Siberia, working as a priest, and had now
come to Krakow to visit his brother. The guest of honour at the reception
was Cardinal Wojtyla and a suitably ornate chair was prepared for him
at the head of the table. But the cardinal refused to sit there. "There is
nothing special in being a cardinal in Poland," he declared. "This man from
Siberia will sit in the place of honour." And so he did, with Wojtyla sitting
beside him.

Another occasion was at the funeral Mass for a professor who had been
friendly with Wojtyla. At the end of the rites, the professor's widow thanked
Wojtyla for the service, but expressed her surprise that the Mass had been
said in Latin instead of the vernacular, which was by now the custom. Wojtyla smiled and said: "I knew Henry's eccentricities". As it happened, the
professor had very much disliked the change from Latin into the vernacular.

In his days as cardinal, no one saw more of Wojtyla than Chancellor
Kuczkowski. As he says, "we lived under the same roof, we met each day,
we ate together each day". Kuczkowski's comments, although tempered by
the fact that Wojtyla is now head of the Catholic Church, are worth
recording.

"We talked," said Kuczkowski, "about the various problems of the archdiocese, about big and small problems, about happy and sad problems. The
cardinal would always listen intensely. From time to time he would interrupt
and ask additional questions in order to get a fuller picture or to bring out
details. He listened to everything, but we knew that first of all he was
interested in a detailed and accurate account of the matter, and not just
a commentary. He left the judgement to himself and was not prone to reveal-
ing whether he shared anyone's opinion or not.

"But my contacts with the cardinal were not reduced to only the matter-

*Karol Wojtyla caught in a candid shot during
a hike through the Tatra Mountains.*

*Bicycle riding was one of Karol Wojtyla's
favourite relaxations.*

of-fact. There were also free informal talks. We, the clerks of the Curia, were close to the cardinal, but the word 'close' might not be accurate. I think a lot of people will agree with me that there was something in his person that set him apart and somehow 'above'. There was a distance. But it was not a 'physical' distance, it was completely natural. It was not caused by high ecclesiastical honours or power. Furthermore he was always able to bridge these distances and talk and get along well with all sorts of people— for these distances were not of an intellectual kind. Of course, his temperament was intellectual, but he knew and valued highly the virtue of simplicity. He had very good contacts with people of quite different background and environment.

"I think that this 'distance' was caused by his rich, deep and powerful personality. It was a peculiar 'distance'—not crushing, but enlarging and enabling everyone around him to grow. It came from the ever-alive springs of religion. He shared all his problems with God, praying alone in his Chapel."

(In fact, Wojtyla would stay for long periods in his private chapel next to his apartments. No one dared enter while he was inside unless it was on a mission of paramount importance.)

"Some of his features not known to the public are worth mentioning. He was hard working and had his own time perfectly organised. And one more feature: he did not 'rule' but directed by creating possibilities for independent people endowed with imagination. He started a new period in the history of our archdiocese."

They are highly complimentary words, but that is the way it is when people speak of Wojtyla. He is seemingly one of those unique persons who leave, like childhood summers, only memories that are good.

Wojtyla still managed to find time to indulge in his private passions of films, theatre, literature and art. He arranged conferences with painters, sculptors, art historians and art critics on the problems of religious art. Wojtyla felt that much could be done to improve the level of ecclesiastical art, and shortly before his election was involved in a conference that was partly devoted to the iconography of St Stanislaw.

And there was also the outdoor life which he followed with equal passion. He loved canoeing on many of the thousands of lakes that dot Poland. There is a story that when he was nominated as a bishop he could not be found. A search for him finally located him on a kayak trip on a lake outside Warsaw. He was summoned back to the capital where he was asked whether he would accept the position. "Yes," he replied. "But that doesn't mean I can't return to my kayak trip, does it?" Within hours he was back on the water.

When he took to the lakes and rivers of Poland regularly each summer, he would travel with a portable altar for prayer on his overnight stops on river banks, and sometimes tied together two paddles to make a cross for an impromptu Mass. With a 50-kilogram pack on his back, he would also

The sparse bedroom of Karol Wojtyla when he was a Cardinal in Krakow.

Sunday at Jasna Gora.

Karol Wojtyla skiing in the Tatra Mountains (pictured right).

find time to tramp through the hills and forests near Krakow.

But skiing was the sport he loved most, describing the swishing rush down a mountain-side on skis as an "extraordinary sensation". He tried to go on a skiing holiday to the Tatra Mountains at least once a year. His favourite spot was Zakopane, placed in a vast valley surrounded by mountains at the foot of the Tatras. The people there are famous for the way in which they have kept their traditional life-style, with their richly-embroidered folk costumes and their dances held to the music of the dudy (a four-toned wind instrument somewhat similar to the bagpipes), the violin and the double bass. Wojtyla also visited this area in spring when the hills became colour-splashed landscapes of wild flowers and the mountain people would perform their astonishingly agile folk dances.

Karol Wojtyla reading the Bible during a skiing trip in the Tatra Mountains.

Karol Wojtyla has his morning shave while on a mountain hike in Bieszczady.

When skiing, Wojtyla would leave Krakow after the midnight Mass at New Year, and would be on the slopes the same morning. Sometimes he would travel to the Chocholowska Valley, the largest valley in the area, with its wooden chalets decorated with exquisitely carved gables and walls made of beams cut from massive trunks of trees. There he would be towed up the hill-sides by horses, but often he would shoulder his skis and walk to the top. As a friend, Father Adam Boniecki, described it: "He would medi-

tate on the Stations of the Cross on the way up, and then permit himself a little bit of joy on the way down". He was known as a daredevil skier, and a fine one at that, who would get his disapproving chauffeur to leave him in the mountains with instructions to meet him again several miles, and many hours, later.

Wojtyla never bothered with the fancy rig worn by skiers today. He stood out in baggy wool pants and old-fashioned lace-up boots. He even preferred his old skis made of Polish hickory instead of new ones friends bought for him in the United States.

But his times in the countryside were much shorter than he would have liked, the business of the Church always demanding his time. He took part in all four sessions of the Second Vatican Council, and he played an important part in the draft of the constitution *On The Presence of the Church in the Modern World*. He was a member of the Vatican Council for Laity, chairman of the Polish Episcopate's Commission for Lay Apostolate and of the Commission for Catholic Education. In 1969 he was elected deputy chairman of the Conference of Polish Episcopate and took part in all Synods of Bishops in Rome where he was twice elected a member of the Council of the Synod of Bishops. In 1970 he led a pilgrimage of Polish bishops and priests, who were former prisoners in German concentration camps, to Rome for the celebrations of Paul VI's golden jubilee of priesthood.

One of Wojtyla's major journeys was to New Guinea, New Zealand and Australia in 1973 where he took part in the International Eucharistic Congress in Melbourne, and, among other things, was photographed with a kangaroo. He left a deep and lasting impression on leaders of other religions, including a Sydney minister, the Reverend Roger Bush. "He impressed me with his humility, deep sense of compassion and the courage to have served his church in Poland during the difficult years," said Bush later. "We talked on 'not for publication' difficulties and the depth of his spirituality literally shone through. He is a man amongst men, with a healthy sense of humour, unafraid to laugh. He says what he thinks. I'm sure this made his tasks in Krakow more difficult than most of us could imagine."

In February 1976, he delivered the Lenten sermons in the presence of the Pope, cardinals, bishops and monsignors of the Roman Curia. Two years later, with Cardinal Wyszynski and Bishops Jerzy Stroba and Wladyslaw Rubin, he visited the Federal Republic of Germany at the invitation of the West German Episcopate. It was an important visit because it symbolised, as far as the Church was concerned, the healing of the old wounds between Germany and Poland.

But from the long-term view his most important journeys outside Poland were to North America in 1969 and in 1976 for the Eucharistic Congress in Philadelphia. On these two occasions some of the most powerful leaders of the Catholic Church were able to gauge the worth of Wojtyla. Their assessments had an important bearing on the conclave held in the Vatican following the death of John Paul I.

CHAPTER TEN

On the last day of August in 1976, Cardinal Karol Wojtyla stood in a pulpit before a congregation of American westerners in a small parish church on the outskirts of Great Falls, Montana, and asked the question: "You probably wonder what I am doing here?"

The congregation reacted with the self-conscious chuckle of an audience exposed, for, yes, they had wondered. Here was this cardinal, all the way from Poland, a communist country whose origins, history and social structure were as alien to the great mountains of Montana as the Polish language itself. During a hectic 37-day visit to North America, during which he had criss-crossed the United States giving lectures, saying masses, addressing Polish communities up to three times a day, Wojtyla had taken for his own pleasure these three days and two nights—and he had chosen to come to the parish of Geyser, Montana.

There were no Poles in Montana to speak of. There was no significant centre of Catholic, Polish or even European studies to which he might speak. No relative, no seminary, no great cathedral. Just the mountains and a man named Joseph Gluszek who was now seated proudly to the left of the cardinal as he spoke.

"Well," continued Wojtyla from the pulpit, "I am in Montana because I have my priest here, and I am his bishop. I told the people at the Eucharistic Congress in Philadelphia that being his bishop, I should see him, where he lives, how he manages there. That is why I am here."

There had been few prouder moments in the 68-year life of Monsignor Gluszek than this one. He may, in fact, be the only Pole in the state of Montana and he is certain there are none among his parishioners. There was no question that the cardinal had travelled these many miles, interrupted such a heavy schedule to see his old friend, perhaps his best friend in this continent, though Gluszek would never suggest a self-importance like that. "But he loves me, yes. Of that I am sure, just as I love him."

Evidence of their love is tied in bundles in Gluszek's study—more than 140 letters, an average of ten a year for the past 14 years. All but one are postmarked Krakow, Poland. The one that is not is postmarked "The Vatican, Rome". It was sent to Joseph Gluszek on 10 November, less than three weeks after Wojtyla's installation as the Holy Father of the Roman Catholic Church. "I know how busy he must be, first as cardinal, and now especially as the Holy Father—and yet he remembers that some little man is lost in the wilderness of Montana. He never forgets me. He is good-hearted. He came here because he wants to make me happy."

Gluszek still retains traces of his Polish accent, and he admits that a large part of his heart is still in his home parish of Krakow, but he is determined to live out the rest of his life in the hills of Montana. To understand Wojtyla's affection for him in his final years it is necessary to go back to the first day of the war, 1939.

"On that day I was taken to the concentration camp," he recalls. "I was in there for six years and when it was over I spent five years and took spiritual care of groups—thousands of Polish people who were in Germany during the war and after the war. We were all waiting to be repatriated or sent someplace, to other countries."

It wasn't until 1950 that Gluszek found his home in the United States. Admissions, even for priests, to the United States were difficult to come by, "so the Holy Father, Pius XII, he sent us here only as visiting priests, for the time being". From that point, Gluszek and others like him remained in America only by renewing their temporary visas, until, in 1956, when the restrictions eased, he applied and became an American citizen. He found his parish in Montana.

"Officially I am still a priest of Krakow, on a loan here. I love the diocese of Krakow very much. It is one of the oldest dioceses in Poland and I was educated there. So my heart is still there, no question."

Not only was Gluszek educated in Krakow, he was educated in the same town of Wadowice where Wojtyla was born. Yet it would not be until 1964 that they would make first direct contact—by letter—and meet face-to-face finally in 1969. "It brought us close together at once", he said. "Wadowice was the place where I attended school for eight years, so I knew his native town and everybody there, because I was at his school. When I went there he was very young, about ten years old, and I don't recall him then. Just a small boy. But I know all the same people."

Through five years of correspondence, and at their first meeting in 1969 when Wojtyla came to the United States on his initial visit, a friendship grew that was more than the normal bishop-priest relationship. It wasn't one that was, or is, mentioned in loud terms, but one shared through deeds. Gluszek returned to Poland to visit him in 1970, and again in 1974 "because we are very friendly".

"But", he added, "perhaps this will show more light on what a kind man he is: He never forgets to send me a card for Christmas, or for Easter, or for a Feast Day, or for my Feast Day, St Joseph's Day. He sends me a card or a telegram congratulating me, always. This means a lot to me. It shows what kind of a man he is, a very thoughtful man, no matter how busy he must be. In our correspondence for 14 years he has never missed answering any letter I wrote. He never forgets."

Wojtyla's letters to Gluszek are not long or political or official, just letters from a friend. "He says not too much of Poland. They never censor his letters but they always could—therefore, he just talks about the church and his priests and what they do. He inquires after my health. Sometimes I mention my health problems and he writes something to give me encouragement or he gives me some advice. His kindness is always there. It is hard to find a man of such a big heart."

For anyone privy to their friendship, then, it might not have come as a surprise that Wojtyla insisted to church officials at the Eucharistic Congress in Philadelphia in 1976 that he be able to visit the town of Great Falls, Montana.

"Those people in Philadelphia told me 'Don't go to Montana because there is nothing to see'," Wojtyla told Monsignor Gluszek's congregation from the pulpit that day. "I told them I don't care if there is anything to see or not—I have my priest there and I want to see *him!*"

They are words Gluszek can still hear. "Boy," he said, "that was really one of my proudest moments. He said that to my people. He came here because I was his priest. He just was anxious to know where I am stationed and what the parish looks like, how is that priest who wrote to him first so many years ago, where does he live and what does he do. He just wanted to show me he is good-hearted I think. Nobody would expect a cardinal to come to Montana where there are no Polish people at all. I am the only one here. Mostly we talked, but I took him for a ride to show him our beautiful mountains. He would have been happy to go and climb some hills. I didn't want him to climb the hills but he was willing to do that. So I just told him 'Those hills are dangerous—there could be some bears up there'. He just said, 'Oh, we have bears' ."

Gluszek confesses he really wanted to show off his hometown cardinal to his American flock. "They were such good people in my parish, I just wanted my people to meet him. They never saw a cardinal before. He said Mass and afterwards he spoke to all my people, blessed their little babies. They just couldn't believe that a cardinal could be so human as he was. Now they know who they have in Rome. They have a most human man in the Vatican. He came just to make me happy."

Wojtyla's visit to America is remembered by Father Bernard Witkowski as one of nervousness as he stood on the platform at Philadelphia's 30th Street railway station on the morning of 2 August 1976, awaiting the cardinal. He was a parish priest, but of Polish background, and therefore assigned by the city's Cardinal John Krol to act as greeter-interpreter for the arriving Polish contingent of seventeen bishops and one cardinal at the Eucharistic Congress. They were the largest group of that nation's Roman Catholic hierarchy ever to travel at one time and had come the previous day on three separate planes—on orders from the Polish prelate, Cardinal Wyszynski. "The cardinal didn't want them all flying in together on one plane because, God forbid, anything would ever happen. So he made them come on three different planes," said Father Witkowski. "Cardinal Wojtyla was leading the bishops and on their first day they had visited the Catholic University. This day they were arriving by train from Washington DC."

When they gathered in Philadelphia it would be the beginning of a six-week journey not only to the Congress, but throughout the heartland of America where they promised to meet and talk with as many of the five million Catholics of Polish background as possible. In retracing the steps of Wojtyla and his fellow bishops during those weeks, it appears likely that they touched, or were heard by, most. They celebrated Masses in Washington, Baltimore, Philadelphia, New York, Cincinnati, Wisconsin, Detroit, Chicago, Los Angeles, Buffalo, Toronto, Hamilton and Great Falls, Montana—and in several different parishes at each city. They held receptions, lectured at universities, were honoured guests at formal banquets and even stood in line for pieces of fried chicken at a midwest barbeque under the stars. They laughed and reminisced with old friends, expatriots and third generation American Poles.

That was what they came for, and Father Witkowski standing on the railways platform in Philadelphia would be the first man in line to see that their itinerary ran smoothly. "I was standing there waiting," he said. "I knew what exit he was coming out of, but there were all these people coming from all over the place. And then I saw him."

Karol Wojtyla wasn't hard to spot. In a country where priests have for many years restricted the wearing of the flowing cassock to the inner sanctums of their churches, the sight of Cardinal Wojtyla on 30th Street station caused a traffic jam of trolleys, people and luggage. "Everybody was looking at him," recalled Witkowski. "He looked so out of place to us. They were staring at him, like, 'What is that? Who is this kook walking around dressed like this?' Heads were turning everywhere. I often think about that moment now. I'd like to answer those quizzical looks. I'd like to say 'That man is the Holy Father'."

So went America's and Father Witkowski's first introduction to the man from Krakow who would in two years be installed as Pope. During the following week Witkowski would come to know Wojtyla better, and understand why he, and most of the bishops who followed him, dressed throughout much of their tour in their full cassocks with red buttons. "In Poland it is worn everywhere, not because it's a convenience, but they are very much concerned about the sign of that cassock and all it means in a communist country. It makes the priest visible, a reminder."

Later, when he spoke in Buffalo, Wojtyla would explain it further. "Life is very difficult for Christians in Poland," he said. "Our country is governed by Marxists whose goal is to restructure human life without religion—yet the church has shown remarkable resilience." He told of the lack of places of worship, and of state control of the media, and of the laws against possessing photocopying or reproduction machinery of any kind. It was a society, he said, where the significance of wearing a cassock in the street was paramount. "Our sermons have also taken on greater importance," he said.

St Mary's Church in Krakow's main square
with the Cloth Hall in the foreground.

"People stand for three hours to hear a sermon by one of the Polish prelates. The traditional practices abandoned in other parts of the world take on special meaning. The Procession With Relics becomes a way of communicating a lesson on Saints. Likewise, the kissing of the bishop's ring becomes a way of communicating solidarity with the church. And a parish priest walking on a main shopping street wearing his cassock becomes a living statement that communist materialism is not the only way of life offered to man."

By the end of Karol Wojtyla's Philadelphia visit, Witkowski said to a friend that "I thought he was going to be Pope one day". It was a feeling he could not shake. "That whole time I was with him, he was just such a very warm person. He sort of reminded me of my grandfather—his concern, his solicitude for everyone, the gentleness about him. All that came through while I knew him to be a man of high intellect and known brilliance in philosophy. But he never pushed that, he didn't even refer to it. I had to find it out other ways. Whether he was talking to a child or a worker or a university professor, he was completely at home and deeply interested in what they had to say. Even when he isn't speaking he comes off as a very special kind of person. In conversation after dinner when people are sitting around talking, he sits and absorbs everything that is said, and then he somehow takes all of it and synthesises it, and comes out with a simple yet profound conclusion. He was truly remarkable."

The freedom of press and technological powers in broadcasting were among the modern aspects of American life that Cardinal Wojtyla noticed first. But he neither criticised the ways of the New World nor preferred the old, according to Witkowski. "He said the church in Poland was living its own life and he felt that the church in America had to live its own life. He was speaking of the economic situation, the morality of society and the condition of government—all had to be taken into account by each church in each country and the church apply itself to those particular situations. He was against making direct comparisons of styles."

By the time Cardinal Wojtyla left Philadelphia he had visited Baltimore, said Mass at the Holy Rosary cathedral, and had been presented with a bouquet of red and white flowers by two small girls dressed in Polish costume. They also presented him with the traditional tokens of greeting in Polish homes, a plate containing bread and salt. Witkowski's appreciation of the man had grown with every day. At that stage, though, he could only hope it was mutual. His answer came the following year when he accompanied Cardinal Krol on a reciprocal visit to Poland. "I met him at an audience at the Chancellory," Witkowski recalled. "I walked up to him

*The traditional sounding of the trumpet
which takes place at midday in Krakow's
main square.*

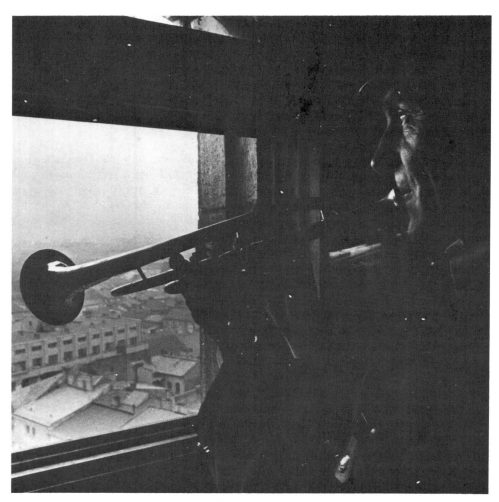

and had gone to take his hand, and to bend over to kiss his ring. But he wouldn't let me pull his hand out to get to his ring. Instead, with his other arm, he just wrapped it around my head and he kissed me on the top of the head.''

Throughout his journey in the United States and Canada, Wojtyla left behind many with a common impression: He is a man before anything. Whether he wore the cloth of a priest, bishop, cardinal—and now Pope— Wojtyla the man always came through. In Chicago he was welcomed by

Cardinal John Cody and the late Mayor Richard J. Daly. He attended the official reception at St Mary of Nazareth Hospital, rode in a boat tour to watch Chicago's Lakefront Festival events and got a first hand look at America's tallest building, the Sears Tower. There may have been some Polish pride in the latter, since Poland's Warszawa radio mast in Konstantynow, at 2120 feet 7 inches (646.5m), was completed in 1974 and became the officially recognized World's Tallest Structure in the Guinness Book of Records.

At the banquet in his honour in the Conrad Hilton, the cardinal made clear that he could enjoy a laugh at his peers' expense. Father Theodore Zarema who was present recalled the sequence of events that led to a thunderous burst of laughter as Wojtyla took over the microphone.

"Cardinal Cody had just spoken and introduced Cardinal Wojtyla," Father Zarema said. "In his address he had mentioned that both he and Cardinal Wojtyla had received their cardinals' hats in the same class. When Cardinal Wojtyla rose to speak he quickly conceded that they had been in the same class and added, 'but we are not of the same age' ". Wojtyla is a good ten years younger, in fact, than the Chicago cardinal.

In Chicago Cardinal Wojtyla faced his biggest congregations and audiences and kept up his most hectic pace. The city has more Poles in its population than any city outside Poland. He spoke to various Polish leagues, visited the Resurrection Mausoleum, stayed overnight with Bishop Alfred Abramowicz, a Pole, at Five Holy Martyrs Church, and with his accompanying bishops said up to three Masses a day in several Chicago parishes. No sooner had he fulfilled his final duty there when he boarded a private jet provided by a Wisconsin insurance company to take him to Stephens Point, home of the heavily Polish University of Wisconsin. The Professor of History at the university, Waclaw Soroka, was one of the locals who took great pride in organising the visit. "We had common friends who approached him in Poland before he left", explained Soroka.

If a priest sworn to poverty ever had a reason to feel uncomfortable among fellow Poles, Cardinal Wojtyla might have had one at Stephens Point. The Polish farmers there are routinely millionaires, with spreads and equipment that are only the dreams of peasants in Poland. "The Poles arrived here comparatively late," said Soroka. "The people from Norway and other countries were already here and stronger when the Poles came, but in 1912 the Poles became a strong factor and in many respects they pioneered the progress of agriculture here. They were responsible for the first irrigation and for the inclusion of electricity to agricultural production. Polish farmers here are extremely prosperous." In short, they are rich and very American, and when they throw a western-style barbecue, they do it with style.

"He had our typical barbecue dinner on a farm under the trees—and he enjoyed it very much," said Soroka. "He was going around with a plate in his hand, waiting in line to get his food, just like everyone else in the crowd. He had to take his place. He loved it. I think it was his first American barbecue."

From all accounts, the Archbishop of Krakow was indeed at home in the midwest and among millionaires. In a local television interview, he saw the experience as a demonstration of the value of private farm ownership, a value, he said, which was obvious to him in seeing the prosperity of these Polish-American men of the land. At the farm he had inspected modern machinery, patted cattle, asked to see horses and given his blessing to wives, children and landowners. He might have been a local himself, except for the everpresent, tell-tale cassock.

His greatest interest, though, might have been in the historic agricultural settlement called Polonia, to which he was driven the next day. Polonia is the home of the Felician Sisters, a religious order first invited to Wisconsin by a hero of the Polish Uprising of January 1863. The freedom fighter fled to the United States when the Uprising failed, and became a priest. He invited the Felician Sisters who came in 1871. The cardinal was extremely interested because the man and the sisters were from Krakow.

Professor Soroka had met Cardinal Wojtyla through friends in Poland and has long been an admirer. "He is a man with natural authority, and at the same time a man with warmth. The authority does not stifle anybody, but it never disappears. He is a man who approaches matters discussed in conversation, not from the point of view of rules and regulations, formalities or dogma—but from the point of view of the meaning of such matters in the light of a person who raised the problem. To him, every issue is separate and needs to be treated in connection with a human being who is troubled by it. He always displays a very fine knowledge of human problems connected with today's civilisation and he has a deep understanding of the East-Central·European problems, of communism, of its aspirations and also of its weaknesses."

Professor Soroka later flew with Cardinal Wojtyla to Boston where the philosophical and theological community was captivated by his lecture on phenomenonology at the Harvard University's Divinity School. Professor George Williams, theologian, noticed particularly the very human man who was always present during even the deepest discussions.

"His own doctrine is of the individual human being", Professor Williams said. "He has this marvellous capacity to listen, a quality which is almost absent by professional disuse in the ministry. I myself am an ordained minister. Ministers generally don't listen—they propound. He is more inclined in conversation with people to ask as many questions as he responds to. He has these wonderful blue eyes that look out at you and you feel that you are taken seriously. I think a child would feel that way, an old lady, a nun, a peasant in the fields or somebody he might meet while climbing on his skis.

"He doesn't radiate, as some of the great princes of the church do, a power of office. He is always the person before he is the cardinal. There is something unusually direct about him. With Wojtyla there is that extraordinary face-to-face swift establishment of that measure of intimacy that is appropriate to the occasion. I am sure he will always be the man as well as the Pope—and I feel we need that. The office itself is so impressive in terms of antiquity that he doesn't have to do anything to enhance it. It carries its own weight."

Professor Williams first met Karol Wojtyla during the Vatican Council of 1962–65 when he attended as an alternate observer. He saw him again when he went to Poland as a Guggenheim Fellow in 1972. Like Father Witkowski of Philadelphia, he came away from all his meetings with the impression that "someday he would be Pope".

"He had physical vigour and a powerful mind. You feel it. He has effortless thinking, in a positive sense. His mind, the machinery, is so well oiled that it is effortless thinking. It's a delight to talk to him, to respond to his questions."

At two dinners at Harvard, Cardinal Wojtyla left behind him academics delighted by his humour, impressed with his intellectual capacity and amazed by his languages. "He addressed the Harvard Ukrainian Institute in Ukrainian", said Williams. "But overall, he came across as a man who has such high esteem for the individual. Even Marxists. Especially Marxists. He can talk to the Marxists through the night and be on top of the situation, remaining genial, magnanimous—and yet adhere to his own deep conviction. He is so well versed in the whole Marxist and Leninist theory, he knows it all."

Again in Buffalo, New York State, and in Hamilton, Canada, Wojtyla left behind impressions of a man at peace with himself and his mission in life, calm, generous and confident. Buffalo's Monsignor Edward Kazmierc- zak, of St Casimir's parish, hosted him in the presbytery and was present at a reception in the Statler Hilton Hotel. "He said Mass at our church and afterward stood for a long time talking to people outside. He has a good sense of humour, but is more of a listener than a talker. A man of great humility, very attentive to children. He was very curious about every- thing in America."

Curious even to the point of asking Kazmierczak for a serving of the stan- dard American bedtime snack. "He asked for milk and cookies in the evening before retiring. He said he was looking forward to something typically American—milk and cookies. And in the morning he had bacon and eggs."

Cardinal Wojtyla told Canadians that their wealth and freedom "strikes our eyes because it is evident everywhere". In the thick of a Polish audience he showed his sadness at the oppression of religion in their native country, but gave them hope with the promise that "our faithful continue to respond to the needs of the church".

"A good example of this is the large number of clergy vocations," he said. "We have as many priests as we need and can even send abroad for mission- ary work. This is a special blessing of God and intercession by Our Lady,

Wawel Cathedral and Castle, Krakow.

Queen of Poland." He told of the solidarity among Poland's 30 million Catholics, but of the need for some 1000 more churches in which to worship. "But the Polish people are almost entirely Catholic and a majority of them support the church. This is our strength."

The kind of solidarity he spoke of is familiar, too, to Father Joseph Kochan, pastor of St Joseph's Church in Radway, Edmonton, Canada. Father Kochan managed to see the Bishop of Krakow in 1976 by flying down to Great Falls Montana where Wojtyla visited his old friend, Joseph Gluszek. But he had also met with him during the Cardinal's 1969 visit, when he came to Edmonton. "I had known him for many years, since I was a pastor in a Polish parish in Belgium," Kochan said. "Later I came to Canada and lost contact, but when he became Bishop of Krakow in 1957, I sent him congratulations. He has written to me ever since."

Kochan is one of many who can say, quite simply, that they have come to love the man. And he gives a clue to the sort of incident that inspires it. "A simple thing", he said, "but it says so much about the man. That same year that he came here, in 1969, I had been in a very bad car accident in Edmonton. I was unconscious for several hours, it was a bad thing. When Cardinal Wojtyla visited me we drove past the place where the accident had happened, and I showed him. I didn't expect the way he reacted. He was shaking, trembling, he was terribly moved with compassion for me. He endured it all over again for me, he has so much compassion. His hands were trembling, as though he lived through the same moment again as me."

And again, in his sermons and his speeches in Edmonton, the cardinal never failed to mention the importance of his local priests from Poland. "He said two Masses, one for all Poles and one for those of us from Krakow", Kochan said. Kochan relates that in a later conversation with Wojtyla, after he had been elected Pope, "He told us of the many things he had to put on the altar of sacrifice in Rome when he became Pope—and one was that he had to leave behind the 600 priests whom he had ordained. He broke down and cried. That is the kind of man he is. He has a genuine feeling for all people, and especially for his priests."

And yet the humour is as much a part of the man Kochan knows as the compassion. He recalled that on that 1969 visit, when the Polish priests from Vancouver expressed their disappointment that the cardinal could not go to Canada's west coast, he made them a promise. "Next time", said Wojtyla, "I will hijack the plane if necessary."

During a 1974 visit by Father Kochan to Poland, he was with Wojtyla and other bishops in a resort ski town for a weekend. "It was raining terribly,

Flower seller in Krakow's main square.

and he wanted to go skiing," he said. "When the rain didn't stop he told us all to start some praying that we get some snow."

Overall, Kochan describes Wojtyla as a man of "kindness and firmness. And he learns and listens. I saw his improvement in the English language just between his visit in 1969 and the one in 1976 when I saw him in Montana. When he first came to Edmonton he just started it. One of the sisters in Poland was teaching him. But when he celebrated Mass in English in Montana, he was clear and fluent—just a little accent."

Our Lady Of The Bright Mount is the only Polish parish in Los Angeles. And the year Wojtyla visited the United States in 1976, it was its golden jubilee. He wasn't about to miss it. "He received the key to the city," recalled Father Zbigniew Olbrys. "He said Mass in our church and met with 300 Polish people in the parish hall."

As everywhere they talked of Poland, of religion, and the cardinal listened to stories of the Californian way of life for Poles. When he talked to the Catholic press, he became the man of firmness that so many had described, in parallel with warmth and kindness. Wojtyla had decided the time was right for strong words.

"Abortion", he said, "is legal in Poland. Its consequences are dangerous not only for Christian morality and family, but also for the nation. Abortion violates the Fifth Commandment—Thou Shalt Not Kill. If children know their parents can kill one of them and if they have already killed one of them, that is a tragic diminution of family stability. The new morality is not compatible with the dignity of man and woman. Married life demands a fruitful continuity. How can human dignity be conserved if a woman is a mere object of use?

"This danger of permissive morality is everywhere. It is in our own country. What is needed is a deeper preparation for marriage, a better consciousness. The church must fight the idea of life and love without responsibility." He went on to say that abortion had been given the respectability of being represented almost as a virtue of the practice of freedom, concluding: "Freedom is not that I can do what I want, but realize and know true good—and then choose the true good."

When the official duties in Los Angeles were over, the cardinal was taken on his first ride up the California coastline. Father Olbrys gave him a brief tour of the city, and as they drove back toward the presbytery, the cardinal who had once aspired to be an actor, was given his first trip through Hollywood.

New Yorkers recall Cardinal Wojtyla from both his 1969 and 1976 visits. The pride of those who shook his hand stays with them now that he is Pope. The Reverend Edward Fus, pastor of the Holy Cross church in Maspeth, Long Island, is one who can boast "The Pope Slept Here". It was in 1969.

"Very few places, even in Poland, can say he stayed overnight at their presbytery," he said. "The thing I remember most is that, for a man who

*Old people waiting for Mass at Jasna
Gora Church.*

was in the United States for the first time, he ate and loved everything
that was presented to him. And the second thing is that, for a cardinal,
he was without any pretensions. He didn't want anybody to serve him or
show any special treatment."

The cardinal's host in 1976, Staten Island's Monsignor Artur Rojek, echoes
the admiration. "When somebody becomes a doctor, the president of a
company, or even a priest, it is natural for him to feel he is something special.
This fellow, who is the greatest in so many ways, thinks about himself as
only human. He is such a wonderful man, as a man."

Women street sweepers in Krakow.

Mrs Christine Keszycka met Wojtyla in Krakow in 1969 when he offici-
ated at her daughter's wedding. "He is a grand, modest and intelligent
man", she said. The Rev Joseph Olinski of Manhattan who was with the
cardinal in 1976 recalled: "When he was here he was dignified and yet
humble, and when he spoke, even in a roomful of people, you felt he was
talking directly to you."

At the Kosciuszko Foundation, before a crowd of Polish doctors, millionaires and business leaders, Wojtyla turned a scheduled 20-minute address
into a three-hour question-and-answer session. He listened to introductory

speeches criticising the Catholic Church in America for not appointing more Polish-American Bishops, to complaints about Polish jokes, about the lack of Polish-Americans in high government positions. When they were all done, Cardinal Wojtyla rose and said: "There are many important things in every-one's life which seem important some of the time. We should always look for peace in the world first, and try to improve relationships and communi-cations between all kinds of people and political institutions. You must help yourselves and attack your problems and you will find improvement. You should never stop talking and discussing your problems. A solution will always come".

During his two days in the city he visited the Polish Soldiers Home and said Mass with Cardinal Terence Cooke at St Patrick's Cathedral and in several Polish parishes. In his final speech in Manhattan, he became serious once again: "We are now standing in the face of the greatest historical con-frontation humanity has gone through. We are now facing the final confron-tation between the Church and the anti-Church, of the Gospel versus the anti-Gospel . . . it is a trial which the whole church must take up. It is a trial not only of our nation and the Church, but in a sense a test of 2000 years of culture and Christian civilisation with all of its consequences for human dignity, individual rights, human rights and the rights of nations. As the number of people who understand the importance of this confron-tation increases in Poland and America we can look with greater trust toward the outcome of the confrontation. The Church has gone through many trials, as has the Polish nation, and has emerged victorious even though at a cost of great sacrifice".

The president of the Polish National Alliance of Brooklyn, New York, Joseph Glowacki, has met often with Cardinal Wojtyla in the past and sums up the new Pope's plan for that "confrontation" as diplomacy. "I'm certain that if he believed a visit to Moscow would help bring peace to the world, he would go there as Pope. He said repeatedly that he believes in diplomacy."

Few of the people travelling with Cardinal Wojtyla during sections of his 1976 visit to the United states were privileged to get a closer, or longer look at the man in action than Father Walter Ziemba, the priest assigned as his companion-helper for seventeen of those 37 days. Ziemba was at the cardinal's side in Washington, Baltimore, Philadelphia, Cincinnati and finally in New York. They began at Orchard Lake Seminary, Michigan.

"Firstly he is a man of tremendous sensitivity," said Father Ziemba. "I don't think I've ever met another man of the hierarchy with such an ability to listen. He can sit there and not say a word—let anyone and everyone have their say first—and then he will make his comment. Secondly, he has a marvellous way of turning a difference of opinion into an acceptable situ-ation so that he doesn't have to contradict, or directly oppose, or conflict with. He uses a sense of humour to cope with paradox and imperfection."

Father Ziemba was also taken by Wojtyla's sense of comedy. "When he looked at the schedule we had prepared he looked at us and said, 'What are you trying to do, kill me?' '' In fact, as Ziemba and Wojtyla both knew, a Polish bishop who toured the United States some years earlier had collapsed and died of pneumonia in New Jersey. The schedule Father Ziemba had drawn up included six cities in seven days.

"In running that schedule he was never rushed," Ziemba said. "We were not always on time. Some of the ten o'clock Masses didn't begin until 10.30, but it was because he would not rush and hurt the feelings of the person he was with. To him the value of the present person always outweighed the value of where we were going, because we'd get there eventually. He's always in complete control, he had tremendous equanimity. I can't ever remember his condemning anybody, on even the slightest of matters."

Every day, in some way, Wojtyla demonstrated his character as that of a man who is poor, genuinely poor. Said Ziemba: "He is detached completely from material things, completely. One of our friends in Detroit offered to buy him an automobile for use in Europe. When we asked him what kind he would like, he thought for a minute and said, 'Ask my secretary.' The type of car just didn't mean anything to him. It was the same with food—whatever you give him he'll eat".

The cardinal's directness extended also to his own needs when they arose. At a three-day conference at the Orchard Lake Seminary, after full day sessions on Wednesday and Thursday, Wojtyla looked at the list of three more sessions listed for the Friday and said, "No, I will not do it. I have to get some exercise. I have to get away. I am cancelling the conference tomorrow afternoon and I'm going canoeing on the lake". And so Cardinal Wojtyla went canoeing on the lake.

"He knew when he had to stop and rest—and it was that simple," recalled Father Ziemba. "He knew when he needed to break away, be alone and rest."

On the last day of Cardinal Wojtyla's 1976 visit, Father Ziemba flew into New York for a final meeting with him to round out arrangements that had been made at Orchard Lake. At the presbytery of Monsignor Rojek on Staten Island, Ziemba found himself seated alone with the cardinal in the final moments before the departure for Kennedy Airport. "We were both physically and emotionally relieved that it was all over, that we had finished with everything. He was sitting on a chair in the dining room across from me. I said to him something that the trip was over, it was a wonderful trip, and he must be looking forward to going back home. Suddenly he leaped from his chair, his cassock flying, jumped into the air and kicked his heels in the manner of the southerner's mountaineer dance, and he shouted: 'I'm goin' home!'

"He was like an excited schoolboy let out of school after his final exam— and he was goin' home." But he was going home for only a relatively short time. In two years he would embark on the most important journey of his life.

CHAPTER ELEVEN

Karol Wojtyla remained alone in his private chapel in the apartments attached to the Krakow Metropolitan Curia after he was told of the death of Pope John Paul I. He had much to occupy his mind, problems, he felt, that only prayer could solve. There is every indication that Wojtyla knew he might not return from his journey to Rome for the funeral of John Paul I and the subsequent conclave ... that he was on a short list of cardinals who could carry the titles that are attached to the office of Pope (Bishop of Rome, Vicar of Jesus Christ, Successor of the Prince of the Apostles, Supreme Pontiff of the Universal Church, Patriarch of the West, Primate of Italy, Archbishop and Metropolitan of the Province of Rome, Sovereign of the Vatican State).

In the conclave which elected John Paul I, seven votes had been cast for Wojtyla and, while this is not a large number, they showed that he already occupied the minds of some cardinals. Also Cardinal Stefan Wyszynski, the Primate of Poland, had told close friends that Wojtyla would never wear the robes of the primate even though they should have rightfully been his. "He is destined to go on to greater things", Wyszynski said. A journalist who travelled to Rome for the funeral of John Paul I was seated close to a European cardinal on the aircraft. He asked the cardinal who he thought would be the next Pope.

"It could very well be a person who has not been mentioned in the newspapers," the cardinal said. "It could even be someone like Wojtyla."

To his everlasting regret, the journalist did not take the cardinal's tip and mention Wojtyla's name when he later wrote a story speculating on who would be elected leader of the Church. A Polish Pope seemed too remote a possibility.

Another journalist, Marek Shwarnichi, who works on Krakow's *Tygodnik Powszechny*, had lunch with Wojtyla in Rome after the funeral of John Paul I. "I had the impression that there was something deeply worrying Cardinal Wojtyla. He was very remote, his mind often absent when he talked. It was visible to those close to him that he felt he might indeed be the next Pope."

These matters troubled Wojtyla as he knelt alone in the chapel. He would, of course, accept the office if it were God's will that it should be thrust upon him, but he repeatedly wondered if he had the strength to carry out the task. He was still stunned at the sudden death of John Paul I, for it seemed only a few days since he had welcomed the election with the words: "Certainly he who has taken on his shoulders the mission of Peter, pastoral responsibility for the entire Church, has also taken on his shoulders a heavy cross. We wish to be with him from the beginning of his road, for we know that this cross—the Pope's cross—is part of the mystery of the world's salvation which has been accomplished in Jesus Christ."

Now he had to prepare a Holy Mass for John Paul I. It took place at St Mary's Basilica in Krakow on 1 October and Wojtyla, his strong voice sometimes quavering with emotion said: "We expected so much, hoped so much from him. He seemed to answer those expectations with his entire human, sacerdotal, episcopal, papal personality. So quickly did be become whom he was to have become by virtue of his calling to the papacy ... Everybody says he inaugurated a new pastoral style at the Holy See. A style full of great simplicity, modesty, respect for man. He had inherited that style from his predecessors, John and Paul, but from the very first minute he gave it an aspect that was his own ... Did the Pontificate of John Paul I fulful itself? Let us ask rather: is ever a man's life, whoever he may have been on this earth, fulfilled, in the dimensions of time, between the hour of his birth and the hour of his death? Faith tells us ... that a man's life is fulfilled only in God. That is why the Easter candle tells us of passing from unfulfilment to fulfilment ... And when our thoughts and reflections now follow the deceased Pope, with all our human powerlessness and hopelessness, let us have hope. If Christ wanted him to be the Pastor of His Church here on earth for such a short time only, we can only accept that inscrutable will of Providence. Answers to our questions will, perhaps, be given by time, by history. Or rather no answer could be the full one. We too must wait for that meeting towards which we are all going, for which we are all living."

Wojtyla flew to Rome to join the other cardinals who were descending on Leonardo da Vinci International Airport at Fiumicino from all parts of the world, then being whisked, without the tiresome formality of going through customs, to the Vatican. Aircraft were bringing in world leaders, politicians, churchmen of many hues, members of religious orders, devout followers of the Church. And scores of journalists were again arriving in Rome, only a month after they had left following the election and inauguration of John Paul I.

It is not an easy task for journalists trying to ferret out information from the close confines of the Vatican. Official information from the Vatican Press Office is difficult to obtain. Richard Dowden, editor of the British weekly *Catholic Herald* says the press office "must make Kremlin spokesmen seem like chatty salesmen and approaches direct to Vatican departments for off-the-record chats are met with: 'I don't give interviews'. The idea of the off-the-record chat not for attribution, by which most journalists gather background information against which they can judge the truth of rumours they may later pick up, is not understood in the Vatican. Perhaps all this will change now."

According to Dowden, journalists were forced to find information from other sources, such as locals and representatives of other denominations working near the Vatican. And there was the Vatican Press Office, the *Gala*

Stampa. "At one o'clock each day Father Jim Roach, an American, announced the day's events and answered what questions he could. Helpful as he tried to be, he sounded like a deputy headmaster facing questions about next week's examination papers which he hadn't set himself. The third source was the restaurants near the Vatican where most journalists interviewed each other over lunch. They were very generous with what little they gleaned and gave freely of quotes, facts, contacts and ideas—all highly prized commodities in the world of the media . . .

"After lunch the fourth source was available at half past three in a basement under the United States Information Office at the far end of the Via della Conciliazione. The contrast with the Vatican Press Office at the other end could not have been greater. Here the Jesuits held forth, answering all the questions journalists could possibly ask. A panel chaired by Father Don Campion, the Jesuits' Press and Information Officer, explained to the press what happened if a Pope went mad or what would happen if they elected a black man or whether it was true that Cardinal Benelli liked driving fast cars."

The arrangements were finalised for the funeral of John Paul I. There were several difficulties because John Paul had died so suddenly, leaving no instructions for his funeral. In fact, historians were searching through the archives to find out if there had been Popes with a shorter reign than that of John Paul. There had. Thirteen Popes did not last as long as John Paul, the one with the shortest reign being a priest called Stephen. He was elected in 752, but died three days later, even before he was consecrated. At the end of the ninth century there were four Popes in 20 months, the most notorious being Boniface VI, a disreputable man who had been dismissed from several ecclesiastical offices. Nor was his successor, Stephen VI, a Pope likely to endear himself to the devout. He had the decomposing body of his predecessor-but-one, Formosus I, disinterred, clothed in papal robes and set on the throne in St Peter's. Then Stephen called a synod to "despose" him, cut off the dead man's blessing forefinger and had the corpse flung into the Tiber. Benedict V lasted only a month before he was deposed by the Holy Roman Emperor in 964. The next Benedict, elected 10 years later, was thrown into prison and later strangled. Pius III was an elderly and sick man who was elected in 1503 for political purposes. He died of gout 25 days later. Marcellus II lived only 22 days after his election in 1555 and Urban VII caught malaria the day after his election in 1590 and died in 11 days.

The cardinals, who were running the Vatican while it was without a Pope, decided on the relatively simple rites of an open-air Mass in St Peter's Square—the same ceremony that had been held for Paul VI only eight weeks before.

But before the funeral, an unseemly, even ghoulish, fuss broke out over demands for an autopsy on the body of John Paul I. Romans, of course, enjoy any hint of scandal, especially in high places and there are none so lofty as the Vatican. The demands were backed by the conservative Catholic group, *Civilta Cristiana*, and the respected Milan newspaper, *Corriere della Sera*. But the rumours faded as the day for the funeral, 4 October, dawned, even though St Peter's Basilica was suddenly closed the previous night when a team of doctors entered. A statement by a Vatican spokesman, Father Romeo Panciroli, explained: "It was a normal check that lasted 20 minutes, conducted by a team of doctors who are in charge of preserving the body of the late Pope and who, since the first day of his death, have checked daily on the body's condition. I am pleased to report that everything was found in order."

The day of the funeral was wet. Rain had been descending on Rome in an almost perpetual torrent since the time of John Paul's death. Vatican officials looked at the dismal sky and consulted with meteorologists and learned that the rain was not likely to cease. Only a miracle would clear the sky and these works of wonder have not been in abundance in recent times. It was decided to go ahead with the open-air arrangement in spite of the weather.

The basilica, where John Paul's body lay, remained open for four hours and 25 minutes to allow the last of around 700 000 mourners to look on the face of the dead Pope. Then the 15th-century bronze doors of the basilica were closed with a hollow boom.

The Pope's body was dressed in robes of red, white and gold, then covered with a white shroud and set on a red blanket fringed with ermine before being placed in the casket. Around his neck was placed his pallium of office, the same simple white woollen scarf, adorned with six black crosses, which he had chosen for his investiture ceremony in place of the usual rich trappings of office. With him in the coffin was placed a cylindrical brass case containing a parchment scroll certifying his death. But missing were the traditional small sacks of gold, silver and bronze coins and medallions minted each year of a papal reign. John Paul had worn the Ring of the Fisherman for too short a time for these to be minted.

Then, in a plain cypress coffin, lined with red damask, his body was carried out of the basilica and placed before a specially built altar on the wide rain-swept steps of St Peter's. On top of the coffin a volume of the New testament lay open. At one side a tall paschal candle, the symbol of resurrection, flickered in the wind.

One hundred thousand people crammed the great square, huddling into raincoats as the chill wind swept across the city, the tears on their faces mixing with the persistent rain. Armed police were everywhere and marksmen crouched on the colonnades that embrace the square. They were concerned that terrorists might seriously embarrass the Italian Government by assassinating one of the scores of representatives of nations and organisations from around the world who sat, somewhat miserably, in the rain near the altar. Near them sat the cardinals in their robes of deep red and white.

Cardinal Carlo Confalonieri, the 85-year-old dean of the Congregation of Cardinals, recited the funeral mass, chanting: "This is the lamb of God who takes away the sins of the world".

The choir, mass servers and mourners answered: "Lamb of God, you who take away the sins of the world, grant us peace".

The rain continued. Vatican attendants held umbrellas over the white-mitred cardinals and placed a portable canopy over Cardinal Confalonieri. On the coffin, the pages of the New Testament, opened at the Gospel of St John, were sodden by the rain and the wind plucked at the paschal candle. And then with the words "Venerable Brothers in Jesus Christ", Cardinal Confalonieri began his homily.

"No one would have thought that less than two months after we celebrated the funeral rites in St Peter's Square of Pope Paul VI, who died suddenly, we would once again be gathered here to say our final farewell to his successor, our Holy Father John Paul I. He died so suddenly after only 33 days of his pontificate.

"We ask ourselves, why so quickly? The Apostle tells us why in the well-known and beloved explanation: 'How deep his wisdom and knowledge and how impossible to penetrate his motives or understand his methods! . . . Who could ever know the mind of the Lord?' Thus is presented to us, in all its immense and almost oppressive greatness, the unfathomable mystery of life and of death. We have scarcely had the time to see the new Pope. Yet one month was enough for him to have conquered hearts—and, for us, it was a month to love him intensely. It is not length which characterises a life in a pontificate, but rather the spirit that fills it. He passed as a meteor which unexpectedly lights up the heavens and then disappears, leaving us amazed and astonished. Already the Book of Wisdom spoke of this when telling of 'the just man: Coming to perfection in such short time he achieved long life. *Consumatus in brevi explevit tempora multa*'. The funeral prayer which we are soon to recite brings this comforting touch of reality: 'Grant O Lord that he may praise you without end in heaven, he who on earth served you with a constant profession of faith'.

"In Pope John Paul we greeted and venerated the Vicar of Christ, Bishop of Rome and Supreme Pastor of the universal Church; but in the brief contact had with him, we were quickly struck and fascinated by his instinctive goodness, by his innate modesty, by his sincere simplicity in deed and word. The very papal allocutions themselves—the few that he was able to give— reflect this quality. It began with the first discourse that he gave in the Sistine Chapel on the day after his election (for him, how unexpected and how painful!). Through his speeches we are able to get a glimpse of the great lines that would have been the programme of his pontificate: the authenticity and integrity of faith, the perfection of Christian life, the love of great discipline in the many activities that lead to the growth of the kingdom of God as well as the spiritual and temporal prosperity of all mankind.

"How could one forget the homily read on the occasion when the Holy

Father took possession of the Cathedral of Rome, St John Lateran? With absolute respect for the liturgical readings, he knew how to illustrate clearly and apply the fundamental concepts contained in them. He applied them to the plans and expectations of the Church in Rome, to the tasks of the spiritual development of the faithful and to the primary duties of his pontifical mission.

"What emerges even more in his loving gift of self was his manner of teaching. He knew well how to translate with ease and joy the lofty theological doctrine into the more accessible language of a catechist. He taught with clarity the way of Christian formation, so necessary (as pastoral experience confirms everyday) in order to keep the sense of the divine in the holy people of God as it daily advances towards the goal of eternal happiness.

"He was the perfect teacher: the time that he spent at Belluno, at Vittoria Veneto, at Venice witnessed to this. His few weeks of ministry as the Supreme Pastor were enough to reveal him as such to the world as it listened both near and afar, to the sound of his fatherly lessons. All understood that he was speaking in order to reach their soul. This was true even when, with wonderful humility and the wisest psychological intuition, he spoke directly to children 'in order that they might help the Pope' (as he so graciously put it). Everybody understood that he was speaking to the little ones in order that the adults would hear and understand. That delicacy, so evident to all, drew from his listeners both attention and action.

"Was it the need for spirituality, now more deeply felt because of the general neglect of spiritual values that pushed the multitudes towards the Pope? How else can we explain the very crowded audiences of Wednesdays? Visitors came from everywhere! How else can we explain the crowds which literally filled St Peter's Square at midday each Sunday, a time dedicated to greeting the family and joining together in the recitation of the 'Angelus'?

"Who has not been moved—and deeply moved—by seeing in these recent days the endless, spectacular lines of the faithful, of Rome and of all the world? They moved step by step, along the entire colonnade of Bernini, whether under a scorching sun or pouring rain. Finally, after two or more hours of patient and heroic waiting, they would reach the Sala Clementina and the Vatican Basilica to see yet once again the Pope of goodness and of the smile.

"Yes, because before a world submerged in hatred and in violence, Pope John Paul has been himself, personally, a message of goodness. He called for peace, he prayed for peace; he had a thirst for justice for all—for the oppressed, the suffering, the poor, the needy in every social category. He exalted labour; he preached charity. And always with a smile on his lips, that smile which never left him, even at the last instant of life. In fact we saw him like that, in the first hours of last Friday. There on his death bed, his head lightly inclined towards the right, his lips were half-open, in his ever present smile. Thus he entered into the peace of the Lord.

The study used by Karol Wojtyla in the
Archbishop's Palace, Krakow.

"Venerable Brothers: Civil leaders, clergy, religious, everyone! Just a while
ago we heard that page of the Gospel which speaks of the threefold question
of Jesus and the triple response of the first Apostle: 'Peter, do you love me?'
'You know that I love you, Lord.' So the pontificate of John Paul was a
dialogue of love between father and children—without pause, without hesi-
tation. On the preceding Wednesdays, reminding us of John XXIII, Pope
John Paul I spoke of faith and hope. Last Wednesday, he spoke of love.
These are the three theological virtues which unite us directly to God. He
said that man must always progress, always progress, in everything that is
good, up to perfection. This is the law of progress which rules life. First
of all one must grow in the love of God and in the love of neighbour. This

The reception room of the Archbishop's Palace, Krakow, with its priceless antique furniture.

is his will and testament. It is the will and testament of the Divine Master, Jesus Christ. Amen."

The ceremony drew to a close in the cold Roman dusk. At five fifty p.m. in the grey light, 12 frock-coated pall bearers gently lifted the coffin and carried it inside the basilica. There it was sealed first into a lead casket, then one made of oak and he was laid to rest in the crypt beneath the basilica, his coffin placed between his two namesakes, John XXIII and Paul VI. On his tomb was placed the simple inscription, Joannes Paulus I.

Eight other traditional Masses for the dead Pope were to be held before the conclave met on 14 October. But the cardinals conducted daily meetings to consider his successor and the problems facing the Church. And the press

The private chapel in the Archbishop's Palace
where Karol Wojtyla prayed daily.

speculated with enthusiasm. The solemnity and pageantry of the funeral Mass having ended, the journalists could now go about their task of selecting the next Pope.

The name Benelli—Cardinal Giovanni Benelli, Archbishop of Florence—was the one mentioned above the others. He presided over one of the most important sees in Italy, was an assistant to Paul VI and wielded enormous power around the Vatican. Then there was Pericle Felici, an expert in church and civil law and a respected Latin scholar, and Corrado Ursi, of Naples, a man, as *Time* magazine noted, "whose easygoing air and ample girth inspire repeated comparison to Pope John XXIII".

Salvatore Pappalardo was also spoken of on many occasions as the man likely to wear the Shoes of the Fisherman. From Sicily, he was knowledgeable in the ways of the Vatican and for a time worked for the Vatican Curia. The name of Giuseppe Siri, of Genoa, was raised, but there were many who were concerned at the description of the cardinal as being "an archconservative's archconservative". And Siri's chances of election faded rapidly when the Turin newspaper, *Gazzetta del Populo*, published an interview with Siri on the day the conclave opened. It was said to have upset many of the cardinals who had already put Siri's name near the top of their lists.

The journalists and the Romans, especially the Romans to whom gossip and intrigue are second nature, continued their speculation as the days went by. They noted with interest the results of a run-through by a computer in America. It produced the names of Ursi and Pappalardo, although it was felt that the computer had been asked only to find another John Paul I.

Of course, the new Pope had to be an Italian. There were few who thought otherwise. Cardinal Paulo Arns, of Brazil, argued that the Third World Cardinals wanted an Italian because a man from Africa would not necessarily understand Latin America or the Far East and a man from Latin America would not necessarily understand the rest of the Third World.

The cardinals knew they would have to be diplomatic in their choice, as Morris West points out in his novel, *The Shoes of the Fisherman*, when describing the attitudes of his fictional conclave: "Nationality was a vital question. One could not elect an American without seeming to divide East and West even further. A Negro pope might seem a spectacular symbol of the new revolutionary nations, just as a Japanese might be a useful link between Asia and Europe. But the princes of the Church were old men and as wary of spectacular gestures as they were of historic hangovers. A German Pope might alienate the sympathies of those who had suffered in World War II. A Frenchman would recall old memories of Avignon and Tramontane rebellions . . ."

An Italian was the easy choice. There was also the important consideration that the Pope is Bishop of Rome, Metropolitan of an Italian see. Again, as West said in his book: "The Romans claimed by historic tradition a preemption on his presence and his services. They relied on him for employment, for the tourist trade and the bolstering of their economy by Vatican investment, for the preservation of their historic monuments and national privileges. His court was Italian in character; the greater number of his household and his administrators were Italian. If he could not deal with them familiarly in their own tongue, he stood naked to palace intrigue and every kind of partisan interest".

Urged on by their editors who wanted a name, preferably one from the country in which the particular newspaper was published, the journalists grasped at any material available. Several studied a new and controversial book, not long on the market, called *The Inner Elite: Dossiers of Papal Candidates*, by Gary MacEoin and the Committee for the Responsible Election of the Pope. The book is hard-hitting in its assessments, saying of one candidate: "On matters political he stands somewhat to the right of Barry Goldwater; on matters ecclesial, to the right of Pius IX".

The book stressed the difficulties faced when trying to assess in national terms the positions the cardinals would take in a papal election. "Up to a century ago, that (national terms) made some sense. Various European monarchs not only had an effective veto to prevent election of a candidate they disfavoured, but often a significant positive influence on the supposedly secret voting. Such is no longer the case. What is of primary importance is the mind-set and values system of those admitted to what is one of the world's most exclusive clubs. There is no longer an Italian numerical majority, as there had been for centuries. Instead, more than three of every four members are non-Italian. All long-lived powers throughout history depended on a controlled infusion of blood and brains to extend their control and maintain their dominance. The Romans, the Turks, and the British, at the height of Empire, not only drew their elite military units but their most brilliant statesmen from that periphery. Having conditioned them and loaded them with honours, they could command total obedience. Far from being a maverick, Henry Kissinger is a typical product of an imperial system. So is it with the typical non-Italian member of the College of Cardinals.

"A study of the processes that bring a man to the cardinalate show the extent to which each has been given a certain mind-set and imbued with a given system of values. A key element is isolation from the normal influences of human experience at an early age and immersion in a homogenised ecclesiastical culture . . .".

The journalists read the book and felt more confused than ever. They did not linger on pages 171 and 172 which gave an assessment of Karol Wojtyla, ending with the words: "At a papal conclave, Wojtyla would still probably agree with other East European cardinals that they would best be served by a Pope who would be socially progressive enough to continue the dialogue with the socialist regimes, a man who at the same time would be conservative theologically and committed to maintain a strong institution capable of bringing influence to bear in moments of crisis".

There was one non-Italian name which was raised frequently during those days of speculation, gentle persuasion, occasional manipulation and always rumour. It was the name of George Basil Hume, of England. A man of eloquence, he was supported by an editorial in the respected British newspaper, *The Times*, which suggested he was the ideal person for the post. In fact, so serious was the speculation that the official Vatican newspaper, *L'Osservatore Romano*, rapidly commissioned a fuller biography on Hume.

Meanwhile the city of Rome continued its daily cacophony of business. The shops were crowded with tourists who had come to the city especially for the funeral and the conclave. Restaurants, charging too much, were packed. Mildly pornographic movies, which seem to be screening at every second cinema, were doing brisk business. So were the souvenirs sellers that cluster like fairground stalls around the Vatican. These specialists in papal kitsch had done handsomely out of the death of John Paul I and, while

*The horse and cart are still remaining forms
of transport in the villages of Poland.*

*A cartload of hares for the restaurants
of Krakow.*

mourning the passing of the man, had also looked with satisfaction at their growing piles of lira notes. Nearly everyone who went to St Peter's during those days seemed to want a souvenir of John Paul I. His reign was so brief that the devout felt an almost desperate need to own a memento of his pontificate. Prices of souvenirs had risen. Before John Paul's death, a first-day cover celebrating his instalment as Pope was available for less than $2. Now it had inflated to $3.

The journalists became even busier as the date of the conclave drew nearer. They rushed from cardinal to cardinal, from church leader to religious expert, in their quest to find a name that stood out above all others. In reply to a question, Archbishop Stanislaus Lokuang of Taipei asked another: "Will it be possible to find a man with the same qualities?" Ladislas Orsy, a Canon lawyer at the Catholic University in Washington, USA, observed: "The very fact that John Paul's election was so successful will inevitably influence the next one. I think the cardinals will look in the same direction as they did before."

One cardinal thought that Eduardo Pironio, of Argentina, would be the ideal person for Pope, and Pironio was of the opinion that the church needed a pastoral man like John Paul I. He had said that at the conclave which elected John Paul the cardinals had agreed that a man was needed with pastoral experience, such as an archbishop who could unify and inspire the Church. "These criteria remain valid" he said, "perhaps more so now. The fleeting but profound mission of John Paul teaches us that the church needs a true pastor".

Cardinal Frantisek Tomasek, of Czechoslovakia, possibly inspired by wishful thinking, came closest to the truth when he said: "I think this time the Pope will not be an Italian".

But there were few who mentioned the name of Karol Wojtyla. He was unknown to those outside the Vatican. And those within the Vatican dismissed him from their list of *papabili* because he was unschooled in the complexities of running the Church.

Wojtyla himself said nothing to fuel the speculation. In fact, he went out of his way to stop any rumours suggesting he could emerge from the conclave as the new Pope.

A news photographer, Franco de Leo, took several pictures of Wojtyla, as he did of all the cardinals who were in Rome for the funeral and the conclave.

"Why are you taking so many photographs of me?" asked Wojtyla, laughing and putting a hand on the photographer's shoulder. "You certainly do not believe I might be the next Pope."

CHAPTER TWELVE

The apartments in the Apostolic Palace were ready to receive the cardinals who would elect the 264th successor to St Peter. But even though the cardinals were princes of the Church, their living quarters for the next few days of the conclave were far from regal. In fact, they had not altered much since 1404 when Innocent VII was elected, when a writer of the day recorded: "It is a close-built place, without anything to divide it, and it is set apart to the cardinals for the election of the Pope; and it must be shut and walled in on all sides, so that, excepting a small wicket for entrance, which is afterwards closed, it shall remain strongly guarded. And therein is a small window for food to be passed in to the cardinals, at their own cost, and this window is so fitted as to open or shut as required. And the cardinals have each a small cell on different floors for sleep and rest".

The lodgings provided for the cardinals were not uncomfortable because it was felt they should wear a hair shirt for such an important Church occasion. No one had set out to make the cardinals follow in the footsteps of Paul the Hermit and sleep in the equivalent of a cave. The austerity and the secrecy were thrust on the conclave for several reasons, some rising out of obscure traditions, but mostly because there must be no outside interference and the cardinals must be allowed to get on with their task without distractions.

The history of papal elections has not always been one of Christian charity and harmony in the name of the Lord. Elections have been blatantly manipulated and violence has sometimes followed in their wake. When Damasus I was elected, the supporters of another candidate, Ursinus, were more than a little upset and there were massacres in the churches of the city. Leo V was thrown into prison, and there tortured and murdered. Eight cardinals and 40 assistants caught malaria and died in the conclave in 1623.

The conclave was first established in 1271 when Gregory X was elected, and the rules and system have been modified 32 times. Before that, the Pope was elected by 25 priests in charge of Roman churches, 13 deacons from Rome and nearby areas and seven bishops of dioceses close to the city. In the 12th century some prelates from more distant dioceses were named cardinals and therefore eligible to vote.

The closed atmosphere of the conclave was such that it would be free from outside interference from sovereigns and members of powerful families who believed their right was equal to any that was divine. But in fact the conclave—from the Latin *cum clave*, meaning "with key"—was often subject to the machinations of those who wanted control of the power of the Church. Money could buy a Pope, as the Borgias showed in the 15th century when their wealth put Alexander VI on the Throne of St Peter. There have been more subtle manipulations, with the governments of such strongly Catholic countries as France and Spain ensuring by vote and by veto that a Pope favourable to their interests would be elected.

Several cardinals were disgruntled by the austerity of the apartments. At meetings after the funeral of John Paul I, they had attempted to get the conclave moved to more spacious and comfortable quarters such as the large Propaganda Fide College where missionary priests are trained. But the move did not gain a great deal of support, especially after Cardinal John Carberry, of the United States, remarked that "some of the cardinals from Africa live in no better conditions back in their archdioceses".

So the cardinals were each given a room—a cell might be a better description—with the only improvement from the previous conclave being that each man had a separate chamber. At the previous conclave, large halls had been divided by wooden partitions into smaller rooms. This caused great discomfort to those cardinals who tried to sleep while, on the other side of the partition, another cardinal smoked, read until late, snored or tossed on his bed as he wrestled with the ungraspable demons of bad dreams.

The rooms were stripped of virtually all decorations. They contained a thinly-padded narrow wooden bed with white sheets and bedspread, a night-table, a prayer stool, for the hours spent on bended knees should be long if the cardinals performed their duties in the rightful manner. There was a clip-on reading lamp, a folder with five sheets of writing paper, two pens, a water jug, a washbasin and a chamber pot for those who had drunk too well of coffee or tea before retiring. Only a few of the cardinals had a private bathroom; the rest were forced to walk down long, cold corridors to reach communal bathrooms. The room also contained a colourful plastic trash can, a bottle of mineral water and a glass, a tiny shaving mirror placed where once had hung a painting, a roll of toilet paper and a thin brown blanket. It was little wonder that Cardinal Guiseppe Siri, of Genoa, commented before entering the conclave: "After three days we shall all go mad. You have to be in there to understand the closed atmosphere". Or as Cardinal William Baum, of Washington, said, perhaps cryptically: "Pray for us".

The dining room where the cardinals were to eat during the conclave was part of the Borgia apartments, but, apart from the frenzied faces of religious paintings of the modern school hanging on the wall, it held nothing of splendour. Mess tables, covered with white cloths, were where the cardinals would eat. Stainless steel knives, forks and spoons would form their cutlery.

God forbid that one of the cardinals, several of whom were not exactly brimming over with health, should become ill. For he would then have to rest in conditions bordering on the miserable. The infirmary consisted of two wrought-iron beds with cheap lights clipped to the headboards. And, as one observer noted: "Two small towels and a bottle of mineral water are the only evidence of first aid and there are no electrical sockets where

*Pilgrims visiting the Monastery of Gora
Paclawska fall postrate on the ground to kiss
the earth at the annual religious ceremonies.*

special equipment might be attached".

The cardinals, of course, are not allowed any contact with the outside world. And to ensure this, the cord was cut from the only telephone in the apartments, an ancient device, incidentally, that seemed to have been made and installed not long after Alexander Graham Bell uttered the first complete sentence over the invention.

But this time the officials organising the conclave allowed the princes of the Church one small comfort. They did not paint over the windows of the long corridors leading to the conclave area. A cardinal, if he was fortunate, and if the weather conditions were ideal, could look out the window and see the moon hanging over the city. Reassuringly, the world outside still existed.

Before they entered the conclave, before the doors were closed behind them to remain so until a Pope had been elected, the cardinals celebrated Mass in St Peter's Basilica. They entered the basilica two by two, singing Gregorian chants, and then the Mass *pro eligendo Pontifice* was conducted by the Camerlengo, Cardinal Villot.

"Once again, Fathers and Brothers," he said, his voice ringing around the magnificent structure, "after just a few weeks, this Gospel is proclaimed in the same circumstances, and we need to draw from it teaching and points for reflection. To the discourse of Jesus, let us briefly call attention to certain words. One: What does it mean 'to remain in his love'? Two: What is the meaning of 'to give his life for his friends'? Three: 'all that I have heard from my Father I have made known to you'? Four: 'you did not choose me, but I chose you'?

"One: One cannot remain in the love of Jesus if one is not in his grace, because each good and meritorious work has its source in the blessing of divine love, that is in grace. Christ obeys the will of his Father.

"A little while before, Jesus had said: 'He who sent me is with me, and he has not left me to myself for I always do what pleases him'. He was speaking clearly as a man, because his divine nature is identical with that of the Father and cannot be apart from it. Thus if Jesus, for the reasons he states, was not left to himself, neither shall we be left alone, if divine love creates in us grace and conformity to his will. It is timely to reflect on this fact: the task that is ours is a serious one; if only we 'do what pleases him', it will not be left to us to do it alone.

"Two: 'There is no greater love than to give one's life for one's friends'. The red vestments appropriate to this body, Eminent Fathers, have their meaning in the obligation—an obligation one assumes when one is made a cardinal—to spend one's life even to the shedding of blood. And since

our bodily lives are so dear to us, to risk life for one's neighbour is a great
sign of love: 'greater' in the words of the Lord. And this, as is clearly understood, on the example of Jesus.

"We must not, however, be led astray by an interpretation of the text
done in haste or heard in the context of a particular occasion. He speaks
of 'friends'. We recall what was said in the letter to the Romans: 'Christ
died for us while we were still sinners . . . while we were still sinners!' Ponder-
ing the text, we find, just as the Fathers before us did, that Jesus died for
his enemies, for sinners, so that they might become his friends. But it would
have been harsh to remind them that they were still in their original human
condition; and so he at once called them 'friends', taking into account the
fact that the work of redemption had begun and had been applied to
them.

"Let us reflect, Brothers, that life—the lives of all of us certainly, but also
in a special way the life of him whom we shall elect—must be given for
the multitude of those redeemed, 'that they may become friends of Christ'.
The entire mystical mission of the Church is contained in that concept. And,
since God uses men as his ordinary instruments, we understand clearly what
spirit should animate one whom he chooses to exercise the office of pastor
and guide, as if announcing for the first time the evangelical message. With
all our failings, we are, to the extent we wish to see ourselves as such, his
friends; but we are such only and exclusively in virtue of his death.

"Three: As a tangible sign of true friendship, Jesus says: 'All that I have
heard from my Father I have made known to you.' That 'all' is surprising.
But the Lord explains it a moment later: 'I have yet many things to say
to you, but you cannot bear them now. When the Spirit of truth comes,
he will guide you into all the truth.' Clearly, that 'all' that the apostles
were then able to receive was in the order of faith, not of science or insight.
We find ourselves in the same situation. Christ has told us what it takes
to follow his way, what is sufficient to act in a manner pleasing to him;
but he has not told us any more than that. He considers us friends, but
he does not give us some sort of total supernatural enlightenment. He leaves
freedom for the working of our intellect and will. It is as men—responsible
men certainly, but always only as men—that we shall have to approach the
task entrusted to us. The result, then, is not a miracle, but the outcome
of the action and prayer of men who, with all their might, wish to be ever
better friends of Christ.

"Four: 'You did not choose me, but I chose you'. Here Jesus intimates
that it was not the apostles' merit which compelled him to choose them,
but that he did so by his own free will. That applies very well to us. We
should not take pride in our abilities—some with more, some with less,
according to human ways of judging—and insist on our own point of view.
Let us recall that our ability to fulfil our task as electors is rooted 'in the
free choice of the Lord', mystically understood, and not in such human merit
as we may individually possess.

"We must elect a bridegroom of the Church; we must elect a Father . . .
It is characteristic of a bridegroom's love for his spouse to love her totally,
while a father loves his children one by one, 'singly'. Thus love for the
Church taken in its totality befits the bridegroom; love for single individuals,
with their faults and defects, befits the father. May the prayer of the People
of God be with us, taking the primary place in this assembly, and may the
Lord be with us now and always. Amen."

In the late afternoon on Saturday, 14 October, the 111 cardinals began
entering the crucible of the conclave. The 88 other persons, such as doctors,
nurses and kitchen staff, were already in the area. So were the technicians
whose job it was to search the apartments and corridors to ensure there
were no hidden devices for recording, receiving or transmitting information.
The staff and the cardinals had all taken a vow of secrecy which barred
them under the extreme penalty of excommunication, from disclosing any
details on the conclave. This was to be the most secret of all the historic
gatherings that had met over the centuries to choose a Vicar of Christ.

Each cardinal took with him small articles and luxuries he thought might
help over the traumatic days ahead. Cardinal Carberry carried with him
eight chocolate bars, with the explanation: "A bishop gave me 10 chocolate
bars before I went into the August conclave. I only managed to eat two.
This time I'm only taking eight." Cardinal Hume took with him several
novels, as he had done in the August conclave when he read books by George
Eliot and Thomas Hardy. And in the battered bag carried by Karol Wojtyla,
as he entered the apartments to find cell Number 91, was a quarterly review
of Marxist theory.

The next day he was thumbing through it when a horrified fellow cardinal
spotted him. "Don't you think that it's sacrilegious to bring that into the
Sistine Chapel?" he was asked.

Wojtyla looked up at him and smiled. "My conscience is clear."

At four forty-six p.m. the doors of the Sistine Chapel were sealed. A search
party, following an old tradition, peered into the dark corners of the conclave
area and reported that there were no persons inside except those who had
business there. The conclave began.

Soon after nine o'clock next morning the cardinals filed into the Sistine
Chapel, possibly the most glorious building erected on this earth in the name
of God. A rectangular hall 131 feet (40 metres) long, 42 feet (13 metres)
wide and 66 feet (20 metres) high, the original structure, ordered by Sixtus
IV, was built between 1473 and 1480. It contains works by Perugino, Bot-
ticelli and Rosselli, but it is the vast soaring paintings by Michelangelo
which give the Sistine its incomparable grandeur. Michelangelo spent four
years lying in agony on scaffolding to paint the ceiling which tells the story
of human events from the Creation through to the revelation of God the
Father and Creator. His other great work in the Sistine Chapel, the magnificent *Last Judgement*, took six years of planning and painting. It was these
golden, glowing works, epics of mystery and imagination, that looked down

*Cardinals gather in the Sistine Chapel
beneath the soaring magnificence of
Michelangelo's famous works.*

on the cardinals as they took their seats for the first vote. Of course, the
cardinals had all seen the Sistine Chapel several times and they were less
occupied with the works of Michelangelo than they were with the 12 wooden
tables set out in two rows. The tables allowed them little elbow room and
not much privacy when it came time to cast their votes.

But they went about their work. After all, they knew that none could
leave here until the Church again had a Pope. And at least the temperatures
were more acceptable than they had been in the sweat-soaked days of the
conclave that elected John Paul I.

The voting began. Each cardinal wrote the name of his choice on a card
beneath the Latin words *eligo in summum pontificem* (I choose as the supreme
pontiff). Then they approached the altar in the chapel, knelt, prayed and
gave the oath: "I call to witness Christ the Lord who will be my judge
that my vote is given to the one whom before God I consider to be elected."
Each card was then placed by each cardinal on a plate placed on the altar.
Three scrutineers recorded the ballots. They were looking for a name that
had a majority of two-thirds plus one—a total of 75 votes.

Even on the first ballot, the cardinals knew this was going to be a conclave
like no other. The brief reign, the sudden death, of John Paul I gave them
the opportunity to be almost revolutionary in their choice. But the first question that had to be settled was whether an Italian would again sit on the
Throne of St Peter. The cardinals went through the ritual of trying to find
a suitable Italian even though they knew in their hearts that the next Pope
would come from another country. The two main Italian contenders were

Guiseppe Siri of Genoa and Giovanni Benelli of Florence. Both men realised it was their last chance to gain the leadership and yet both men knew it was almost hopeless from the start because of the way they split the votes of the conservatives.

Siri and Benelli attracted large blocs of votes, but both were a long way from gaining the necesssary majority of two thirds plus one. It was obvious that Siri's conservatism was against him as well as his condemnation of many aspects of the important Vatican Council which sat from 1962 until 1965 and introduced the theme of collegiality into the Church. As for Benelli, there still lingered against him some resentment from the days when he wielded power, sometimes not wisely, in the key Vatican position of Substitute Secretary of State.

It was at this stage, as one cardinal later put it, that "the Italians began tearing each other to pieces". With Siri and Benelli out of the running, other Italian names were put forward—such men as Corrado Ursi of Naples, Salvatore Pappalardo of Palermo, Ugo Poletti of Rome, Giovanni Colombo of Milan and the Vatican-based cardinals, Pericle Felici and Sergio Pignedoli. The 26 Italian cardinal-electors could not make up their minds, prompting one cardinal to say: "You don't deserve the papacy the way you are divided".

The name of Karol Wojtyla began coming more to the fore in the minds of many cardinals, especially those from Germany, the United States and Third World Countries. But the ritual of trying to select an Italian went on, for tradition is not an easy thing to discard. Four centuries of Italian domination could not be tossed aside in a few hours, although its end was by now inevitable.

Outside, the vast square of St Peter's was jammed with people—with tourists, Romans, journalists, police, pickpockets, nuns, priests, and every now and again, like a wave, a rumour would ripple through the crowd.

"Ursi has the numbers."

"No, I heard Colombo is gaining a lot of support."

Shortly before noon, the stovepipe chimney on the roof of the Sistine Chapel was the focal point for every eye. Smoke began to emerge. The crowd bubbled with excitement. It looked white and some in the crowd shouted "*Viva il Papa*", but it soon turned black. There had been no result in the two morning ballots. To avoid confusion with the smoke signals—black for no result, white for a new Pope—the conclave had broken with tradition by burning a chemical pellet with the voting papers. Wet straw had been used previously to produce black smoke.

After lunch, the cardinals returned to the Sistine Chapel for the next ballot. The crowd in the square grew rapidly. The weather was now warmer and the scene between the colonnades was like a fiesta, a Sunday afternoon filled with well-being and excitement, people from all countries of the world talking to strangers, chattering among themselves, shouting, sometimes singing, sometimes praying. In the evening, washed by the brightness of tele-

*Through this chimney will come the smoke
signals to tell whether a Pope has been elected.*

*The far-from-luxurious quarters where the
Cardinals stayed during the conclave.*

vision lights, the chimney once more produced smoke. But it was puzzling.
It was at times white, brown and dark grey, but after a while everyone agreed
it was black. Some suggested that, in an age of satellite communication,
the use of smoke was an archaic way to tell the world of such an important
event, that a simple electronic device would be more in keeping with modern
times. But the system of smoke signals added a carnival air to the scene
and looked dramatically effective on the world's television screens.

In the conclave, the cardinals continued their deliberations, each one
paring down the list of 111 candidates, each one wondering what his reaction
would be if he was thrust into the limelight. There are many who profess
that the papacy is too rich a diet, and yet in their inner selves they hunger
after it. That evening, as the cardinals dined and talked and speculated,
the move towards Wojtyla grew stronger. It was agreed that he was a man
of towering intellect, a supporter of the Vatican Council, a fighter for human
rights and was not soft on communism, seen by many cardinals as the greatest of all threats to the Church. Wojtyla was prepared for the move. He
realised he was gaining support and, although doing nothing to push himself
forward, was preparing himself, almost with reluctance, for the moment
when he would be the popular choice.

The fifth ballot took place on Monday morning. Wojtyla attracted a large
bloc of votes and went even further into the lead on the sixth ballot. But
he still did not have the necessary majority.

The crowds outside gave mixed cheers and groans when at midday first
white, then black, smoke puffed from the chimney above the Sistine Chapel.
They settled down to an afternoon of waiting. Some speculated on the name
the new Pope would use. There was a vast list from which to choose, but
some names, such as Peter, were considered untouchable because Peter was
the name Christ gave his apostle Simon, the man who was the first Pope.
No other pontiff has dared call himself Peter II.

John has been the most popular papal name, used by 21 Popes, followed
by Gregory (16), Benedict (15), Clement (14), Innocent and Leo (13) and
Pius (12). Of course, there was no reason a Pope could not use his own
name, but in fact that had not been done since Hadrian was elected in
1522. Popes quite often retained their baptismal names in the early days
of the Church, giving rise to such awkward-sounding pontiffs as Telesphorus,
Eleutherius, Zephyrinus, Melchiades and Agapitus. The Pope who had
changed that was John II in 533, who was christened Mercury and considered it irregular for the Vicar of Christ to have the name of a heathen
god. Sergius IV, who was elected in 1009, was also anxious to change his
name. He was called Pietro Boccaporca, which meant he would have been

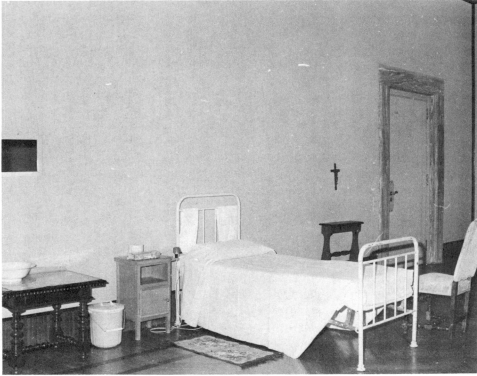

known as Pope Peter Pig Mouth I.

Those speculating on the names agreed that the new Pope would call himself either John or Paul, or possibly a combination of the two as his predecessor had done.

The first ballot of the afternoon, the seventh since the conclave began, showed that Wojtyla was the man likely to be named. Some cardinals still held back, but in the eighth ballot they accepted the inevitable. Wojtyla won an impressive 90 votes.

The conclave burst into applause.

Karol Wojtyla wept.

Outside, the crowd once more gazed towards the chimney, tense and excited as though they knew that this time the smoke would be white. It was.

"Bianca, bianca," the crowd shouted, pointing towards the chimney. They cheered, shouted, whistled and clapped. Thousands more began running to the square as the word spread with astonishing speed around Rome. "Bianca, bianca." It was six eighteen p.m.

The white smoke continued to billow from the chimney and the crowd could see that inside the Apostolic Palace there was important activity. Lights were being turned on. Flurries of movement could be seen. Now the crowd, buzzing with excitement, waited for the name to be announced as the band of the Swiss Guards marched up and down the centre of the piazza playing the bouncy, brassy pontifical march.

Inside the conclave, Wojtyla said he would accept and that he would be called John Paul II. After praying, he changed into the papal vestments, of which there was a variety of sizes provided by Gammarelli's, the official tailors to the Vatican, and then blessed the kneeling cardinals from whose numbers he had just stepped.

The crowd outside saw the preparations, the lights coming on in the Hall of Benediction, the tapestry being uncoiled over the balcony, the papal assistants emerging and waving. And then appeared the figure of Cardinal Pericle Felici, standing in the bright glare of television lights, facing the multitude below.

"I announce to you a great joy," he said in Latin. "We have a pope."

A roar went up from the crowd. Some wept, others sang, then there was a hush as Felici announced the name. "Carolum Cardinalem Wojtyla . . . who has taken the name of John Paul."

It was a curious and rare moment in the history of the Church. During the announcement the crowd was alternatively stunned into silence and spurred into cheering. The silence was because they knew nothing of the name Wojtyla except that it wasn't Italian. The cheering was because this man, this stranger with a strange name, had taken the same title as the much loved John Paul I. Journalists in the crowd heard a wide variety of comments.

"My God, it's a Pole."

"How old is he?"

"Is he a communist?"

"Well, why not a foreigner? Why not a Pole? They've always been good Catholics."

"The Church is universal. He is not a Pole any longer. He is our Pope."

The journalists themselves were as confused as the crowd. Checking to see if they had the name correct, they rushed to find out something about the man. Anything. So little was known. Their understandable confusion was summed up in a leading article in Rome's *International Daily News*, one of two English language newspapers published in the city:

"A picture of Pope John II, unknown to the world at large until Monday evening, is emerging in hundreds of reports and articles being disseminated by the media. It is still blurred, a surreal canvas in words so packed with information, or a distortion of it, that the man recedes into the background to be replaced by a creature of fable. Consider some of the 'facts'. The pope was a dullard who worked in a factory until he bumped his head in an accident and became a genius (*Corriere della Sera*). He has written 'more than 300 books' and is a noted poet. He is a liberal. He is a moderate. He is a conservative. He is a hard-liner. He supports *Humanae Vitae*, Paul VI's encyclical on birth-control. (Which cardinal didn't?). He opposes Paul's encyclical. He and Cardinal Benelli, the head of the curia, are friends. They dislike each other intensely. He wanted to be an actor, which is probably true: he handled the crowd in St Peter's Square on Monday night with a skill that would not be despised in the West End.

"He is so devout that he sometimes prays all night lying on the ground spread out like a cross—an antic, one imagines, which would be more appropriate to a Billy Graham (or an Elmer Gantry) than to a pope. In between writing more than 300 books, he canoes, skis, climbs mountains and, in the words of a news agency, plays 'Ping Pong', the trade-name for one of the companies producing table tennis equipment. (The Ping Pong people might now fairly advertise their products as being 'by appointment to his Holiness the Pope'). He is inept in diplomacy, never having worked in the curia. He is an expert in diplomacy having dealt for years with an inimical communist regime. He detests socialist economic principles. He approves of socialist economic principles, believing that the worker is the mainstay of any state. He will favour rapprochement with the Italian Communist party. He will oppose any such move. There is much more in similar vein, including wild stories that he was once married.

"The scramble for information about the new pope has been such that we can no longer see the man—he is being buried under a mountain of trivial recollection ('An old school friend who lives in Toronto remembers . . ., and the like) and conjecture. That is the curse of the 20th century—information is so plentiful and so easy to transmit that we are overwhelmed by it, and perhaps want to be. This is a superficial age and the adjective

Men of the small town of Kalwaria
Zebrzydowska, near Krakow, carry a cross to
instal in front of their church.

extends to the media. Albino Luciani becomes pontiff and dies 33 days later. He did nothing but smile and, to be kind, tell a few corny jokes. Yet in just over a month he became a figure of fable, a man eulogized in thousands of metres of third-rate, lachrymose verse, elevated to ludicrous heights of saintliness in uncountable newspaper articles and television programs. The 'cult' appears to already be in a state of atrophy.

"Everyone, of course, is interested in John Paul II. But, as we said, all that has emerged so far, except for the basic outline of his life, is conjecture and trivia, much of it contradictory. Meanwhile the Vatican 'experts', the men who failed to include the former Cardinal Wojtyla in a list of 50 possible popes, continue to make solemn judgments. Probably the only man who knows anything qualitative about John Paul II is John Paul II himself, and in time the man will emerge, leaving behind the prefabricated instant hominid created by the press, this newspaper included. All that can be said on first acquaintance is that he appears to be a fine man who has the potential of becoming an outstanding pope—provided (the jibe is directed against the press and not the pontiff) he doesn't bump his head on a Ping Pong table and revert to his 'former state'."

The journalists also consulted their history books to find out when the last non-Italian pope had been elected. They discovered it was a Dutchman, Hadrian VI, who had a brief and unhappy reign from 1522 until 1523. He took office at a time when the reforms of Martin Luther were causing considerable discomfort to the Church and did nothing to help his position by confessing to ecclesiastical errors. It was said that when he died after a pontificate of 20 months, someone hung laurels on the door of the papal physician who had failed to save his life. But throughout its long history, the church has stubbornly stuck to Italian popes. A total of 205 have been Italians. The rest were made up of 15 Greeks, 15 Frenchmen, six Germans, six Syrians, three North Africans, three Spaniards, two Dalmatians, two Goths, a Thracian, an Englishman, a Portuguese, a Dutchman and one of unknown nationality.

And now a Pole. The crowd waited tensely until at seven twenty-one p.m. the stocky figure of John Paul II appeared in the harsh glare of television lights. Countless flashbulbs exploded. A cheer went up from the crowd, mixing with the deep tolling of the Vatican bells. Flanked by Vatican officials and wearing the white and gold papal vestments and the gold seal of the Ring of the Fisherman, he seemed almost shy and somewhat nervous as he stood before the vast crowd.

And then he began to speak. "Blessed be Jesus Christ . . . May Jesus Christ be praised." The words were in Italian, with only a slight accent, and the crowd cheered as he spoke. They were thrilled that he could address them in their tongue, delighted he had the understanding to soften the blow that their Church was no longer led by an Italian. He paused while the cheering died down. He was now in total command.

"Dearest brothers and sisters, we are still all grieved after the death of the most beloved John Paul I and now the most reverend cardinals have called a new bishop of Rome. They have called him from a distant country, distant but always so close for the communion in the Christian faith and tradition.

"I was afraid to receive this nomination but I did it in the spirit of obedience to our Lord and in the total confidence in His mother, the most Holy Madonna. Even if I cannot explain myself well in your . . . our Italian language, if I make a mistake you will correct me . . . And so I present myself to you all to confess our common faith, our hope, our confidence in the Mother of Christ, and also to start anew on that road, the road of history and of the Church—to start with the help of God and with the help of men."

It was a superb performance, a Hollywood production helped by a bright orange moon hanging over the city. In a few words, John Paul II had won over the people, the doubters, the disappointed. Their cheers again soared towards the dark Roman sky. After reading the text of a Latin benediction, he waved and then disappeared inside. Thousands among the jubliant crowd remained in the square, savouring the words they had heard, some wondering about the impact on the Church of a Pope from Poland.

John Paul II.

The congratulations from around a surprised world soon began pouring into the Vatican. Said President Jimmy Carter of the United States: "I add my congratulations and my sense of joy to that felt around the world at your selection as Pope. Twice in eight weeks, the College of Cardinals has had to choose a new leader for your church and a spiritual guide for the world—and twice they have given us choices which have filled the Church and the world with new hope. Like your predecessor, Your Holiness has shared the experiences of working people, and understands the daily victories and defeats of human life. As a theologian, a pastor, and a worker, you also understand the most extreme tests that life presents. You know what it is to struggle for faith, for freedom, for life itself; and your insight into these modern dilemmas will enrich, and be enriched by the enduring traditions of your Church. During our visit to Poland early this year, Rosalynn and I gained a sense of the spiritual resilience of the nation that has given you to the world. All Americans share my sense of warmth and gratitude at your election."

Those of other faiths joined in the congratulations. Hafez Al-Assad, president of the Syrian Arab Republic, said: "On the occasion of your election I have the honour to present in the name of the Syrian Arab people and in my own name our sincere congratulations and wishes for your success. We highly appreciate the mission placed upon your shoulders by this election and the role attached to your high office with regard to the service of the church and the service of the sublime principles and aims of humanity. We hope that the Almighty will support Your Holiness in carrying out this mission to the good of the peoples of the world at large."

And even those rulers of countries where religion was not encouraged on the grounds that it was the opium of the people, added their congratulations. Said Tito of Yugoslavia: "On Your Holiness' election as Head of the Catholic Church, I extend to you my cordial congratulations and best wishes. On this occasion I wish to express my conviction that the Holy See will be further giving its important contribution to the efforts exerted by the international community to safeguard peace, better understanding and equitable co-operation among peoples, to the benefit of overcoming the economic underdevelopment in the world and of establishing more equitable relations among states and peoples. I am also convinced that the good relations and the co-operation existing between the Socialist Federal Republic of Yugoslavia and the Vatican will be further promoted successfully."

Some newspapers were less enthusiastic about the choice of Wojtyla. In London, *The Times*, possibly disgruntled that their choice, Cardinal Hume, was not elected, suggested that the new Pope would unleash human, political

and religious forces that the College of Cardinals who elected him could not control. It moaned that the choice "has the imaginative rashness that one might expect from a college of students rather than the weighty caution that one associates with a College of Cardinals." The cardinals had "elected a Pope to face the problem of communism . . . they have started the church on a journey the end of which cannot be known".

The liberal British newspaper, the *Guardian*, also questioned whether the reasons needed to elect a non-Italian Pope were met "by reaching out into the gavotte between Church and State, between Christianity and Communism in Eastern Europe". It said the conclave of cardinals "risks being accused of harking back to the stubborn battles everyone has become familiar with instead of preparing for those which are to come".

The British communist newspaper, the *Morning Star*, accused Wojtyla of being "outspoken in his criticisms of the Polish United Workers' Party and Polish government", and of "atheistic education" in his country.

But more reasoned assessments of the man took over from the instant editorials of newspapers. The noted British commentator on Catholic affairs, Patrick O'Donovan, summed up the feelings of many when he wrote: "It will take many months before the Catholic Church breathes easily with its new Pope. It will take many years—if ever—before it is known how, or why, precisely he was elected . . . No pundit, no Vatican-watcher predicted this man. He came like a thunderclap. It seems to be an act by the College of Cardinals, locked away in a great chapel decorated with Michelangelo images of the penalties of getting and doing things wrong, that is at once imaginative and rash and significant and wildly exciting for the world . . . they chose a Pole and a Pope who was not in the Third World but one who hovers between the East and West, and who comes from a nation which has a government that the people would not have freely chosen and who have suffered too much at the hands, not of nature but of men, and now deserve this spiritual recognition".

After his election on Monday and his appearance before the vast crowd in St Peter's Square, John Paul II sat down with the 110 cardinals who had elected him for a last meal together in the Borgia apartments. His health was toasted in French champagne.

And then Karol Wojtyla retired to pray for the strength needed to face whatever lay ahead.

CHAPTER THIRTEEN

It was a cold evening in Wadowice. The autumn nights were growing longer, the temperatures dropping until in the coming weeks they would slide below zero, and old men were thinking of warming fires and plates of steaming hot borscht. Dr Edward Zachar, the priest in charge of the parish, ignored the cold as he knelt to pray in St Mary's Church. He was, as he sometimes told people, getting old, but the 44 years he had spent in Wadowice had taught him that nothing could be done to alter the fact that his parish just happened to be one of the chillier spots on the map of Europe. He was still on his knees when a priest from the presbytery ran breathlessly into the church.

"We've got a Pope," he shouted to Zachar.

"Who is that?" asked Zachar rising from his knees.

"It's Lolek," the priest said.

Zachar blinked, heard his heart thump, and then shouted with joy: "Thank's to heaven."

The old prelate, still half fearing it was a mere rumour that Karol Wojtyla, the man he had given religious instruction to those long, sometimes bleak years ago, had been the choice of the cardinals, ran across the road to the presbytery and switched on the radio. It was true. The news was repeated again and again by the state-controlled radio station.

Hurrying back across the road, Zachar began ringing the church's five bells, sending out a joyous, jubilant cacophony over the town. People, also hearing the news on the radio, and now the ringing of bells, ran from their homes towards the church, shouting, singing, crying. Within minutes the church was overflowing, but Zachar, choked with emotion, could not find the words he wanted to say. Several times he tried, but finally he had to let another priest make the announcement.

At the rectory the telephone began ringing. It would not stop ringing for the next few days, and Zachar would learn, in one exhausting, overwhelming lesson, that the media are no respecters of age when it comes to a story of international importance. The old prelate was virtually run off his feet, his tongue over-worked and his brain reeling, as journalists poured into Wadowice to seek information about the man now called Pope John Paul II. Zachar confided later that some rather foolish questions were asked of him by representatives of the media. "They inquired about such stupid things," he said. "One journalist, for instance, wanted to know if the new Holy Father would abolish celibacy. They also wanted to pick up some sensational things from his life, from his childhood and his youth."

Zachar toiled mightily to cope, at one stage remembering only at dinner time that he had not yet had breakfast. The journalists, having gleaned what they could from Zachar, descended on anyone else in the town, old school friends, teachers, neighbours, in an attempt to gain further insights into the mystery that was Karol Wojtyla.

In Krakow the news that Wojtyla was the new Pope was greeted by the tolling of Dzwon Zygmunta, the great bell on top of Wawel Cathedral that rings only on historic occasions. This was deemed to be one of the most historic of all. People ran into the streets, hugging each other, singing, cheering, sometimes weeping with emotion, waving Polish flags and holding lighted candles. The old grey city was transformed into an instant carnival. Thousands poured into Krakow's dozens of churches, including St Mary's Church, with which Wojtyla has been closely associated, in the corner of the vast city square. Others ran to the archbishop's residence on Franciszkanska Street where Wojtyla had lived when a cardinal.

The journalists were not long in arriving in Krakow, either. They all demanded to see the apartments where Wojtyla had lived as a cardinal, and were, perhaps, a trifle disappointed when they were shown his bedroom. It was ... well ... so ordinary. So lacking in the opulence that one would expect to surround a prince of the Church.

The only luxury was a pair of Polish hickory skis standing in one corner. The bedroom itself was boarding-house plain. There was a narrow bed, one large chair and two small chairs, a bedside table, a wardrobe, a writing desk and a rack on which to place his red hat of office. Eight pictures of no particular merit hung from the walls. A coloured picture of Paul VI was under the glass that lay on top of the writing desk. A pair of black shoes and a pair of well-worn slippers were tucked neatly beneath the bedside table.

The journalists looked, took notes and photographs, and then rushed elsewhere in their search for snippets to fill out the life of Karol Wojtyla. Unfortunately, one journalist rushed out with Wojtyla's old shaving brush in his pocket. An intimate memento of the new Pope! Some of Wojtyla's friends took offence at the theft, but they later had their revenge when they demanded—and got—more than $100 each for early snapshots of Wojtyla. The Pope had suddenly become a minor but lucrative industry in Krakow.

All Poland, it seemed, went a little mad the day Wojtyla was elected. The news hit the country when the last Mass of the day was being held. Even though it was a Monday, the churches were crowded, because that is the nature of Polish religious life. The devout do not worship God on only one day of the week. Streams, then rivers, then floods of people poured into the streets. Flags were hung out, monuments to old heroes were adorned with ribbons and free liquor was willingly handed over in many bars.

Thousands went immediately to the Jasna Gora monastery at Czestochowa, one of the most revered shrines in the country. And there they prayed before the sombre picture of the Black Madonna, scarred by the twin slashes made by a Swedish sword during an invasion in the 17th century.

The news was received with mixed feelings by the Polish government. As Poles, the leaders were patriotically pleased that one of their countrymen had been thrust into the world spotlight, but as communists they were disturbed at the impact on the country. Several top government officials met that night and spent hours discussing how the news should be treated and what the official line should be. Earlier in the day, the Minister for Religious Affairs, Kazimierz Kakol, who is responsible for the unenviable task of standing between Church and State, had been talking to a party of visiting journalists. He joked that he had an open line to the Vatican and would buy them all champagne if the new Pope should be Polish. Everyone thought it was a fine joke, then went about more serious business. A few minutes later he was handed a note saying the impossible had come true. He bought champagne.

The Government later announced that those who wished to travel to Rome for the investiture of John Paul II would be allowed to do so. "We will set up an airbridge between Warsaw and Rome to give the pilgrims a chance to witness this event," boasted Minister Kakol. "We have had numerous applications for passports and we will issue them as fast as we can." In fact, the Government was not as generous in allowing people to leave Poland as it made out. Several close friends of Wojtyla, some of whom could be loosely connected to the dissident movement, could not obtain permits to leave the country. One Krakow friend was personally invited by Wojtyla to the inauguration Mass. Six weeks after the event he was still waiting for his permit.

After much discussion, the Polish Government decided to send a telegram of congratulations to the Vatican. Signed by party secretary Edward Gierek, President Henryk Jablonski and Premier Piotr Jaroszewicz, it read: "In connection with the election of Your Holiness to the post of the new pope we send you on behalf of the Polish nation and the highest Polish authorities cordial congratulations and best wishes. This significant decision of the conclave brought great satisfaction to Poland. For the first time in history a son of the Polish nation was elected to the highest post in the church. We express our conviction that the election of the new pope will contribute to the further development of relations between Poland and the Vatican". Then the Polish government went about devising ways of telling the world that the new Pope was the product of a good socialist state. A couple of weeks later, the government-sponsored literary weekly, *Literatura*, carried an article by Jozef Winiewicz, a retired deputy foreign minister. Talking of Wojtyla, the article said: "We must underline that such a frame of mind and such a personality was shaped in a socialist country . . . it is proof of the continuation of Poland's tradition of tolerance even under our changed political structure. But we have never been a society of backward, simple men. It was Copernicus who published in Poland his theory on the structure of the universe". Another literary magazine, *Kultura*, added support to the government's thinking by saying: "It is not a paradox but simple logic that socialist Poland should give the world its first Polish pope". The magazine stressed that, despite its strong Catholic tradition, Poland had never produced a pontiff in pre-communist days.

In Rome, John Paul prepared his first speech. People hoped it would give some indication of the path along which the new pontiff would travel, but this was not to be so. Clad in his robes of office, which were slightly ill-fitting because there had been no time for a tailor to properly measure him, and dwarfed by the overwhelming splendour of Michelangelo's *The Last Judgement* in the Sistine Chapel, John Paul celebrated Mass with the College of Cardinals, and then told the world:

"Our Venerable Brothers, beloved children of the Holy Church, and all men of goodwill who listen to us. One expression only, among so many others, comes immediately to our lips at this moment, as after our election to the See of the Blessed Peter we present ourself to you. The expression, which, in evident contrast with our obvious limitations as a human person, highlights the immense burden and office committed to us, is this: 'O the depth . . . of the wisdom and knowledge of God! How unsearchable are his judgments and how inscrutable his ways!'

"In fact, who could have foreseen, after the death of Pope Paul VI whom we always remember, the premature decease of his most amiable successor, John Paul I? How could we have been able to foresee that this formidable heritage would have been placed on our shoulders? For this reason, it is necessary for us to meditate upon the mysterious design of the provident and good God, not indeed in order to understand, but, rather, that we may worship and pray. Truly we feel the need to repeat the words of the Psalmist who, raising his eyes aloft, exclaimed: 'From whence does my help come? My help comes from the Lord.'

"These totally unforeseen events, happening in so brief a time, and the inadequacy with which we can respond to that invitation, impel us to turn to the Lord and to trust completely to him. But they also prevent us from outlining a programme for our Pontificate which would be the fruit of long reflection and of precise elaboration. But to make up for this, there is to hand a certain compensation, as it were, which is itself a sign of the strengthening presence of God. It is less than a month since all of us, both inside and outside these historic walls of the Sistine Chapel, heard Pope John Paul speaking at the very beginning of his ministry, from which one might have hoped much. Both on account of the memory that is yet fresh in the mind of each one of us and on account of the wise reminders and exhortations contained in the allocution, we consider that we cannot overlook it. That same address, as in the circumstances in which it was given, is truly apposite and clearly maintains its validity here and now at the start of this new pontifical ministry to which we are bound and which, before God and the Church, we cannot avoid.

"We wish, therefore, to clarify some basic points which we consider to be of special importance. Hence—as we propose and as, with the help of God, we confidently trust—we shall continue these not merely with earnestness and attention but we shall also further them with constant pressure, so that ecclesial life, truly lived, may correspond to them. First of all, we wish to point out the unceasing importance of the Second Vatican Ecumenical Council, and we accept the definite duty of assiduously bringing it into effect. Indeed, is not that universal Council a kind of milestone as it were, an event of the utmost importance in the almost two thousand year history of the Church, and consequently in the religious and cultural history of the world? However, the Council is not limited to the documents alone, neither is it completed by the ways of applying it which were devised in these post-conciliar years. Therefore we rightly consider that we are bound by the primary duty of most diligently furthering the implementation of the decrees and directive norms of that same Universal Synod. These indeed we shall do in a way that is at once prudent and stimulating. We shall strive, in particular, that first of all an appropriate mentality may flourish. Namely, it is necessary that, above all, outlooks must be at one with the Council so that in practice those things may be done that were ordered by it, and that those things which lie hidden in it or—as is usually said—are 'implicit' may become explicit in the light of experiments made since then and the demands of changing circumstances. Briefly, it is necessary that the fertile seeds which the Fathers of the Ecumenical Synod, nourished by the word of God, sowed in good ground—that is, the important teachings and pastoral deliberations—should be brought to maturity in that way which is characteristic of movement and life.

"This general purpose of fidelity to the Second Vatican Council and the express will, in so far as we are concerned, of bringing it into effect, can cover various sections: missionary and ecumenical affairs, discipline, and suitable administration. But there is one section to which greater attention will have to be given, and that is the ecclesiological section. Venerable Brethren and beloved sons of the Catholic world, it is necessary for us to take once again into our hands the 'Magna Carta' of the Council, that is, the Dogmatic Constitution *Lumen Gentium*, so that with renewed and invigorating zeal we may meditate on the nature and function of the Church, its ways of being and acting. This should be done not merely in order that the vital communion in Christ of all who believe and hope in him should be accomplished, but also in order to contribute to bringing about a fuller and closer unity of the whole human family. John XXIII was accustomed to repeat the following words: 'The Church of Christ is the light of the nations'. For the Church—his words were repeated by the Council—is the universal sacrament of salvation and unity for the human race.

"The mystery of salvation which finds its centre in the Church and is actualised through the Church; the dynamism which on account of that same mystery animates the People of God; the special bond, that is collegiality, which 'with Peter and under Peter' binds together the sacred

Pastors; all these are major elements on which we have not yet sufficiently reflected. We must do so in order to decide in face of human needs, whether these be permanent or passing, what the Church should adopt as its mode of presence and its course of action. Wherefore, the assent to be given to this document of the Council, seen in the light of Tradition and embodying the dogmatic formulae issued over a century ago by the First Vatican Council, will be to us Pastors and to the faithful a decisive indication and a rousing stimulus, so that—we say it again—we may walk in the paths of life and of history.

"In order that we may become better informed and more vigilant in undertaking our duty, we particularly urge a deeper reflection on the implications of the collegial bond. By collegiality the Bishops are closely linked with the Successor of the blessed Peter, and all collaborate in order to fulfil the high offices committed to them: offices of enlightening the whole People of God with the light of the Gospel, of sanctifying them with the means of grace, of guiding them with pastoral skill. Undoubtedly, this collegiality extends to the appropriate development of institutes—some new, some updated—by which is procured the greatest unity in outlook, intent, and activity in the work of building up the body of Christ, which is the Church. In this regard, we make special mention of the Synod of Bishops, set up before the end of the Council by that very talented man, Paul VI.

"But besides these things, which remind us of the Council, there is the duty in general of being faithful to the task we have accepted and to which we ourself are bound before all others. We, who are called to hold the Supreme Office in the Church, must manifest this fidelity with all our might and for this reason we must be a shining example both in our thinking and in our actions. This indeed must be done because we preserve intact the deposit of faith, because we make entirely our own the commands of Christ, who, after Peter was made the rock on which the Church was built, gave him the keys of the kingdom of heaven, who bade him strengthen his brethren, and to feed the sheep and the lambs of his flock as a proof of his love.

"We are entirely convinced that in no inquiry, which may take place today into the 'ministry of Peter' as it is called—so that what is proper and peculiar to it may be studied in greater depth every day—can these three important passages of the holy gospel be omitted. For it is a question of the various parts of the office, which are bound up with the very nature of the Church so that its internal unity may be preserved and its spiritual mission placed in safe hands. These parts were not only committed to St Peter but also to his lawful successors. We are also convinced that this high office must always be related to love as the source from which it is nourished and, as it were, the climate in which it can be expanded. This love is, as it were, a necessary reply to the question of Jesus 'Do you love me?' So we are pleased to repeat these words of St Paul, 'The Love of Christ constraineth us', because we want our ministry to be from the outset a ministry of love, and want to show and declare this in every possible way.

"In this matter we will strive to follow the meritorious examples of our immediate predecessors. Who does not remember the words of Paul VI who preached 'the civilization of love' and almost a month before his death declared in a prophetic way: 'I have kept the faith', not indeed to praise himself but after 15 years full of apostolic ministry to examine his conscience more strictly? But what can we say of John Paul I? It seems to us that only yesterday he emerged from this assembly of ours to put on the papal robes—not a light weight. But what warmth of charity—nay, what 'an abundant outpouring of love'—which came forth from him in the few days of his ministry and which in his last Sunday address before the Angelus he desired should come upon the world. This is also confirmed by his wise instructions to the faithful who were present at his public audiences on faith, hope and love.

"Beloved brothers in the Episcopate and dear children, fidelity, as is clear, implies not a wavering obedience to the Magisterium of Peter especially in what pertains to doctrine. The 'objective' importance of this Magisterium must always be kept in mind and even safeguarded because of the attacks which in our time are being levelled here and there against certain truths of the Catholic faith.

"Fidelity too implies the observance of the liturgical norms laid down by ecclesiastical Authority and therefore has nothing to do with the practice, either of introducing innovations of one's own accord and without approval, or of obstinately refusing to carry out what has been lawfully laid down and introduced into the sacred rites. Fidelity also concerns the great discipline of the Church of which our immediate predecessor spoke. This discipline is not of such a kind that it depresses or, as they say, degrades. It seeks to safeguard the right ordering of the mystical body of Christ with the result that all the members of which it is composed united together perform their duties in a normal and natural way. Moreover, fidelity signifies the fulfilment of the demands of the priestly and religious vocation in such a way that what has freely been promised to God will always be carried out in so far as the life is understood in a stable supernatural way.

"Finally, in so far as the faithful are concerned—as the word itself signifies—fidelity of its very nature must be a duty in keeping with their condition as Christians. They show it with ready and sincere hearts and give proof of it either by obeying the sacred Pastors whom the Holy Spirit has placed to rule the Church of God, or by collaborating in those plans and works for which they have been called. Nor at this point must we forget the Brethren of other Churches and Christian confessions. For the cause of ecumenism is so lofty and such a sensitive issue that we may not keep silent about it. How often do we meditate together on the last wish of Christ who asked the Father for the gift of unity for the disciples. Who does not remember how much St Paul stressed 'the unity of the spirit' from which the followers of Christ might have the same love, being 'of one accord, of one mind'? Therefore one can hardly credit that a deplorable division still exists among Christians. This is a cause of embarrassment and perhaps a scandal to others. And so we wish to proceed along the road which has happily been opened and to encourage whatever can serve to remove the obstacles, desirous as we are, that through common effort full communion may eventually be achieved.

"We turn also to all men who as children of almighty God are our brothers whom we must love and serve, to make known to them without any sense of boasting but with sincere humility our intention to really devote ourself to the continual and special cause of peace, of development and justice among nations. In this matter we have no desire to interfere in politics or to take part in the management of temporal affairs. For just as the Church cannot be confined to a certain earthly pattern, so we in our approach to the urgent questions of men and peoples, are led solely by religious and moral motives. Following him who gave that perfect way to his followers, so that they might be the 'salt of the earth' and the 'light of the world', we wish to strive to strengthen the spiritual foundations on which human society must be based. We feel that this duty is all the more urgent the longer that discords and dissensions last, which in not a few parts of the world, provide material for struggles and conflicts and even give rise to the more serious danger of frightful calamities.

"Therefore it will be our constant care to direct our attention to questions of this kind and to deal with them by timely action—action forgetful of our own interests and motivated by the spirit of the Gospel. One may at this point at least share the grave concern which the College of Cardinals during the interregnum expressed concerning the dear land of Lebanon and its people. For it we all greatly desire peace with freedom. At the same time we wish to extend our hand to all peoples and all men at this moment and to open our heart to all who are oppressed, as they say, by any injustice or discrimination with regard to either economic or social affairs or even to political matters, or even to freedom of conscience and the freedom to practise their religion which is their due. We must aim at this: that all forms of injustice, which exist today, should be given consideration by all in common and should be really eradicated from the world, so that all men may be able to live a life worthy of man. This also belongs to the mission of the Church which has been explained in the Second Vatican Council, not only in the dogmatic Constitution *Lumen Gentium*, but also in the pastoral Constitution *Gaudium et Spes*. Brothers, dear sons and daughters, the recent happenings of the Church and of the world are for us all a healthy warning: how will our pontificate be? What road will mankind take in this period of time as it approaches the year 2000? To these bold questions the only answer is: 'God knows'.

"The course of our life which has brought us unexpectedly to the supreme responsibility and office of apostolic Service is of little interest. Our person, we ought to say, should disappear when confronted with the weighty office we must fill. And so a speech must be changed into an appeal. After praying to the Lord, we feel the need of your prayers to gain that indispensable, heavenly strength that will make it possible for us to take up the work of our predecessors from the point where they left off.

"After acknowledging their cherished memory, we offer to each one of you, our Venerable Brothers, whom we remember with gratitude, our greeting. We extend a greeting which is both trusting and encouraging to all our brothers in the Episcopate, who in different parts of the world have the care of individual churches, the chosen sections of the People of God and who are co-workers with us in the work of universal salvation. Behind them, we behold the order of priesthood, the band of missionaries, the companies of religious men and women. At the same time we earnestly hope that their numbers will grow, echoing in our mind those words of the Saviour 'The harvest is great, the labourers are few'. We behold also the Christian families and communities, the many associations dedicated to the apostolate, the faithful who even if they are not known to us individually, are not anonymous, not strangers, nor even in a lower place, for they are included in the glorious company of the Church of Christ. Among them we look with particular affection on the weak, the poor, the sick, and those afflicted with sorrow.

"Now at the beginning of our universal pastoral ministry, we wish to open to them our heart. Do not you, brothers and sisters, share by your sufferings in the passion of our Redeemer and in a certain way complete it? The unworthy successor of St Peter who proposes to explore 'the unsearchable riches of Christ', has the greatest need of your help, your prayers, your devotedness or 'sacrifice', and this he most humbly asks of you.

"We also wish, most beloved Brothers and sons who hear us, because of our undying love for the land of our birth, to greet in a very special way all the citizens of Poland, 'ever faithful', and the bishops, priests, and people of the Church of Krakow. United in this greeting by an indissoluble bond are memories, affections, the sweet love of the fatherland and hope.

"In this grave hour which gives rise to trepidation, we cannot do other than turn our mind with filial devotion to the Virgin Mary, who always lives and acts as a Mother in the mystery of Christ, and repeat the words 'Totus tuus' (all thine) which we inscribed in our heart and on our coat of arms twenty years ago on the day of our episcopal ordination. We cannot but invoke saints Peter and Paul and all the saints and blesseds of the universal Church.

"In this same hour we greet everyone, the old, those in the prime of life, adolescents, children, babes newly born, with that ardent sentiment of fatherhood which is already welling up from our heart. We express the sincere wish that all 'may grow in the grace and knowledge of our Lord and Saviour Jesus Christ', as the Prince of the Apostles desired. And to all we impart our first Apostolic Blessing, that it may procure not only for them but for the whole human family an abundance of the gifts of the Father who is in heaven."

In his first full day as pontiff, John Paul showed he was not going to be trapped inside the walls of the Vatican, that he was not going to be a prisoner of tradition and no one would be his jailer. Less than 24 hours after assuming office, he left the Vatican, much to the concern of cautious officials, and went to a Roman hospital to visit an old friend, Polish Bishop Andrzej-Maria Deskur, who had suffered a stroke. After seeing him in private, he spoke for a few minutes to a group of hospital officials, doctors, nurses and patients. And once more he fell foul of tradition, of the old established order of doing things. As he left the group, he waved to them, saying: "Praise be to Jesus Christ".

But Bishop Giuseppe Caprio, the Under-Secretary of State for the Vatican, who had accompanied the Pope, reminded him with a whisper in the ear that he had not performed his duties properly.

John Paul broke into a grin. "The Under-Secretary tells me this is not enough. I still have to give the benediction. He tells me how a Pope should behave."

The group burst into laughter and applause. And John Paul gave the Latin benediction that Popes intone when they visit outside the Vatican.

John Paul also had to learn to navigate his way through the vast labyrinth of corridors, halls and courtyards that make up the Vatican Palace. When trying to find the St Damasus courtyard where his car was waiting to take him to the hospital, he took the wrong turning. Instead, John Paul found himself outside the Vatican Bank with the car, a black Mercedes, nowhere in sight. The driver, on the other side of the palace, realised what had happened and raced through the narrow streets in an urgent search for the lost Pope. He spotted John Paul, waiting patiently and unruffled, outside the bank.

Lawrence Elliott, in his book *I Will Be Called John*, tells of a similar incident that happened soon after Pope John XXIII was elected. A visitor became lost and wandered into a huge and splendid chamber of mirrored walls. "It was a room in which an outsider clearly had no business, but once he had closed the ornate door behind him the hapless soul could not find his way out. Wherever he turned, his own agonised image gaped back at him until, defeated, he watched his reflection helplessly. There he stood in terrified expectancy, as one of the great mirrors slowly swung towards him, and into the room stepped the Pope. Evaluating the situation at a glance, John roguishly put a finger to his lips and whispered, 'Shh, I'm lost too'."

John Paul was determined not to become lost again in what was, after all, his new home and place of work. The next day he left his office and asked a Swiss Guard the way to the elevator.

"On the left around the corner, Your Holiness," said the guard.

"Show me," said the Pope.

"I can't leave my post," the guard replied.

Gripping him by the elbow, John Paul pulled the astonished guard along with him. "Your job is to protect me, no? So come along, show me the way and protect me." And he said it in German so that there would be no misunderstanding by the Swiss Guard.

Within days John Paul was discovering corridors, opening doors to see what lay behind, questioning people about their jobs. Instead of merely greeting top officials and then withdrawing, as other popes had done, John Paul refused to be accompanied by the ranking prelates and walked from one office to another asking each individual priest exactly what was his job. On his first "voyage of discovery", he covered about one-third of the Secretariat and promised that he would return to visit every other office.

His new duties kept John Paul busy. He spent long hours in conferences with Vatican officials, filled his head with the complexities of running both the State and the Church, received a variety of visitors, and worked on plans for his inauguration on the following Sunday. He insisted that it be a simple occasion in keeping with the informality established by his predecessor, John Paul I. And, being a practical man, he changed the time of the ceremony from the afternoon, when it would conflict with televised soccer matches, to the morning.

But already he was feeling that great loneliness which is the burden all popes must carry. Though he was surrounded by officials and forever meeting people, he was still a solitary figure, thrust on to an isolated peak by protocol and tradition. It went against his gregarious nature and caused him inner anguish, especially when he remembered the old buildings of Krakow, the green rolling foothills of the Tatras, the friends with whom he could exercise his mind.

He reached frequently for the telephone in those first few days, on one occasion talking to 10 of his former staff and colleagues in Krakow. "I am so sad, I feel so far away from you all," he said to one of them. "Please come and see me soon."

At another time, a nun picked up the telephone when it rang in the Metropolitan Curia in Krakow. "Who is speaking?" she asked.

A voice from far away, a voice thinned by loneliness so that it was almost a whisper, said: "It's me". The nun almost collapsed when she realised she was talking to the new Pope.

But he was delighted when he discovered that many old friends from Poland, the United States and other parts of the world, were coming to Rome for his installation. He later met many of the 5000 Polish pilgrims who had been allowed out of the country, and he had to fight back tears as he said to them: "It is not easy for me to leave my beloved countryside of Poland. But if it is God's will, I accept".

Nor did he forget those with whom he had become friendly while touring North America. After his installation, he spotted a familiar face in the crowd. It was that of Father Joseph Kochan, pastor of St Joseph's Church in Radway, Edmonton, Canada. He had officials bring Kochan out of the crowd for a private audience. "Then Pope John Paul had the Vatican photographer come and make five pictures which they have now sent me," Kochan recalls.

Also in the crowds that swarmed to meet the new Pope was Monsignor Joseph Gluszek, of the small and unlikely parish of Geyser, Montana, which the Pope had visited when a cardinal. Gluszek was just one of scores of Catholic priests and bishops of Polish descent who were waiting to be blessed as a group by John Paul.

Gluszek recalls: "There was a vast crowd of Polish people there before him. Many faces packed together. He looked over to me in that big crowd and saw me, and he picked me out. He called to me, 'Monsignor Gluszek! Come to me at 7.30—to my place'."

That night Joseph Gluszek dined in private with the new Pope of the Roman Catholic Church. "We sat down and we dined in the Vatican and we talked about friendly things. He was interested in how the world accepted his election as Pope. I said a few words about what I see and hear in my own parish in Montana and I told him that the people were very happy there. We just talked quietly about things. I was very proud."

On the day before his inauguration, there occurred an event, instigated by John Paul, that was unique in the history of the Church. It astonished some, amused others and shocked the more conservative members of the hierarchy. It began traditionally enough, with John Paul meeting in the Hall of Benedictions those members of the international press, television and radio who had covered the funeral of John Paul I and the conclave, and who were now waiting for the inauguration. Preceded by six bearers of the pontifical gestatorial chair and followed by members of the Pontifical Household, John Paul took his place and, after hearing a homage delivered by Father Romeo Panciroli, Secretary of the Pontifical Commission for Social Communications, addressed the media representatives, first in French, then switching to English.

"Ladies and Gentlemen, I bid you welcome! And thank you heartily for everything you have done, and for everything you will do, to present to the general public, in the press, on the radio, and on television, the events in the Catholic Church which have gathered you several times at Rome within the last two months. Certainly, at the mere professional level, you have lived through days as tiring as they were moving. The sudden, unforeseeable character of the facts that followed one another, obliged you to appeal to a sum of knowledge in the area of religious information that was, perhaps, unfamiliar to you; and then to meet, under conditions that were sometimes feverish, a requirement marked by the malady of the century: haste. For you, to wait for the white smoke was not a restful hour!

"Thank you in the first place for having echoed so widely, with unanimous respect, the extensive and really historic labour of the great Pope Paul VI. Thank you for having made so familiar the smiling face and the evangelical attitude of my immediate Predecessor, John Paul I. Thank you again for the favourable coverage you gave to the recent conclave, to my election and to the first steps I have taken in the heavy office of the pontificate. In any case, it was an opportunity for you not only to speak of persons—who pass— but of the See of Rome, of the Church, her traditions and her rites, her faith, her problems and her hopes, of St Peter and the role of the Pope, of the great spiritual stakes of today: in short, of the mystery of the Church. Allow me to dwell a little on this aspect: it is difficult to present well the true face of the Church.

"Yes, it is always difficult to read events, and to enable others to read them. In the first place they are nearly always complex. It is enough for an element to be forgotten inadvertently, omitted deliberately, minimised or on the contrary emphasised disproportionately, to distort the present vision and the forecasts to come. Ecclesial events, furthermore, are more dif- ficult to grasp for those who contemplate them—I say it in all respect for everyone—outside a vision of faith, and even more difficult to express to a large public which has difficulty in perceiving their real meaning. You must, nevertheless, arouse the interest and win a hearing from this public, while your agencies ask you often and above all for the sensational. Some are then tempted to drop into the anecdote: it is concrete and it may be very good, but on condition that the anecdote is significant and really related to the nature of the religious phenomenon. Others plunge courageously into a very advanced analysis of the problems and motives of ecclesial persons, with the risk of not considering sufficiently the essential which, as you know, is not of a political but of a spiritual nature. Finally, from this last point of view, things are often more simple than is imagined: I hardly dare speak of my election!

"But this is not the time to examine in detail all the risks and merits of your task as reporters of religious news. Let us note, moreover, that here and there some progress seems to be visible in pursuit of the truth, and in understanding and presentation of the religious phenomenon. I congratu- late you on the part you have played in it.

"Perhaps you yourselves have been surprised and encouraged by the im- portance attributed to it, in all countries, by a very wide public which some people thought was indifferent or allergic to the ecclesiastical institution and to spiritual things. In actual fact, the handing down of the supreme office, entrusted by Christ to St Peter, with regard to all the peoples to be evan- gelised and to all the disciples of Christ to be gathered in unity, really appeared as a reality transcending habitual events. Yes, the handing down of this office has a deep echo in spirits and in hearts which perceive that God is at work in history. It was loyal to acknowledge it and to adapt to it the media of social communication which, in different degrees, you have at your disposal.

"It is my wish precisely that craftsmen of religious information may always find the help they need from competent ecclesial organisms. The latter must receive them in respect for their convictions and their profession, supply them with very adequate and very objective documentation, but also propose to them a Christian perspective which sets facts in their true significance for the Church and for mankind. In this way you will be able to tackle these religious reports with the specific competence that they demand.

"You are very concerned about freedom of information and of expression: you are right. Think yourselves lucky to enjoy it! Use this freedom well to grasp the truth more closely and to admit your readers, your listeners or viewers into 'whatever is true, whatever is honourable, whatever is just, whatever is pure, whatever is lovely, whatever is gracious', to repeat the words of St Paul; into what helps them to live in justice and brotherhood, to discover the ultimate meaning of life, to open them up to the mystery of God, so near each of us. Under these conditions, your profession, so demanding and sometimes so exhausting—I was going to say your vocation—so topical and so beautiful will elevate further the spirit and the heart of men of good will, at the same time as the faith of Christians. It is a service which the Church and humanity appreciate.

"I am happy at this first contact with you. I assure you of my understanding and I take the liberty of relying on yours. I know that in addition to your professional problems, to which we will come back another time, you each have your personal and family cares. Let us not be afraid to entrust them to the Virgin Mary, who is always at Christ's side. And in Christ's name, I willingly bless you."

It was here that John Paul switched with remarkable ease into near-perfect English.

"I would like to offer my greetings and my blessing, not only to you, but to all your colleagues throughout the world. Although you represent different cultures, you are all united in the service of truth. And the corps that you make up here today is, in itself, a splendid manifestation of unity and solidarity. I would ask to be remembered to your families and to your fellow-citizens in your respective countries. Please accept—all of you—my expression of respect, esteem and fraternal love."

At the end of his address, John Paul began breaking almost every rule in the papal book of etiquette, which had been written so long ago that it was about time for drastic revision. Instead of leaving the hall after giving a blessing, as had been the custom, John Paul, a grin on his face, plunged into the crowd of journalists. He shook hands, exchanged remarks and ignored Vatican officials who tried to get him to return to his chair on a raised dais. He was thoroughly enjoying himself and he was not going to allow stuffy protocol to stand in his way.

As Hugh Mulligan of Associated Press reported: "It took Pope John Paul II forty minutes to pass down the splendid hall of the benedictions after his formal talk, as he took the hands reaching out frantically to him, smiling and making conversation like Lyndon Johnson moving along an airport fence at campaign time.

" 'Holy Father, the Associated Press of America,' this reporter called out to him from behind the wooden barrier.

"The pontiff from Poland turned in mild surprise from the Italian nuns begging a blessing and said, 'I love America, I thank you Associated Press.' His hand clasp was firm and his English perfect with only a trace of a Slavic accent as he fixed this reporter with a warm unblinking gaze from his deep-set blue eyes.

"At one point, when it seemed the pope would be crushed by the surge of photographers following in his wake, a Swiss guard came on the run to his rescue with a silver halberd at the ready.

" '*No, no, non e necessario*'—no, no, not necessary—one of the papal noble guard in a brown cutaway morning suit intercepted him."

John Paul answered questions in the language in which he was asked—in Polish to the Polish journalists, in German to the Germans, in English to the Americans, British, Australians and Irish, in French to the French and in Italian to the Italians. He attempted to answer as many questions as possible, not an easy task with 1500 journalists jostling to be near him, each one hoping to extract new information from the man.

"Would you like to visit your native Poland?" one journalist asked.

"If they'll let me," he replied.

Would he continue his favourite sport of ski-ing? "If they'll let me."

Would he like to visit Russia? "When they'll let me."

He was asked if he would be prepared to meet journalists once a year.

"Willingly," he said, then after a pause he added: "Let's see how you treat me."

At that stage journalists would have treated him with nothing but enthusiasm. If he had been a sporting hero he would have been called "the greatest", if he had been a play or a movie he would have been proclaimed "a hit". In 40 minutes of chatting he had said more to reporters than his three predecessors had done in their combined pontificates.

And as he was leaving, John Paul again forgot the traditions. He was almost out the big bronze doors when he remembered he had not delivered the usual blessing that comes at the end of every Papal audience. Cupping his hands into a megaphone, he shouted "I forgot" and then proceeded to give the Latin benediction over the heads of the noisy, bustling crowd.

Brisk, biting winds were whipping across the city of Rome as thousands of people began pouring into St Peter's Square on the morning of Sunday, 22 October for the inaugural Mass of John Paul II. They were from all parts of the world: famous, wealthy and privileged people like King Juan Carlos and Queen Sophia of Spain and Prince Rainier and Princess Grace of Monaco; people who had sought fame such as the President of Poland, Henryk Jablonski, and the Prime Minister of France, Raymond Barre; those who walked with the famous, like the United States national security adviser Zbigniew Brzezinski; and people who knew neither fame nor wealth but only devotion to the faith. An important figure, eyed by many Catholic leaders was Britain's Anglican Archbishop of Canterbury, Dr Donald

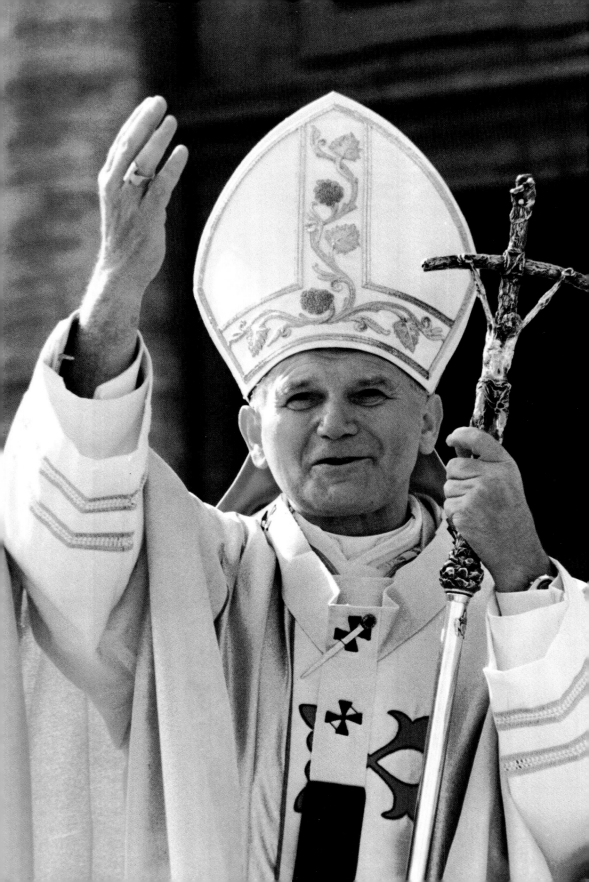

John Paul II at Inauguration.

Coggan, the first Primate of England to attend a papal inauguration since the final break between Anglicans and Catholics in the 16th century.

With so many attending the Mass, security was a problem. More than 5000 armed police mixed with the crowd, kept an eye on guests who could be possible targets for assassination, while overhead clattered a police helicopter. By the time the Mass began, 300 000 people were packed into the square, overflowing down the broad expanse of the Via della Conciliazione. An estimated one billion people would watch the Mass on television including millions in Poland who had never before been allowed the freedom to see such an event.

Soon after ten o'clock the vast crowd exploded into a thunder of applause as John Paul appeared at the doors of St Peter's. An observant and painstaking reporter later noted that during the Pope's homily, he was interrupted 47 times by applause.

The reign of John Paul II was officially inaugurated at ten eighteen a.m. when the senior Cardinal Deacon, Pericle Felici, placed a white wool pallium, adorned with six black crosses, around the shoulders of the new pontiff. And then during the Mass of three hours ten minutes, emotion took over the great piazza. John Paul wept quietly, as did thousands in the crowd, and then wiped away the tears to smile and wave. A warm sun replaced the previous chill wind.

Age prevented many of the cardinals falling to their knees in the traditional act of obeisance, but John Paul leapt from his throne to embrace them. And then Cardinal Stefan Wyszynski, the tough and stern Primate of Poland, the man who had guided Karol Wojtyla up through the ranks of the church, at times crossing swords with him, stepped forward. The crowd was hushed. As he bent over to kiss the papal ring, John Paul lifted him up with his ski-strong arms, embraced him and kissed the primate's own ring.

John Paul's homily was another dazzling virtuoso performance. He spoke in Italian, then followed it with Polish, French, English, German, Spanish, Portuguese, Russian, Lithuanian, Czech and Ukrainian, a stunning reminder of the universality of the Church.

" 'You are the Christ, the Son of the living God' These words were spoken by Simon, son of Jonah, in the district of Caesarea Philippi. Yes, he spoke to them with his own tongue, with a deeply lived and experienced conviction—but it is not in him that they find their source, their origin: '. . . because it was not flesh and blood that revealed this to you but my Father in heaven'. They were the words of Faith.

"These words mark the beginning of Peter's mission in the history of sal-

Cardinal Wyszynski embraces John Paul II at
the inauguration.

vation, in the history of the People of God. From that moment, from that confession of Faith, the sacred history of salvation and of the People of God was bound to take on a new dimension: to express itself in the historical dimension of the Church. This ecclesial dimension of the history of the People of God takes its origin, in fact is born from these words of faith, and is linked to the man who uttered them: 'You are Peter—the rock—and on you, as on a rock, I will build my Church'. On this day and in this place these same words must again be uttered and listened to: 'You are the Christ, the Son of the living God'. Yes, Brothers and sons and daughters, these words first of all.

"Their content reveals to our eyes the mystery of the living God, the mystery to which the Son has brought us close. Nobody, in fact, has brought the living God as close to men and revealed him as he alone did. In our knowledge of God, in our journey towards God, we are totally linked to the power of these words: 'He who sees me sees the Father'. He who is infinite, inscrutable, ineffable, has come close to us in Jesus Christ, the only begotten Son of God, born of the Virgin Mary in the stable at Bethlehem.

"All of you who are still seeking God, all of you who already have the inestimable good fortune to believe, and also you who are tormented by doubt: please listen once again, today in this sacred place, to the words uttered by Simon Peter. In those words is the new truth, indeed, the ultimate and definitive truth about man: the son of the living God—'You are the Christ, the Son of the living God'.

"Today the new Bishop of Rome solemnly begins his ministry and the mission of Peter. In this city, in fact, Peter completed and fulfilled the mission entrusted to him by the Lord. The Lord addressed him with these words: '. . . when you were young you put on your own belt and walked where you liked; but when you grow old you will stretch out your hands and somebody else will put a belt round you and take you where you would rather not go'.

"Peter came to Rome! What else but obedience to the inspiration received from the Lord guided him and brought him to this city, the heart of the Empire? Perhaps the fisherman of Galilee did not want to come here. Perhaps he would have preferred to stay there, on the shores of the Lake of Genesareth, with his boat and his nets. But guided by the Lord, obedient to his inspiration, he came here!

"According to an ancient tradition (given magnificent literary expression in a novel by Henryk Sienkiewicz), Peter wanted to leave Rome during Nero's persecution. But the Lord intervened: he went to meet him. Peter spoke to him and asked. 'Quo vadis, Domine?'—'Where are you going, Lord?'

And the Lord answered him at once: 'I am going to Rome to be crucified again'. Peter went back to Rome and stayed here until his crucifixion.

"Yes, Brothers and sons and daughters, Rome is the See of Peter. Down the centuries new Bishops continually succeeded him in this See. Today a new Bishop comes to the Chair of Peter in Rome, a Bishop full of trepidation, conscious of his unworthiness. And how could one not tremble before the greatness of this call and before the universal mission of this See of Rome! To the See of Peter in Rome there succeeds today a Bishop who is a son of Poland. But from this moment he too becomes a Roman. Yes—a Roman. He is a Roman also because he is the son of a nation whose history, from its first dawning, and whose thousand-year-old traditions are marked by a living, strong, unbroken and deeply felt link with the See of Peter, a nation which has ever remained faithful to this See of Rome. Inscrutable is the design of Divine Providence!

"In past centuries, when the Successor of Peter took possession of his See, the triregnum or tiara was placed on his head. The last Pope to be crowned was Paul VI in 1963, but after the solemn coronation ceremony he never used the tiara again and left his Successors free to decide in this regard. Pope John Paul I, whose memory is so vivid in our hearts, did not wish to have the tiara; nor does his Successor wish it today. This is not the time to return to a ceremony and an object considered, wrongly, to be a symbol of the temporal power of the Popes.

"Our time calls us, urges us, obliges us to gaze on the Lord and immerse ourselves in humble and devout meditation on the mystery of the supreme power of Christ himself. He who was born of the Virgin Mary, the carpenter's Son (as he was thought to be), the Son of the living God (confessed by Peter), came to make us all 'a kingdom of priests'.

"The Second Vatican Council has reminded us of the mystery of this power and of the fact that Christ's mission as Priest, Prophet-Teacher and King continues in the Church. Everyone, the whole People of God, shares in this threefold mission. Perhaps in the past, the tiara, this triple crown, was placed on the Pope's head in order to express by that symbol the Lord's plan for his Church, namely that all the hierarchical order of Christ's Church, all 'sacred power' exercised in the Church, is nothing other than service, service with a single purpose: to ensure that the whole People of God shares in this threefold mission of the Christ and always remains under the power of the Lord; a power that has its source not in the powers of this world but in the mystery of the Cross and Resurrection.

"The absolute and yet sweet and gentle power of the Lord responds to the whole depths of the human person, to his loftiest aspirations of intellect, will and heart. It does not speak the language of force but expresses itself in charity and truth. The new Successor of Peter in the See of Rome, today makes a fervent, humble and trusting prayer: Christ, make me become and remain the servant of your unique power, the servant of your sweet power, the servant of your power that knows no eventide. Make me be a servant.

Indeed, the servant of your servants.

"Brothers and sisters, do not be afraid to welcome Christ and accept his power. Help the Pope and all those who wish to serve Christ and with Christ's power to serve the human person and the whole of mankind. Do not be afraid. Open wide the doors for Christ. To his saving power open the boundaries of States, economic and political systems, the vast fields of culture, civilisation and development. Do not be afraid. Christ knows 'what is in man'. He alone knows it.

"So often today man does not know what is within him, in the depths of his mind and heart. So often he is uncertain about the meaning of his life on this earth. He is assailed by doubt, a doubt which turns into despair. We ask you therefore, we beg you with humility and trust, let Christ speak to man. He alone has words of life, yes, of eternal life. Precisely today the whole church is celebrating 'World Mission Day'; that is, she is praying, meditating and acting in order that Christ's words of life may reach all people and be received by them as a message of hope, salvation, and total liberation.

"I thank all of you here present who have wished to participate in this solemn inauguration of the ministry of the new Successor of Peter. I heartily thank the Heads of State, the Representatives of the Authorities, and the Government Delegations for so honouring me with their presence. Thank you, Eminent Cardinals of the Holy Roman Church. I thank you, my beloved Brothers in the Episcopate. Thank you, Priests. To you, Sisters and Brothers, Religious of the Orders and Congregations, I give my thanks. Thank you, people of Rome. Thanks to the pilgrims who have come here from all over the world. Thanks to all of you who are linked with this Sacred Ceremony by radio and television."

John Paul now spoke in his native tongue: "I speak to you, my dear fellow-countrymen, pilgrims from Poland, Brother Bishops with your magnificent Primate at your head, Priests, Sisters and Brothers of the Polish religious congregations—to you representatives of Poland from all over the world. What shall I say to you who have come from my Krakow, from the See of Saint Stanislaw of whom I was the unworthy successor for 14 years? What shall I say? Everything that I could say would fade into insignificance compared with what my heart feels, and your hearts feel, at this moment. So let us leave aside words. Let there remain just great silence before God, the silence that becomes prayer. I ask you: be with me! At Jasna Gora and everywhere. Do not cease to be with the Pope who today prays with the words of the poet: 'Mother of God, you who defend Bright Czestochowa and shine at Ostrabrama'. And these same words I address to you at this particular moment.

"That was an appeal and a call to prayer for the new Pope, an appeal expressed in the Polish language. I make the same appeal to all the sons and daughters of the Catholic Church. Remember me today and always in your prayer!

And then he delighted the French in the crowd by speaking in their language: "To the Catholics of French-speaking lands, I express my complete affection and devotedness. I presume to count upon your unreserved filial assistance. May you advance in the faith! To those who do not share this faith, I also address my respectful and cordial greetings. I trust that their sentiments of goodwill may facilitate the spiritual mission that lies upon me, and which does not lack repercussions for the happiness and peace of the world".

With no apparent difficulty, John Paul switched to English: "To all of you who speak English I offer in the name of Christ a cordial greeting. I count on the support of your prayers and your goodwill in carrying out my mission of service to the Church and mankind. May Christ give you his grace and his peace, overturning the barriers of division and making all things one in him".

Then he repeated the same message in German, Spanish, Portuguese, Czech, Russian, Ukrainian and Lithuanian, finally adding: "I open my heart to all my Brothers of the Christian Churches and Communities, and I greet in particular you who are here present, in anticipation of our coming personal meeting; but for the moment I express to you my sincere appreciation for your having wished to attend this solemn ceremony. And I also appeal to all men—to every man, and with what veneration the apostle of Christ must utter this word: 'Man'!

"Pray for me!

"Help me to be able to serve you! Amen."

At the end of the Mass, the sun now shining warmly, the crowd elated, John Paul walked towards the people and triumphantly thrust his heavy, crucifix-topped staff into the air. A small boy, clutching flowers, rushed out of the edge of the crowd. Vatican officials tried to push him away, but John Paul called him forward and embraced him. Then, with a last wave, he disappeared inside the Vatican Palace. But the crowd was reluctant to go. The people stood in silence, breaking it only to pray. It was as though they wanted, needed, one more glimpse of their new Pope, one more look at the man who had electrified them that morning.

At one twenty-five p.m. the window to the Pope's private study opened, and John Paul appeared, smiling. He wanted to recite the Angelus Domini with the thousands who remained, even though it was an unusual hour for the prayer.

"I wish," he said in a strong voice, "to resume the magnificent habit of my predecessors and recite the Angelus together with you, dear Brothers and Sisters.

"The solemn Mass for the inauguration of my ministry as Peter's Successor has just ended. To live intensely this historic moment, we had to make the profession of faith in common, which we recite every day in the Apostles' Creed: 'I believe in the Holy Catholic Church', and in the Nicene-Constantinople Creed: 'I believe the Church to be one, holy, catholic and apostolic'.

"All together we became aware of this marvellous truth about the Church, which the Second Vatican Council explained in two documents: in the dogmatic Constitution *Lumen Gentium* and in the pastoral Constitution *Gaudium et Spes*, on the Church in the modern world.

"Now, we must go even deeper. We must arrive at this moment in the history of the world, when the Word becomes flesh: when the Son of God becomes Man. The history of salvation reaches its climax and, at the same time, begins again in its definitive form when the Virgin of Nazareth accepts the announcement of the Angel and utters the words: 'fiat mihi secundum verbum tuum' (Let it be to me according to your word).

"The Church is, as it were, conceived at that moment. So let us go back to the beginning of the mystery. And in it let us embrace once more the whole content of today's solemnity. In it let us embrace the whole past of Christianity and of the Church, which has found her centre here, in Rome. In it let us try to embrace the whole future of the pontificate, of the People of God and of the whole human family, because the family begins with the Father's will, but is always conceived under the Mother's heart.

"With this faith and with this hope let us pray."

After reciting the prayer in Latin, with a few added words in Polish, John Paul still seemed reluctant to take his leave of the crowd. He turned away for a moment, then said he would like to speak to the young people in the square. "You are," he said, "the future of the world, the hope of the Church. You are my hope."

He caused laughter and applause by finally saying: "We must close now, for it is time for lunch. For you and for the Pope."

The pastoral ministry of Pope John Paul II had begun.

CHAPTER FOURTEEN

Pope John Paul II walked into his weekly general audience and so thunderous was the applause of the crowd that he put his hands over his ears in a gesture of mock discomfort. But his smile showed how delighted he was, not only at the response but also at the size of the crowd. More than 30 000 people, overflowed St Peter's Basilica and packed the nearby Vatican audience hall. They were mostly young people, the sort of crowd that could be expected at a rock concert, eager—no, wildly enthusiastic—to see the new Pope. Teenagers, whose heroes are John Travolta or Rod Stewart, stretching out their arms to try and touch the man from Poland, tearing at his cassock, scratching his hands and, embarrassingly, leaving lipstick on his sleeves when they tried to kiss his hands.

Looking over the mass of young people, John Paul told them: "Go back to your homes, your schools and your associations and tell everyone that the Pope counts greatly on young people. Tell them that young people are the comfort and strength of the Pope, who wants to see them all".

The size of the crowds who have turned up to the general audiences have surprised, and gratified, Vatican officials. The first few weeks of his reign indicated that John Paul could become the most popular Pope in the history of the Catholic Church. As veteran Vatican-watcher, Michael Wilson, put it: "There is a spirit of vitality, of youthful energy blowing through the centuries-old Apostolic Palace".

And that is not just because the Pope is keen on fresh air, much to the discomfort of Italian priests who shivered in the winter breezes blowing through wide-open windows. "Polish air conditioning" they muttered as they pulled up their collars.

The freshness comes as a contrast to the slowed-down pace of Pope Paul VI, who was ailing in the last years of his pontificate, and to the brief reign of John Paul I. A new decisiveness seems to have imbued the papacy, stemming to a large extent from the pure energy of a 58-year-old man in the prime of physical condition. "Papa Wojtyla is the complete man," says one of his friends. "He is pious, a scholar, a sportsman, a lover of music and art, and a boy at heart. All generations find they have something in common with him."

Especially the young. They are spellbound by him and, in turn, they fascinate the Pope. John Paul, at the public audiences, always zeroes in on the young. True, he shakes hands and talks with anyone within reach; he takes the letters they hand him (and they always get an answer); he listens and replies. But it is the children who get his special attention.

At one audience, he walked by waving at a group when he noticed an eight-year-old boy with tears in his eyes. Turning back, he asked the reason for the tears.

"My father died three days ago," said the boy. "But they told me, too, that you were also my father. Is this true?"

"Certainly it is," replied the Pope, hugging the boy. "And you may call on me as you would your father."

He signalled an usher to get the boy's name and address. "You may be sure he will keep in touch with him and his family," the papal secretary said later.

John Paul still retains the compulsive need to touch people which was characteristic of his days in Krakow. He hates to sit aloof on the gestatorial chair, the portable throne, preferring to plunge into crowds, an action that gives his security men nightmares. Crowds are not crowds to John Paul. They are made up of individuals and he wants to show each one that he feels and cares for them as persons. He finds a great consolation in the public audiences, as did Pope Paul, although Paul was more reserved. Said one observer: "Paul would cancel many events, but never an audience unless it was physically impossible for him to attend".

John Paul's approach caused much consternation at first among Vatican officials. A protocol prelate, keeping to the old ways, would in the early days of his reign lay a hand on the Pope's arm and say "basta", which meant that the Pope had talked enough, that he had to press on to the next person. John Paul merely shrugged off their hands and continued talking. Now the word "basta" is no longer heard in his presence. Vatican officials also at first tried to get him to walk rapidly through the audiences or be carried in his gestatorial chair. But a muscular papal arm, strong from skiing and canoeing, held the protocol prelates back and he simply ignored the gestatorial chair. It takes John Paul more than half an hour to walk from the door of St Peter's to the chair at the altar from which he talks. Paul did it in three minutes.

At times John Paul's determination to be independent has caused some misgivings among Vatican officials who have long run things the way they wished. They have noted there has not been such a tough and decisive Pope since Achille Ratti (Pius XI), a mountaineering man from Milan who was reputedly as "tough as nails", an absolute sovereign-pontiff during his reign from 1922 until 1939. Once, when Pius was displeased with Cardinal Billot, he stood up, snatched off the prelate's red skull cap, and said: "You are no longer a cardinal".

John Paul's way of doing things was expressed in a remark to a friend: "They won't tie my hands". Monsignor Virgilio Noe, papal master of ceremonies, found out how independent—and brusque—John Paul could be when he kept pointing to paragraphs in the missal to be read by the Pope and indicated where and when he should sit or stand. He had performed the same duty for the two previous Popes, but John Paul snapped at him: "I'm the Pope and I know how to behave."

Other traditions have been cast aside by John Paul. Up until and during the pontificate of Pius XII, it was common for prelates and priests called in by the Pope to kiss his ring and the toe of his slipper. John XXIII could not abide such ceremonies, once telling an aide who, several times a day, would genuflect thrice in front of the Pope: "Surely once is enough. Don't you think I believe you the first time?" John did away with the toe-kissing ceremony, but allowed his ring to be kissed in private audiences, although he often pulled back his hand at public ones. Paul VI tried to avoid ring-kissing as much as possible. In fact, in public audiences he learned from experience not to let anyone even hold his hand. Twice he was almost pulled into the crowd and after that he used to slap lightly at people's hands to avoid being grabbed. John Paul II has the strength to pull his hand away and twist it sideways before any eager-beavers can get their lips down on the ring. But he still allows, possibly with reluctance, the ring to be kissed in such official ceremonies as cardinals making obeisances. Old traditions stretching back centuries cannot be wiped out overnight, even though John Paul seems to be making a supreme effort to rid the Vatican of some of the more dubious ones.

But in the minor battle of wits between John Paul and tradition-bound Vatican officials, the victories have not all been on the side of the Pope. There was, for instance, the skirmish over clothing. Officials were dismayed at the clothing he brought with him to the Vatican. The material was patched, darned and frayed. When he lifted his arms at early audiences they were further alarmed to see his sleeved Polish undershirt or, even worse, his bare arms. He was forced to wear new clothes provided by the papal tailors, Gammarelli, who made him white cassocks and a dozen long-sleeved white shirts with French cuffs. Now no one is embarrassed when he raises his arms at audiences; one sees a flash of tailored cuffs fitted with cufflinks. Gammarelli also provided John Paul with a sleeveless lambswool cardigan which he wears over his cassock and under his cape for appearances in the open when the weather is cold.

One of the first things John Paul faced up to after being elected was the fact that the papacy is an extremely demanding job. For 365 days a year he must be available, for a Pope cannot delegate his responsibilities or his signature. Determined that the job will not get the better of him, he made it known that he intended to run the Vatican, and not let the Vatican bureaucracy or Curia run him.

"They told my predecessor (John Paul I) what he should do and when", the Pope said to one of his Polish friends. "This may have led to his early death. They will not tell me what to do or when. I will decide. They will not kill me."

But even though the work is so demanding that few politicians or business-men would put up with the conditions, John Paul has found he can cope. His physical fitness and utter dedication to the Church keep him going. "I don't work any harder than I did in Krakow," he said. "The only strain I find is that while at Krakow I worked mainly in Polish, here I am constantly switching languages. I may be reading a document in Italian, then I receive people in German, followed by more papers in French or English, and audiences in all these languages. I suppose I will get used to it and won't find it such a strain after a few months."

John Paul's day begins at five a.m. Half an hour later he is in his private chapel for Mass. The Pope insists that a priest should spend at least an hour a day in meditation, and he sets his example before breakfast. Then he sits down to a meal of fried ham and sausages before going to his desk in his study in the papal apartments to read documents and newspapers. By eight thirty he has gone down one floor to the official papal study and library where he begins the day's work. He prefers to get a great deal of the Holy See's workload out of the way before he meets people and rarely has an audience before eleven a.m.—even on Wednesdays when his weekly public audiences begin with one in St Peter's at eleven a.m., a second in the Nervi-built audience hall at noon and continue with semi-private audiences until around two thirty p.m. Lunch for the Pope is more of a snack than a meal, usually a bowl of soup and sandwiches. Then, much in the style of Winston Churchill during the war years, he allows himself a 15-minute catnap. This mere 15 minutes has caused some nervousness among the Italians working in the Vatican who have a siesta lasting for an hour or more. They fear he could completely cut out the traditional siesta—which is needed, at the most, only in the hot days of summer. It would be a move that would be strongly fought, even though it tends to whittle away the efficiency of the Vatican bureaucracy.

Another cause for consternation is the walk he takes after his catnap. He covers at least two miles at a brisk pace, a physical feat that never entered the minds of other Popes. They were often elderly men, sometimes not in the best of health, and their pace through the Vatican was a leisurely one. But not the new Pope. "He's a fanatic for fitness," said one worried priest, "and it wouldn't surprise me if he has us all doing physical exercises."

The Pope does not keep to the tarmac roads when he goes walking in the gardens, but cuts off into the bylanes and shrubbery that stretch from the Vatican museum. Walking at a fast athletic pace, he moves off behind the Vatican radio tower of St Lee, always pausing to pray and kneel at the Grotto of Lourdes, a copy of the grotto in France. Then he heads behind the Grotto around the tower of St John and the Chinese pavilion and back via the Ethiopian College, altering this route as the whim strikes. Only a secretary accompanies him on these walks; because of the pace he sets, it is usually his Polish secretary from Krakow, Don Stanislau Dziwisz, who used to ski with him in Poland. When the Vatican security men wanted to go with him, he sent them packing. But they still try, from a distance, to keep track of the white skullcap bobbing above the shrubs.

He meditates again in the afternoon and works on papers in his private study until close to six p.m., when he sees Bishop Jacques-Marie Martin, Prefect of the Apostolic Palace, about the next day's audiences, calls in a cardinal for consultation, and then sees or discusses over the telephone any pending business with the Cardinal Secretary of State, Jean Villot.

In his dealings with the Vatican and Curia staff, he is brisk and efficient. There is no small talk, no skimming around the main topic, which is a much-loved and somewhat irritating Italian custom. John Paul gets right down to business, sometimes scheduling as many as four 15-minute sessions within the hour. Cardinals and archbishops arriving in the Pope's study find that John Paul has the files right in front of him, contained in stiff white folders addressed to His Holiness. If the sender of the file is a cardinal prefect of a congregation or cardinal president of a secretariat or commission, that person's name is printed in red on the folder. The name of a lesser prelate is in blue. Using this system, the Pope knows at a glance the importance of the sender. Opening the folder, he begins immediately with the business, and at the conclusion he says goodbye with a firm twist of the hand that rejects the ring-kissing ceremony. Out goes the visitor. In comes the next.

This style of wanting to personally meet those who have prepared reports is one of the major changes that have occurred in the Vatican since John Paul's election. Under previous pontifs, documents were presented to the Pope from the various congregations and other bodies via the Secretariat of State. They were given a file number and the Pope would then answer back through the same channels. If he wanted further information he would call the prefect of the body concerned. But John Paul asks to see, not the prefect or the secretary, but the person who actually drew up the text. Before signing his message to the United Nations Secretary General for the 30th anniversary of the UN's universal peace declaration, he called in the four members of the Justice and Peace Commission who had been instrumental in preparing the outline and "had a real business session with us", as one of them said later.

His method of personal talks and interventions has caused some problems in that they leave wide gaps in the files and archives of the Holy See. For example, he talked personally to the recalcitrant and suspended French archbishop, Marcel Lefebvre, but no one else was present nor is there any record of what the two discussed. Paul VI, on the other hand, would have left careful notes of the meeting.

Although John Paul rarely has guests to lunch, making exceptions only for elderly or infirm prelates or visitors, he likes companionship at dinner. Before John XXIII, it was the custom of Popes to eat alone, mainly because centuries ago it was feared the pontiffs might indulge in unseemly behaviour if several people were present. John changed the tradition. If he had not done so, it would certainly have been changed by the present Pope. The apartment into which dinner guests are ushered is not regal. There are two living rooms, one somewhat stiff and formal but the other, in which guests take their pre-dinner drinks, has easy chairs and a sofa, and a stereo system installed by Paul VI. John Paul likes music, and in fact has a fine-sounding basso voice which he exercises when he is happy or satisfied over the way work is proceeding. He can be heard in his study, singing to himself his beloved Polish religious songs which are set to polka or mazurka music.

John Paul does not drink aperitifs and rarely takes wine, which prompted one cardinal to joke: "If the Italians had known of his taste in wine, he would never have been elected Pope". The Polish Pope prefers an occasional glass of Polish Pilsener-type beer. At dinner, he sits alone on one side of an eight-foot table, his two secretaries usually occupying each end. The two or three guests sit opposite the Pope on the other side of the table, and if he has more than three guests the secretaries have their dinner in a smaller adjoining dining room. No one sits beside the Pope.

For a man in such an important position, a man who is leader of the biggest Christian denomination in the world as well as head of a state, John Paul has a small personal staff. Only five nuns, one of whom acts as his private secretary for private correspondence, look after his needs. The nuns are "sister servants of the Sacred Heart", an order founded in Poland in the middle of the last century to act as housekeepers and secretaries to Church leaders. All are highly trained: his secretary-nun, for instance, being able to take rapid dictation in English, French and Italian, as well as in her native Polish. All his nuns speak Italian for they have worked in Rome at various times.

John Paul brought few personal goods with him from Poland, only his books, records and holy pictures. He uses the same simple bedroom and bed that served John XXIII, Paul VI, and in which John Paul I was found dead.

One of the first, and to him one of the most important, things John Paul did after taking office was to win over the Italians, and especially the Romans. There was some initial disappointment, even a little bitterness, that a foreigner was made Bishop of Rome. After all, Americans would not be exactly delirious with joy if, say, a Frenchman took over operations at St Patrick's Cathedral in New York.

John Paul went to considerable trouble to remove any discontent among Italians. He let it be known that he is only the Pope because he is Bishop of Rome. He always speaks Italian and has spared no effort in getting to know his new diocese of Rome, with special audiences for Roman priests, nuns and seminarians and frequent trips outside the walls of the Vatican. He has told Vatican officials: "I intend to do something every Sunday for the diocese".

In speech after speech, he has made references to the fact that he is not an Italian, but that he has a love for the country, a desire to be made a part of it, and a willingness to learn about the Italian way of life. Soon after his election, he said: "Since I was not born on this soil, I feel all the more need here for a spiritual birth".

On another occasion, he paid a tribute to Italy with these words: "All the more do I feel the need to insert myself in this new land that Peter chose . . . this land has always been near to me; now it has become my second homeland. I desire to be part of Italy in all its historical richness, and at the same time in all its current reality".

It worked. Within days John Paul was being greeted with enthusiastic cheers and exuberant cries of "Viva il Papa!" He quickly moved around Rome and within a few weeks had visited two shrines; taken possession of the Bishop of Rome's basilica, St John Lateran; visited a Rome suburb, the one to which Mussolini moved the inhabitants of the two borgos, or Vatican area streets, when he tore them down to build the imposing Via Della Conciliazione which sweeps from the Tiber to St Peter's; went to the papal summer residence at Castelgandolfo; laid a wreath at the statue of the Virgin Mary off the Spanish Steps; and celebrated Mass in St Mary Major, the largest basilica dedicated to the Virgin.

"At last we have a Bishop of Rome," a priest said after watching John Paul's efforts. It was true, for since 1870, when King Victor Emanuel II overthrew the papal states, until 1929, when Mussolini signed the Lateran Pact, the Popes had considered themselves as prisoners of the Vatican. Even when Pius XII ventured forth after the Pact, it was in the pageantry of state and not as a bishop.

One of the more interesting duties John Paul had to perform in his early days, and one eagerly awaited by Romans, was his meeting with the communist Mayor of Rome, Giulio Carlo Argan. The dedicated Catholic and the dedicated communist met at the foot of Capitol Hill before thousands of cheering people who were divided almost equally into supporters of the Church and supporters of the mayor. It was a reasonably affable meeting of two opposing creeds. Earlier the mayor had plastered the city with posters carrying a message, somewhat rewritten from history, to the public.

"Citizens: the warmth and cheerfulness of the greeting which the citizens and municipality respectfully extend to the new Pontiff as he assumes charge of the Diocese of Rome are not diminished by a still lively sense of mourning for the two popes who have died in so short a time. John Paul II comes to us from a country which, always our friend, was during the last war and the appalling Nazi occupation an object of loving anxiety and fraternal solidarity to the Romans. Among the nations devastated by the last war none was so crushed by the Nazi oppression as Poland, none so constant in resistance, none so heroic in liberation. With admirable faith in civilisation it has almost miraculously rebuilt its destroyed cities and its national unity. And Rome will never be able to forget the Polish soldiers who died for her liberation. For such moral strength and generosity it is a fitting reward that today she should have one of her noblest sons ascending the chair of Peter. It is in the higher logic of history that a citizen of a nation which was above all others victim and martyr of the war should today become here in Rome the defender, the apostle, the guarantor of a peace which is still disastrously threatened by inhuman armaments. The gladness of the Roman people expresses the hope of the entire world and Rome is glad to be such an interpreter. Wishing John Paul II a long, strong and glorious pontificate, from the Capitol, 12 November 1978, the Mayor, Giulio Carlo Argan."

The Mayor, a man of intellect, an art historian of international repute, continued his Polish theme when he met the Pope.

"Among the nations laid waste in the last world war", he said, "none suffered enemy oppression so much as Poland, but none was so staunch in resistance and heroic in liberation. Today Poland sees its sacrifice justly compensated with the accession of a noble son of hers to Peter's Chair. It is part of the just pattern of history that the citizen of a nation that was a victim and martyr of the war, should become, from Rome, the defender, apostle and guarantee of peace in the world."

The Mayor then pointed out to the Pope "the thirst for justice and human solidarity" which animates a city like Rome, harassed by multiple spiritual and material needs. "Too often," he said, "uncertainty and loneliness drive disillusioned youth to drugs, crime, violence and terrorism."

Argan then emphasised that "religious sentiment, the bond with the Church, the presence of her visible Head, have been elements of cohesion of the Roman community for centuries," observing that "this sentiment, which is still alive, does not contradict the desire for progress, emancipation, and the moral, civil and political dignity of the working people."

"Our Administration," he concluded, "is, and wishes to be, respectful of the distinction between religious and civil powers, being certain that their parallelism cannot but benefit social balance, just as it contributed to maintain it during the pontificate of the preceding Popes, mourning for whom does not diminish in citizens' spirits the joy at the election of Your Holiness. A balance which is important both for the Church, of which Rome is the centre, and for the Italian State, of which Rome is the capital. For this reason Roman citizens want an order that will guarantee, with the fullness of the religious and of the political function, the dignity of persons and the freedom of consciences."

The Pope thought there were some fine sentiments, and absolute truth, in what Mayor Argan had to say, thanked him for expressing them, and then decided he better get in a plug for his new position as Bishop of Rome and the Catholic Church in general.

"This first meeting with those on whom it falls to interpret, protect and serve the interests of a city like Rome—whose glorious and mysterious destiny is so closely interwoven with the events of the Church of Christ, which has here, by providential disposition, her visible centre—arouses in me a surge of feelings, of memories, of solemn and weighty thoughts, difficult to restrain. In this City, which was the sovereign ruler of peoples, an admirable teacher of civilisation, an unequalled maker of wise laws, there once arrived the humble fisherman of Galilee, the Apostle Peter. He was ill-equipped and defenceless on the human plane, but inwardly sustained by the strength of the Spirit who made him the courageous bearer of the Glad News, destined to conquer the world. In this same City there has now arrived a new Successor of Peter, also marked by so many human limitations, but trustful in the indefectible help of grace, and coming from a country of which you, Mr Mayor, have kindly spoken with sympathy and cordiality.

"Today the new Pope officially begins his ministry as Bishop of Rome and Pastor of a diocese which has no equal in the world. I feel deeply the responsibility deriving from the complex problems that the pastoral care of a community, which has expanded at a bewildering speed in the last few years, brings with it. And I cannot but look with sympathy on those who, bearing the honour and the weight of the civil administration of the City, are doing their utmost to improve the environmental conditions, to overcome inadequate social situations, and to raise the general living standards of the population.

"Hoping that these goals, at which this important service of the citizens aims, will be successfully reached, I also express the wish that the Administration, adopting a view of the common good which includes all true human values, will give open and cordial attention also to the requirements raised by the religious dimension of the City, which, owing to the incomparable Christian values which characterise its features, is a centre of attraction for pilgrims from all over the world.

"With these sentiments, I invoke God's blessing on this City, which I now feel mine, and I wish to you, Mr Mayor, to your Collaborators, and to the whole large family of the Roman people, serene prosperity and civil progress in hardworking concord, mutual respect and sincere aspiring to a peaceful, harmonious and just society."

Everyone agreed it was a splendid meeting between two of the most powerful men in Rome. There was no confrontation. In fact, it was rather a pleasant exchange of views.

From his first days on the Throne of St Peter, John Paul emerged as a pillar of the Second Vatican Council and a staunch supporter of every encyclical, constitution and document produced by Paul VI—even though he may couch his endorsement in terms more understandable to today's world. The significant lesson to be learned from his speeches is: There will be no change in the teaching of the Church as handed down by the Council. Those seeking modification of conciliar or Pauline doctrines may look for no easy way out. He will make no changes in the present teaching of *Humanae Vitae*, on confession, on absolution, on the indissolubility of marriage, on divorce, on abortion.

Many liberal Catholics misinterpreted John Paul's earlier thoughts expressed when he was in Poland. They felt he would stick less rigidly with orthodox doctrines; for instance, that he might be more liberal on the vexed question of contraception. But, in fact, he has always taken the conservative line with contraception, condemning out of hand artificial methods. He has also spoken out against the prolonged avoidance of offspring, even by legitimate means, while allowing that responsible parenthood may entail limiting the number of children.

He has pointed out that marriage and the family are invariably at the

Within a few days John Paul II defied the traditions and travelled outside the Vatican. Here, he boards a helicopter.

The sun sets over one of Krakow's 200 churches.

root of all the affairs of human beings and society. But although the family is the smallest social group, "the fate of nations and continents, of humanity and the Church, depend upon it".

John Paul has made the observation that while some countries were worried by their high birth rates, others faced a decline in birth rates. Therefore it was not the number of people born but the methods used if birth control was involved. "For these matters are very deeply a part of the meaning of human life—they speak of the very value of man and also constitute it." He stressed that the Church's pronouncements have the aim of "forming an upright and mature conscience in husband and wife".

Arguing that the human conscience was at the centre of the meaning of parenthood, and in particular responsible parenthood, he reiterated that the rhythm method of birth control only may be used, and then only if there was good reason to employ it. He said that Paul VI, in *Humanae Vitae*, was conscious of the psychological difficulties "and perhaps even the intellectual ones which the standpoint of the Church may meet . . . That is why those who take up this standpoint must have a clear understanding . . . In practice, especially, they must not allow the morality of the action to be confused with the technique of the action, the principle to be confused with the method. One of the fundamental errors in the interpretation of *Humanae Vitae* proceeds precisely from this confusion. The modern 'technical' mentality wants to see, above all, a 'technique' also in the case where two people, a man and a woman, as husband and wife, must face each other in the whole truth of their mutual gift, guided by their upright and mature conscience. The Church wants to save the true sense of love for them, and the mature dignity of behaviour proper to persons. That is also the true reason of continence, which constitutes an indispensable condition not only of responsible parenthood, but also of responsibility for conjugal love itself".

Those words hold little comfort for the spreading movement among certain Catholic groups for a more liberal approach to sexual matters. Nor has John Paul given any hope to those priests who wish to lift the 1500-year-old ban on marriages, said by some to be one of the main causes for the steady defection of priests in recent years. "We must retain the sense of our unique vocation," declared John Paul. "We are in the world but we are not worldly."

He has come firmly out against abortion and divorce when after his election he said: "While respecting those who disagree, it is very difficult—even objectively and impartially—to countenance those who violate the sanctity of marriage or destroy life conceived in the womb. It is impossible to say that the principle of divorce or the principle of abortion help mankind and make life more humane and dignified and make society better. The family carries with it the most fundamental values of mankind. Too often those values are crushed by socio-economic tendencies that prevail over Christian feeling and humanity. These values must be sustained with tenacity and firmness, because to violate them is of incalculable damage to man and society. It's easy to destroy values but far more difficult to reconstruct them".

Many priests, especially those in Latin American countries, had hoped that John Paul's experiences with a totalitarian regime might lead him to support radical, even revolutionary movements against oppressive governments. In Nicaragua, for instance, the Sandinistas who are fighting the right wing dictator, Somoza, are supported and partially led by Catholic priests. Priests throughout Latin America want the Church to follow what they believe are the footsteps of Jesus and become a revolutionary leader of the poor. They have demanded nationalisation of foreign-owned property and land reform and justice for those who at present have nothing but the ache of an empty belly.

Those priests could well be disappointed because John Paul has made it clear that he will not radically change Paul's insistence that the Church must eschew politics or involvement in politics—but that it remains the guardian of justice and peace. He will not tolerate an "armed" priesthood preaching revolution or taking part in such revolutions; there will be no priest-fomented revolutions or uprisings. John Paul believes that justice and peace can be obtained by a realisation of what the Church means in the world. As he has already told his bishops, priests, religious and laity: Your job is to preach the Gospel and show the way; not to start uprisings. Maybe you will be persecuted and die, but you will not start popular revolts in the name of the Church and Christianity.

Of course, this does not mean he approves of dictatorships, either of the right or the left. Four days after his election, he told the diplomatic corps that diplomatic relations with the Vatican did not necessarily mean Vatican approval of their regimes. "That is not our business", he said. What the church seeks is dialogue to redress abuses.

John Paul has made it clear there will be no "stalemate" in the church's relations with communist or other totalitarian regimes. He believes that for Catholics, in fact for all Christians, the final chapter of the book of existence has already been written: Christ triumphs in glory. The Church will win out in the long run. What he is making clear, and he is basing it on his experiences in Poland, is that ideological and practical dealings with communists are on different levels. Ideologically there can be no compromise with Marxism. In practice the Church deals with the authorities of whatever land they may work in, whether those authorities are communist or not. So long as there is no compromise with the faith.

In several speeches since he was elected, John Paul has hammered these points, calling for freedom and justice and at the same time telling the followers of the Church not to be afraid, informing governments he does not wish to interfere in their politics. Soon after his election he said: "With sincere humility our intention is to really devote ourselves to the continual and special cause of peace, of development and justice among nations. In this matter we have no desire to interfere in politics or to take part in the management of temporal affairs. For just as the Church cannot be confined to a certain earthly pattern, so we in our approach to the urgent questions of men and peoples, are led solely by religious and moral motives ... we wish to strive to strengthen the spiritual foundations on which human society must be based. We feel that this duty is all the more urgent the longer that discords and dissensions last which, in not a few parts of the world, provide material for struggle and conflicts and even give rise to the more serious danger of frightful calamities.

"We wish to open our hearts to all who are oppressed, as they say, by any injustice or discrimination with regard to either economic or social affairs, or even to political matters, or even to freedom of conscience and the freedom to practice their religion which is their due. We must aim at this: that all forms of injustice which exist today should be given consideration by all in common and should be really eradicated from the world, so that all men may be able to live a life worthy of man."

Three weeks after his inauguration he told members of the papal Justice and Peace Commission that "the Church is neither a stranger nor a rival" in the lives of nations. He asked all nations not to fear religion, saying that the Church's concern is chiefly to ensure that "men open to Jesus Christ". He added: "Do not be afraid. Open wide the doors for Christ. To his saving power open the boundaries of states, economic and cultural systems, the vast fields of culture, civilisation and development. Do not be afraid ... We are living in a time when everything should push us to open our doors: The keener awareness of the universal solidarity of men, the need to protect the environment and the common heritage of mankind, the need for reducing the burden and deadly threat of armaments, the duty to free from poverty millions of men who would find, along with the means to lead a decent life, the chance to contribute fresh energies to the common effort".

In his 1978 Christmas message, John Paul again referred to the lack of freedom, and in particular, religious freedom, when he said: "On this night let us think of all the human beings that fall victim to man's inhumanity, to cruelty, to the lack of any respect, to contempt for the objective rights of every human being. Let us also think of those who on this night are not allowed to take part in the liturgy of God's birth and who have no priest to celebrate Mass".

John Paul is not so worried about the Church in his native Poland, because it has shown over the years that it is strong enough to fend for itself, although it always welcomes moral support from the Vatican. Poland today has 20 000 priests and 32 000 nuns, the seminaries are full and the Churches are packed at every Mass. Yugoslavia has a relatively active Catholic

Church, although it is outnumbered by the Orthodox churches. There has been a thaw in Church-State relations in Czechoslovakia and Hungary, but in Bulgaria and Rumania only limited freedom is allowed. In the USSR the Church has, in many cases, been forced to go underground and Albania has declared itself the "first atheist state".

It is with these nations, and with Cuba, Kampuchea, Vietnam, North Korea and China, that John Paul will continue the Vatican's policy of dialogue. And the communist nations know that when John Paul speaks it is with the voice of experience. They could well be prepared to listen to him more than they have done with previous popes. But at the same time John Paul is unlikely to go along with Paul VI's view that Apostolic Succession, or the need to fill all dioceses, is paramount. All the dioceses in Hungary are now filled, but at least two of the bishops are considered to be "peace priests", or those that "string along" with the regime. John Paul, it is said, would prefer to see these sees vacant rather than be filled by peace priests. This may well complicate matters for the future of the Church in Czechoslovakia.

There is one other form of communism that John Paul must face, and that is the so-called Eurocommunism. The powerful Italian communist party is foremost in this movement. When he was Cardinal Wojtyla, the Pope was asked what he thought about Eurocommunism. He replied, sardonically: "Fine words!" Yet he will face this question during Italian political elections. The Italian Episcopal Conference is not yet strong enough to speak out with any great clout and previous popes have done the talking, either directly or through the Vicar General. John Paul has said that the Holy See must not get into temporal politics, but if he says nothing about communism during Italian elections people are apt to criticise: "The Pope says nothing. He doesn't care". On the other hand, too, his efforts to spark a religious renewal, and more particularly his approaches to youth, are being seen by many as direct political interference. For if the youth follow papal exhortations they may well vote against the left. The wisdom of Solomon will be needed.

Another vital issue the Pope must face is that of ecumenism. He has already indicated that he will pursue the ecumenical goals set by Paul VI by reconfirming Cardinal Jan Willebrands as president of the Secretariat for Christian Unity. And on his first speech after his election he declared that "the cause of ecumenism is so lofty and sensitive an issue that we may not keep silent about it. How often do we meditate together on the last wish of Christ who asked the Father for the gift of unity . . . therefore one can hardly credit that a deplorable situation still exists among Christians. This is a cause of embarrassment and perhaps of scandal to others. And so we wish to proceed along the road which has happily been opened and to encourage whatever can serve to remove the obstacles, desirous as we are that through common effort such communion may eventually be achieved."

It was significant that the Archbishop of Canterbury, Dr Donald Coggan, head of the Anglican Church (the equivalent church in the United States is the Episcopal Church) attended the inauguration of John Paul, the first such leader to do so since before the Reformation in the 16th century. After meeting the Pope, Dr Coggan said the prejudices between Catholics and Anglicans could be overcome by education. He said the Pope's determination to pursue and develop the findings of the Second Vatican Council were significant, with the next steps being the continued study by the Catholic and Anglican churches of the three documents already issued. Two questions needed a decision: the question of Rome recognising Anglican orders and the progress towards inter-communion. Asked whether he would be willing to regard the Pope as "first among equals", Dr Coggan replied that he would agree on historical grounds that the Pope was first among equals. Dr Coggan said he thought that the infallibility of the Pope as proclaimed by the First Vatican Council would not prove a stumbling block to future unity because "the Roman Catholic Church is looking at this doctrine very hard in the light of the emphasis of the present Pope on collegiality". But Dr Coggan was concerned over the Anglican Church's decision to accept women priests, because John Paul has indicated that he saw no role for women as priests. "We are dealing," said Dr Coggan, "with a *fait accompli*, and this does present difficulties. But it is not inaccurate to say that a good many in the Roman Catholic Church hope for this, and I think it may come before too long."

The British Catholic leader, Cardinal Hume, also saw ecumenism as one of the more important issues facing John Paul. He said in an interview with the London-based *Catholic Herald* that the Pope must "heal divisions within Christianity, both within the Catholic Church and between the different Christian Churches . . . I have felt for a long time that some new initiative needs to be taken to bring the Churches closer together. I am by no means certain what it should be. It is really encouraging to know that many share the same view. I believe that Christ has offered and is offering the gift of unity; we probably need more time, more prayer and more work to see the way forward. The Holy Father is well aware of the importance of ecumenical work. It has his support and that is very important."

Although John Paul believes in the basic principles of the Second Vatican Council, his conservatism has made him call a halt to the experimentation that followed in the council's wake. Immediately after his election, he hauled back on some issues. For example, there will be no relaxation on the status of priests, religious or nuns. The first thing he stopped was the laicisation of priests and religious, that is, the request by priests and others to return to lay life. He feels strongly about the obligations of priesthood, so much so that a Vatican official said: "The Pope was horrified when he was presented with papers for the laicisation of some 200 priests. He told the congregation official, 'Leave them here. I want to think out my policy on this'." During his time in Krakow only two priests had asked for laicisation and he refused both. Added the Vatican official: "I think that he genuinely considers the post-Vatican Council policy on granting laicisations too easy and that many priests have regretted their departure and are wanting to return. If he makes it hard for them to leave they will reconsider and stay on".

Several other problems face John Paul. There are positions to be filled around the Vatican, and several Church leaders to be selected to wear the red hats of cardinals. And there is the continual worry of Vatican finances. In fact, the Vatican's serious financial situation was one of the important issues discussed by the College of Cardinals in the period prior to John Paul's election. The Vatican argument is that most people come to Rome to see the Pope, the Vatican and St Peter's, and not just the ancient monuments. But the city of Rome and the Italian government benefits from these visitors with taxes on their travel, board and lodgings and purchases made. The Vatican gets only the museum entrance fees, but nothing from the city or government. So, stresses the Vatican, if the city or government want to levy real estate and other taxes on Vatican property, then they should hand over to the Vatican a percentage of the taxes from visitors. To date, the fees collected for entry to museums, and the sale of stamps and coins have served to meet only the expenses of the physical upkeep of the Vatican City State. It does not pay for the huge outlays for staff, donations and so on. Peter's pence have dropped and most archdioceses and dioceses are too much in debt themselves to make regular contributions to the Holy See.

John Paul, a practical realist who knows full well that he must call on his staff for help, is not a monarch in the sense that former popes were, even to the degree Paul VI was. He desires collegiality with his bishops, but as one observer said: "Let there be no mistake, his whole past shows that he will be prepared to swing those Keys of Peter to devastating effect should he deem it necessary".

The major difference between Paul VI and John Paul II is that Paul was a nuanced Pope who always appeared wary of compromising his successor. John Paul, on the contrary, comes out straight and may offend some people. Some observers consider that the Polish Pope may have difficulty in understanding and adjusting to a Western secular mentality. They also see a danger in the Church becoming more authoritarian in spite of John Paul's talk about collegiality. In the past, the papal influence has been of a west-European philosophical approach which stressed the freedom of the individual and his rights. John Paul comes from a tradition where the value of authority is greatly respected.

There is one thing that John Paul might never overcome during his reign as Pope and that is the longing for his homeland. Time and again he has shown that he is homesick, that the memories of mountains, forests and lakes, of the old buildings of Krakow and the little villages that surround it, have stayed strongly with him.

At a pre-Christmas celebration, he spent two hours with Polish

John Paul II at the end of his inauguration.

seminarians singing Polish folk-songs. But after they sang the traditional *Goralu czy ci nie zal* (Mountain Man, Aren't You Sad at Leaving Your Home) he asked them not to sing it again.

"I get very sentimental," John Paul said. "Don't sing it again or I shall start crying."

BIBLIOGRAPHY

Attwater, Donald. *Penguin Dictionary of Saints*. Penguin Books, London, 1965.

Dal Maso, Leonardo B. *Rome of the Popes*. Bonechi, Florence, 1974.

Dziewanowski, M. K. *Poland in the 20th Century*. Columbia University Press, New York, 1977.

Elliott, Lawrence. *I Will be Called John*. Fontana, London, 1976.

Hajdukiewicz, Leszek and Mieczyslaw Karas. *The Jagiellonian University*, Wydawnictwo Uniwersytetu Jagiellonskiego, Krakow, 1978.

Hoess, Rudolf. *Commandant of Auschwitz, The Autobiography of Rudolf Hoess*. Pan Books, London, 1961.

Kimche, John. *The Unfought Battle*. Weidenfeld and Nicholson, London, 1968.

Kydrynski, Juliusz. *Tapima*. Krakow, 1969.

Livingstone, E. A. *The Concise Oxford Dictionary of the Christian Church*. Oxford University Press, Oxford, 1977.

MacEoin, Gary, and the Committee for the Responsible Election of the Pope. *The Inner Elite: Dossiers of Papal Candidates*. Sheed Andrews and McMeel, Inc. Kansas City, 1978.

Nagel's Encyclopedia Guide to Poland. Nagel Publishers, Geneva, 1974.

Pallenberg, Corrado. *The Vatican from Within*. Pall Mall Press, London, 1968.

Piekarski, Adam. *The Church in Poland*. Interpress Publishers, Warsaw, 1978.

Smolen, Kazimierz. *Auschwitz 1940–45*. Krajowa Agencja Wydawnicza, Katowice, 1978.

West, Morris. *The Shoes of the Fisherman*. Fontana, London, 1976.

Wojtyla, Karol (John Paul II). *On The Possibility of Constructing Catholic Ethics on the Basis of the System of Max Scheler*. KUL, Lublin, 1959. *Love and Responsibility*, Znak, Krakow, 1962. *Person and Action*, Polish Theological Society, Krakow, 1969. *The Foundation of Renewal: A Study of the Implementation of Vaticanum II*, Krakow, 1975. *Segno di Contradizione*. Rome. 1976.

The author has also drawn on articles in *Tygodnik Powszechny* and *Znak*, published in Krakow; *The Catholic Herald* and *The Tablet*, published in London, and reports from United Press International and American Associated Press, as well as such journals as *Polish Perspectives*, *Poland* and *Catholic Life in Poland*.